Praise for *The Living In Her Dying*

"What does it mean to let go of a parent? To finally not be the child? With this searing memoir, Sara Bragin approaches these questions with raw honesty and intelligence. Her language is that of the poet and the seeker, rich with aching emotion and keenly observed life. Every moment of this story engages the reader in a fresh understanding of what it means to be the dutiful daughter, and what it means to create an identity out of the shadow of the past."

— Monona Wali, *My Blue Skin Lover*

"In Sara Bragin's *The Living in Her Dying*, Bragin takes on the sacred task of helping her mother Hannah through the end of her life. This memoir of relationship - mother-daughter, woman-woman, self-other - is written with remarkable insight and authenticity. As each of us moves along our own path, Bragin's story serves as a fine example of how to discover deeper meaning for ourselves and our loved ones. An outstanding book, this one is exactly right for our time."

— Holly Prado, *award-winning writer*

"I have just finished reading Sara Bragin's memoir, *The Living In Her Dying*, and have come to love the characters. As they struggle to find connection and intimacy with each other, an amazing intimacy is created with me, the reader. I am eager to know the unique love that exists between this mother and daughter.

Sara is a straightforward narrator whom I quickly trust and want to be friends with. The sensual details with which she writes draw me in; the pace so quick and smooth, I don't want to stop reading. I feel that I am living the story right alongside her.

All along, we know that Hannah will die — and soon. But there is so much life in this story of dying, there is nothing morbid here, nothing sentimental. The limitations and frustrations Sara shares with us about her old, old (as she writes) mother and the plight of other elderly people are generously sprinkled with humor and compassion.

I am moved by Sara's commitment to provide the best care possible for her mother. Not just because I have cared for elders myself, or because I may someday be an elder needing care: the writing itself feels nourishing.

The Living In Her Dying is one of those books that shows the miracle of everyday life, with its moments of suffering and beauty, and all so very worth living. As I continued to read, I felt myself coming more alive. I will miss being with Hannah and Sara."

— Michael Richter, *Dance Educator*

The Living In Her Dying

ISBN Print 978-0-578-45601-0

Book Design by Blue Jay Ink
Ojai, California
bluejayink.com

Cover design by Richard Nanaumi
Cover photo by Sammie Vasquez on Unsplash
Author photo by Enric Bruguera Marti

Published in the United States by
Broken Buddha Press
sarabragin.com
sarabragin@gmail.com

The Living In Her Dying

How a mother and daughter
come to know each other and themselves
so the mother can die
and the daughter can live.

Sara Bragin

Broken Buddha Press
California, USA

Dedication

A bow to each of us who has had the chance, or will, to walk with another person in their dying time. A bow, too, to those of us who live with the certainty of our own death. Which, of course, means all of us.

To Bill, my brother, for being the kind of *mensch* who understands this is my story, the one *I* need to tell.

Finally to Mom for sticking it out with me.

“Wayfarer, there is no way,
you make the way as you go.”
—Antonio Machado

“Be kind.
Everyone you meet is fighting a fierce battle.”
—Philo of Alexandria

"Hurry up," my mother would say ...

... and the supper plates would be washed and dried before the sweet taste of fruit cocktail had vanished from my mouth.

To keep up, I learned to step out in front of myself, leaving the core of me behind. Other times, to hold back, still betraying what the real me knew to be true.

My mother, with her *own* hurried ways, her *own* holding back, is now very old. To step out of this life she is so fiercely holding onto into whatever is next, if indeed there *is* anything next, she will have to feel secure enough in her own footing to let go into whatever death actually is. And me? To walk on without her, I will have to discover how to live on an earth that no longer reverberates with her particular footfall. I will have to discover my own center, stand on my own ground, step out at my own pace.

The Beginning Of The End

September 25, 2002

I open the car door, step out of the two tons of steel that have been holding me together and into an emergency. Though I'd spoken with my mother by phone every day during the month I was away, I had no idea how much ground she'd lost.

The Transitional Care Unit of The Jewish Home, where my mother has been recovering from the second of two major pneumonias, either one of which would have done in a less feisty woman, is about to be torn down. Everyone else has already been moved back to Eisenberg Village, either to the new Alzheimer's building or to some other level of nursing care. My mother had been due for months to move back to the campus where, until the pneumonias hit, she'd been walking to meals, playing the piano for Friday afternoon services, watching *Jeopardy* on her own tv.

I find her sitting behind a tray table picking at a plate of cottage cheese, half a canned pear, half a canned peach, a bran muffin. There is only one bed left in the room, only bare springs at that.

Both she and Georgina light up when they see me. Georgina, who has just returned from El Salvador where her own father, 89, is recuperating from a heart attack, has stayed with my mother for a few hours a day since before her move to The Jewish Home four years ago. Mom had been living in her own home in Camarillo and started to need help driving. My mother loves Georgina "like family."

Mom is trying her best to look normal, the way she'd want to look, seeing her daughter for the first time in a month. Her smile is watery, even a little silly.

Before I can give her a kiss, a nurse pulls me away, tells me they've had to take her off the antidepressant that has been keeping her on an even keel, more or less; that the level of sodium in her blood is precariously low; and Dr. Smith wants to admit her to the Geriatric Psych Ward at UCLA, until she can be stabilized on new medications. Quite a mouthful.

"Not today," I say. "Not after all these weeks of looking forward to moving back. Not after watching everyone else leave and waiting for me to come and drive her there."

What I don't say is this. That fifteen years earlier, I'd walked by that very same psych ward just as someone opened the door and I heard people crying out, cries that seemed to move toward me along the shiny tile floor. I was a student then, getting my master's degree in clinical psychology, and we were being shown around UCLA's psychiatric hospital. Since then, I've feared that my mother would, one day, be a patient there.

"Hannah isn't showing life-threatening symptoms yet," Dr. Smith tells me, "but she might. And there's the question of how to manage her depression, the increase in anxiety."

But I'm adamant and he's willing to go along with me: to keep her at The Jewish Home and watch her. Which means I'll have to watch her. Even in a skilled nursing facility for which she pays $6,000 a month, not including medications, which add up to another seven or eight hundred, there will be very few people to watch her. Even here at The Jewish Home which, I have no doubt, is one of the best.

Georgina walks out to the car with us, my mother moving slowly behind an aluminum walker. It's a hot San Fernando Valley day and the air conditioner in my old Acura is pumping lukewarm air. "I'll pay to fix it," my mother says. "Can you have it done today, can you have it done NOW!" The hard look around her mouth only gets harder as we're unable to pass through the gate of Eisenberg Village. Though we've called ahead, no one has come to open it for us.

"There's no air. Get me some AIR!" I begin to see a

side of my mother the nurses have been telling me about. Demanding. Inflexible. Angry.

To prevent the sodium in her blood from moving even lower, she's on a regimen of limited water and is threatening she will die unless I give her a sip from the bottle of Arrowhead she's spotted on the back seat of my car. Her voice has risen to a shout, her half-closed eyes digging into me like arrows. I reach back, hand her the bottle.

A Bingo game is going on in the dining room of the Factor Building. After watching for a while from the sidelines, she acquiesces to join the other women. Women. No men.

When I say I'm going to leave to get some lunch, she asks if I can take her home. "Can you take me to somebody's home?"

Here it is, the question I've been afraid to hear since my brother and I sold her house a month ago. I'd stayed there as long as I could so she would have the security of knowing there was a home she could return to. I imagine stowing her away with me in the home of a friend where I've been invited to stay until I can find a place of my own.

When I come back, her dinner hasn't arrived — the kitchen wasn't expecting her — and she is demanding her salad, Italian dressing that seems to have taken on the importance of life itself.

Leaving, I ask for a kiss. Her lips on my cheek are hard.

That night, Ginger and I lie on facing sofas in her cozy living room talking about mothers. Hers, recently dead, having chosen not to go back on dialysis. Mine, still alive and, literally, kicking.

Ginger's guest room could be the favored bedroom in a New England inn — honey-colored wood floors; a maple sewing basket on spindled legs; a crystal vase filled with Double Delight roses cut from the garden; to cover me, a quilt of complicated fans in pastel colors.

Before laying my head on the pillow, I call The Jewish Home to find out how things are going. The administrator is sitting with my mother in the hallway of the nurses' station. I hear Mom's voice, loud. Very loud. I ask to talk to her. She tells me about everything that has gone wrong, including the part about not getting her dinner on time. The salad. The Italian dressing.

"Can you possibly go to sleep?" I ask.

"How can I?" she answers.

I ask the nurse to give her a Tylenol.

I wake in the middle of the night and call again. When I hear that my mother is sleeping, I turn over, go back to sleep myself.

I am in a car with my mother. She is in the driver's seat. I get out and watch her try to park it by herself. The motor's been turned off. She steps out and tries to steer it into a space by walking the car backward. I keep yelling to her, at her. "Get back in," I say. "Turn the motor on. Go!"

When I call in the morning, Mom is in the dining room eating breakfast. I make myself a cup of strong coffee, melt soy cheese on a slice of good whole wheat bread and climb back into bed to savor the early morning peace. A precious respite. On my way to where?

Where does she end and I begin?

Wasn't it supposed to happen when Dr. Fine cut the umbilical cord? Okay, if not then, then during the Terrible Twos when my job was to say "no" to Mommy, establish myself as a separate being. Okay, if not then, then as a rebelling teenager who came in past curfew, sneaked a Chesterfield, had sex. But I never had a curfew. Never sneaked a Chesterfield — well, except for those times on the hill behind Joy Lawrence's house. Didn't have sex 'til

I was well out of my mother's house.

Wasn't I supposed to find, as I gazed up from my crib into my mother's blue eyes, the security I would need to walk my own path, whether she was with me or not?

Supposed to doesn't always happen the way it's supposed to.

Some of us — can it be that I'm the only one? — never leave the home of our mother's arms, feel our own connection to the earth, take off in our own direction at our own pace. At least not until we're fully grown, with children of our own.

And if we don't have children of our own?

Now, well into the graying of my own hair and sometimes shaky on my own feet, I've feared I was still my mother's baby, needing to find myself in the steadiness of her gaze, needing to know she'd be there to catch me if I fell. These thoughts and fears sat next to me on the passenger seat as I drove back to Los Angeles.

Needing some recovery myself from seeing my mother through the two pneumonias, I'd said yes to the chance to go to Santa Fe for a month to house-sit a fine adobe, take care of two dogs: Sebastian, a tall, golden German Shepherd and Thor, part Pit Bull, part Labrador with the purple tongue of a Chow.

One day, walking in the Sangre de Cristo mountains with Sebastian and Thor, a rock caught my eye — one side round, the other side sharp, a deep V in the middle. A rock in the shape of a heart. Light, it fit easily in the palm of my hand. I decided to take this heart-shaped rock back to California with me, where my own heart is often heavy.

I'd learned to love California's ocean and mountains, to feel freedom in their wide openness, so different than the New England I'd grown up in. But, unlike the dogs who would run off to celebrate their freedom, only now and then turning around to make sure I was still there, I didn't feel the kind of security that makes freedom possible. Something about my father having died when I was ten. Something about not being able to find myself in my mother's eyes. Who would I be when she was no longer here?

Thanks to the miracles of medicine, my mother's will to live and my commitment to see her through to her dying, I would have this one last chance to discover what I need to go on without her. As it turned out, we had five months to get our work done. Hers, mine, and ours.

I Pray For A Hummingbird

September 26

I catch sight of Mom through the front window of the Factor Building. She is wearing navy pants and a black cotton cardigan over a pink flowered top, none of which belong to her. This happens. Other people's clothes appear in her closet, and she doesn't say they're not hers.

Her short white hair is uncombed. She doesn't have on her usual rouge, eyebrow pencil, powder, lipstick. She's 92 and, today, looks every year of it. To hell with all that. She's participating in the afternoon's activity.

She and five other women are sitting around a table. An enthusiastic volunteer holds up a greenish-yellow fruit the size of two large lemons, the *etrog*, and a palm branch, the *lulav*, both symbols of Sukkoth, a holiday celebrating the forty years Jews spent in the desert after escaping from slavery under Pharaoh.

The conversation takes a sharp turn to the women's early lives. My mother offers that she went to P.S. 51, then stops. Mom was never one to expand much on her childhood. Still, Tiffany Street and The Bronx were always staples. Now, we're down to a meal of one dish.

Miriam, her new roommate who has bright red hair and wears shocking pink everything, is dozing in her wheelchair. It hurts my neck to see how heavily her head hangs on her chest. Lauretta, in a pastel zip-up-the-front housecoat, isn't finished talking about the *lulav* and how old-fashioned it seems to her, this ritual of shaking a palm branch in six directions.

I watch my mother disappear into herself as if listening to a conversation going on inside her head. She's done this as long as I can remember. At some point, she'll re-emerge and, having a lot to say, will say it directly into the space in front of her as if no one else is around.

"Let's go outside," I say, hoping fresh air will wake her up. Air — or a hummingbird. I pray for a hummingbird.

When Mom moved to The Jewish Home, she had to decide which few possessions she would bring with her. One was an antique plate with an iridescent hummingbird hovering over a trumpet flower. I make a mental note to free the plate from the top drawer of the bureau where, with the pneumonias and all the moves, everything precious has been stored away.

She sucks the juice out of a Tangelo and spits the rest into her hand. I retrieve a tissue from the mesh bag hanging from her walker.

At dinner that night, which arrives on time, she chews on the corned beef until all the juice is gone, spitting out whatever's left. I break off small pieces of meat from her plate to see for myself whether chewing and chewing, as it reduces the meat to salty liquid, might allow for easier swallowing. If I can swallow it, could she be swallowing it, too? Is this habit of not swallowing the fibrous parts of food why she has been so constipated? I am working to fit together the pieces of the puzzle that has become my mother.

I'm reminded of a phone conversation we'd had while I was away. Mom was sitting on the toilet, and a nurse brought a cell phone into the bathroom in hopes that I would be able to convince her to get up. Not being able to move her bowels had become the center of her existence, and she was insisting on staying right where she was until her "stomach worked," an expression I knew well.

Between bladder and bowels, she'd been spending a good part of each day on the toilet, and no amount of explaining or cajoling was enough to convince her it was okay to get up. She'd become well known for this behavior among the nurses and aides, even among the other residents. Nobody believed her anymore so, in addition to being uncomfortable, she was angry.

"You're obsessing," I'd said from where I was, a thousand miles away, seeing her, in my mind's eye, sitting on the toilet, an exasperated nurse holding a cell phone up to her ear.

"It's not an obsession!" she'd shouted, ending the conversation by pushing the phone away with a swipe of her chin.

Now, there are these food peculiarities, too.

After the last pneumonia, when the breathing tubes had been removed and she was breathing on her own again, all her food had come puréed. Chicken, turkey, calves' liver, chopped steak — all shades of the same pale brown. Green beans, broccoli, limas — each a slightly different shade of green. Mashed potatoes, every meal mashed potatoes.

Soups, juices, coffee, tea — they all had to be thickened, too, in the hopes of preventing food from "going down the wrong pipe," causing another aspiration pneumonia.

Well over a year after she returned from the hospital, I'd wondered why she was still being served a soft diet and asked that she be given regular food again.

It's hard to watch her, lips bulging over a slug of chewed corned beef. How she expels it into her hand, adding it to the pile of pale pink mush building up on the side of her plate.

"Swallow, Mom, please swallow," I say. Has she forgotten how? Have the muscles in her throat become too weak? Is it her teeth? Something else her old flesh is heir to?

So much of my life, I've tried to get my mother to do things she didn't want to do. Take a walk, watch a made-for-tv movie all the way through to the end instead of getting up to leave before it's over.

Suddenly, I can feel in *myself* what the source of that impulse to get up might be. The chance to leave while she still can, still has some power to exert before having to face the inescapable end. The chance to get up and leave before feelings arise she may not know what to do with. Leave before she's lost the chance to keep moving, keep herself alive. I feel my own fear of endings and the pain of not knowing whether anything will be there after. A fear of dying before my time.

My mother has not wanted to die. As frail as her body is, her mind, for the most part, has been strong. And, though she freely admits to being 92, she says she feels young. "I'm not like those old ladies over there," she tells me.

But, more and more, she suffers. Her bladder sags, muscles not strong enough to hold it in place, leaving her with the press of urine, even after the second and third streams have passed. Now, too, the ever-present sensation that a bowel movement is waiting.

"I'm jumping out of my skin," I remember her saying from the time I was a child. I was always too slow for her. She had no patience for the way I would set the table. She'd fold the paper napkins in half herself, make my bed, vacuum the rug. Younger and stronger in those days, she'd found ways to manage her anxiety, found a friend in "phenobarb."

I'd found ways, too, to manage *my* obsessions, *my* anxiety. Moved from career to career — from physical therapy to writing advertising to helping elders record their life stories, to becoming a therapist in an effort to understand my own story. Stayed too long in a marriage that offered false security. Went on diets where I would eat nothing but asparagus one day, watermelon or potatoes the next. Immersed myself in books and more books that promised philosophical or psychological or spiritual or bodily or literary salvation. And trusted in The New Age. Until a divorce and the 1994 Northridge earthquake shook me loose from whatever illusion of stability I was hiding behind, depositing me in my mother's house out beyond the northern edge of the San Fernando Valley.

She was already old by then, collecting dents in the bumpers of her red Honda Accord. She'd taken some falls, broken her shoulder, her wrist, her thumb. And, at 88, decided on her own, thank god, to move to The Jewish Home.

I stayed on in her house for four years — after all, I told myself, what if she needed a home to return to?

A month ago, I taped up a big box and labeled it Memorabilia; boxed the Limoges for twelve and the full set of Spode stoneware, both of which she'd inherited from her sister Doris; in another box, nestled a score of antique cups and saucers in scrunched-up newspaper, the oyster plates that had been a wedding gift from her best friend, Fritzi (hold them up to the sun and you can see light coming through); and moved it all into storage, together with whatever was left of my own things after years of winnowing. I moved myself out, too, with all the physical and metaphorical meaning that moving out of your mother's house can bring, and off I went to Santa Fe.

Under the huge New Mexico sky and with the strange freedom of having no home of my own to return to, a thought came like a flash: when I return to California, I'll be on my own for the first time.

In 1948, my mother and father, my three-year-old brother and I (I was eight) had arrived in North Hollywood from Connecticut, whatever we would need to begin a new life strapped to the top of our 1939 Buick. Years before he would become my father, a young man named Irving had hitchhiked across America and back, vowing to return to California someday to find himself there. Two years after we arrived, he had a first heart attack and died. He was just forty.

Now, it was time for me to let go of my father's dream, begin the hard work of finding myself. Maybe, too — just maybe — I would begin to understand the inordinate attachment I've felt to my mother. Not by looking back — there's been enough psychology for a while — but by seeing clearly whatever life was offering up right in front of me. Around and under me. Right here and right now.

Right here and right now, Mom is finding fault with everything.

Her room – "No air!"

The food – "Where's the Italian dressing?!"

Her roommate – "She's stupid!"

And me.

"I guess I just don't have taste," she says, spitting out words she'd been chewing on since she heard me say — was it just this morning? — that I knew she didn't pick out the clothes she was wearing, that she would never put on a black jacket with navy pants.

I wondered: Are the peculiarities I'm witnessing proof of what we've all heard — that those quirks we use to get by increase as we get older, so we better get used to them now? Or, still wanting to give her the benefit of the doubt: how much of what's making her so hard to be with might be caused by the latest chemical imbalance in her system?

At dinner, she insists that she is wearing her "partial" — denture, that is. Seeing spaces where teeth should be, I go to her room and find the teeth in a container of water on the sink. Unable to find a brush and, in a hurry to get back, I wash them with my hands, scraping off the whitish film with my thumbnail. I bring them to her, ask her to rinse her mouth with the coffee and put her teeth in for the rest of the meal.

After dinner, I get her a toothbrush and we walk to the bathroom, so she can give her mouth and teeth a proper cleaning. She brushes and brushes and brushes. I become impatient at how long it's taking, at the same time proud and admiring of how clean my mother keeps herself.

I'm getting ready to leave, don't want her to go to her room. "*Jeopardy* isn't even on yet," I say, bringing her back into the dining room to a seat in front of the tv.

The news is on. War about to break out in Iraq.

I kiss her goodbye and drop off an extra toothbrush, some paste in her bathroom. As I'm walking back down the hall for one more goodnight kiss — maybe this one will be sweeter — I see her walking toward me.

I leave her in her room, sitting on the toilet.

Please Don't Call Me Honey

September 27

Mom is sitting, still or again, on the toilet, her pants down around her ankles. The smile on her face is sickeningly sweet; if she were diabetic, it would speak of sugar eating away at her. Her legs, white with splotches of pink in various sizes, look sturdy; despite the splotches, she could be a bobbysoxer.

"I'm so happy to see you," I say, relieved she's still alive after how hard I was on her over the corned beef. At least I didn't kill her. I was nine when Daddy died and I took on the job of making sure my mother would stay alive. Maybe it was even before that, maybe it was when I was born.

She says she's happy to see me, too. It's another day to love her daughter.

While I'm waiting at the nurses' station to find out if her prescriptions have been called in to Costco, I see her coming down the hall toward me, pushing her aluminum walker — her wagon, as she calls it.

In the dining room, a watered-down version is taking place of the Sabbath extravaganza that Howard, an angel in white, orchestrates most Friday afternoons. He cajoles each resident into choosing an instrument from his bag of tricks – a tambourine, maracas, bells, an African gourd filled with seeds. Jokes with them in Yiddish and sings Yiddish songs, accompanying himself on the accordion. There is nothing old Jewish women love more than a young Jewish man with an accordion. Today, a woman volunteer is banging out melodies on an upright piano, as Izzy, the token male and "a dresser," in taupe patent leather loafers, tan pants and a light blue sports coat, launches into his favorite medley: *If I Were A Rich Man, My Yiddishe Momme* and *L'Chaim, L'Chaim, To Life*. My mother gestures at clapping, her small bony hands coming half-an-inch away from each other and back in soundless semi-participation.

As the entertainment departs for the next floor, leaving the dining room quiet and expectant, I take the opportunity to move the piano around so its side, rather than its bare, unpainted back, faces toward the women, hoping that will hide, too, how bad it sounds.

"I thought you were going to ask me to play," Mom says.

"Mom, I'd love you to play." She sends me to get her music.

I return with her book of exercises and place it on the piano. Its front cover is long gone, the corners of its pages soft from years of turning. I help her up from her chair and onto the bench. Before taking the time to center herself behind the pedals, and without a glance at the music, she begins to play one of her old standbys, a Russian folk melody. From there, she picks out *Hatikvah*, Israel's national anthem, then signals to me she is done. I ask her to play one more and she hurries through *Für Elise*. She's tired, she says, wants to go to her room to lie down.

I don't want her to be tired, I want her to be well. I

stay and talk with some of the residents who are relatively well.

I'd grown up hearing my mother's fingernails clicking against the keys of her own piano, a black baby grand, "1927" burned into the unfinished wood of its heavy cover. She was seventeen the year her piano teacher walked her over to Steinway Hall on 57th Street in Manhattan, around the corner from his studio in Carnegie Hall, to help her pick out the Mason & Hamlin she would pay for, week by week, from her paycheck as a stenographer for a man who ran an import/export business downtown. That piano would follow her from The Bronx to Brooklyn, to Old Greenwich when she married Irving, to North Hollywood, to Long Beach and back to Connecticut when Daddy died.

When I was a child, she'd arranged for me to take piano lessons from Mr. Cable. Mr. Cable, who always wore a navy blue suit when he came to our house for my lesson and was very tall and thin with thick white hair. Abe Lincoln if Abe Lincoln had had the chance to grow old. I got as far as playing *The Minuet in G*, precisely but passionless, as part of a recital in a church basement. The piano never felt like my instrument, not helped by the fact that Mom had no patience for my mistakes, quick to stand behind me, show me what I was doing wrong.

Back in her room, Mom is sitting on the toilet again,

says she'll be able to get up soon.

At the nurses' station, I get into a long, drawn-out conversation with Adrienne, the psychiatric nurse, and Marla, the psychologist. They are both concerned about the increase in Mom's anxiety. I say I wonder how much of it is due to her medical conditions — the low sodium, a prolapsed uterus that presses on her bladder, and is her bladder pressing on her rectum, too? Might she be anxious with good reason?

By the time I get back to her room, Mom has a wild look in her eye and is drinking water, cup after cup of it, from the blue container that stores her dentures at night. "If I don't drink, I'll die," she tells me. "I have to keep drinking so it'll work through me." I try to get her to lie down and rest. "If I rest, I'll die," she says. "You'll see. I won't see, but you'll see." She's drinking and drinking and won't ... can't ... stop. "It won't come out. The water won't come out," she says.

She is adamant. She wants to live. She knows what she has to do. And she is at the point of exhaustion doing it.

"My poor Mom," I say out loud. I've said it many times over these last two years. In the ICU with a breathing tube down her throat and a feeding tube strung through her nose to her stomach. As blood gushed when a nurse tore an impaction away from the wall of her rectum. As she was coming out from under weeks of sedatives and screaming orders from her bed into an empty hospital room about something known only to her that needed to be done. "Now! Hurry up! Hurry UP!"

"Hannah, are you going to sleep on the toilet?" Adrienne asks.

"Yes! I have to!" my mother says, throwing her head back, coming close to banging it, in emphasis, on the steel pipe that extends up the wall behind the toilet seat. Adrienne returns to the nurses' station and writes orders for Mom to be admitted to UCLA's Geriatric Psych Ward.

Completely done in, my mother agrees to get into bed if I will promise to keep giving her water. She doesn't dare to close her eyes. If she does, she will fall asleep and she is sure that, if she falls asleep, she will die.

I feed her ice chips, one at a time. "Get another one ready," she orders, through ice in her mouth still melting.

I begin to knead her stomach, which turns out to be an inspired intervention. If the kneading is able to push "water" out, it might distract her from taking water in. She tells me where to press and how hard. I do exactly what she says. Her voice is loud as she belts out orders, her blood pressure life-threateningly high. "Don't stop! Maybe it's coming a little."

The ambulance team arrives — two men and a woman in fire department uniforms. I can't believe I'm hearing right, but, twice now, one of the men has called me honey. "Please don't call me honey," I say, turning from my task at my mother's belly. He rolls his eyes and stops calling me honey.

I show the woman, who will be riding with my mother in the back of the ambulance, how to knead her belly. Even without traffic, the trip will take half-an-hour.

As Mom is being wheeled out past Miriam, whose eyes, pink with tiredness, are glued to the tv next to her bed, I apologize for all the agitation. "I wasn't agitated," she says, hardly looking up.

I catch up with the ambulance as it's going east on Victory Boulevard and ride alongside it. The woman has her hands on my mother's stomach. The man who called me honey sits behind them.

As we wait to be admitted to the inner sanctum of UCLA's Emergency Room, I make repeated visits to the restroom to re-wet the washcloth my mother is demanding to have over her nose. The cool, wet cloth is somehow helping her to breathe. She resumes telling me how and where to press on her stomach.

For the next seven hours in the ER, a uniformed security guard sits outside Mom's room, making small talk with the nurses. I make some small talk with him myself, find out he's stationed there because my mother came in on an involuntary admission, a 5150, and, as such, is deemed potentially harmful to herself or others. It's his job to make sure she doesn't get away.

Oh, I'm a bad one for rules and regulations. My mother is 92; she is lying on a high gurney with the side rails up, one wet washcloth over her forehead to shield her eyes from the overhead lights, another over her nose and mouth to help her breathe and keep her lips moist; it's the middle of the night; her walker is nowhere in sight; and she needs a burly security guard, in uniform with a badge, to make sure she doesn't get away.

A nurse inserts an IV to draw blood. Another inserts a catheter, drains 400 cc of urine from my mother's bladder. I am awed, as I have been many times before — as she's gotten old, I've seen her undressed again and again — to see the sparse blonde hair over my mother's pubis, the pink-brown lips of her vagina. I imagine myself being borne out of her.

It turns out she has a urinary tract infection, and this may be why she's delirious; at least, it's part of the reason for her being so demanding of water. I tell myself never to forget this: If you ever again find yourself with an old woman on the verge of delirium, your mother or anyone else, and you're not ready to chalk it up to dementia when everyone else is, remember to ask that she be checked for a urinary tract infection! Don't forget!

A young doctor, very tall and very thin, with curly

black hair and three names, asks my mother if she knows what year it is. I glow when she gets it right. "O two," she says.

A young psychiatric resident comes in, drags herself to a chair. Not sure who to address, me or my mother, her words land somewhere in the space between us. She speaks so softly Mom has to ask her to repeat every question she asks. At some point, the resident begins to repeat herself — it's the middle of the night for her, too — and I quietly cheer when my mother tells her to stop asking such stupid questions.

A man comes to take her (my mother, not the resident) for a CT scan. When I question the need for it, a nurse tells me it's because the chest X-ray isn't of good enough quality to determine whether or not Mom has pneumonia. It seems her old hiatal hernia, the too-big opening in her diaphragm through which her stomach protrudes upward, is in the way. I follow alongside the gurney on the long trek to Radiology. The tech, it turns out, is a saint. He asks me if I'm sure I want my mother to undergo the injection of dye needed for the contrast scan the doctor with three names has ordered. He explains it'll make her feel hot all over and, at 92, her kidneys may have trouble excreting the dye. I ask him to call the doctor, who agrees that a non-contrast scan will be just as useful. I thank the tech for being awake. He hands me a lead apron and an extra piece to put around my neck to protect my thyroid gland, and I stay in the room as my mother is slid back and forth into the round hole of the scanner. My brother, Bill, who is finishing up his twenty-eighth year at General Electric and is on vacation in Hawaii, will be happy to hear that the scanner was made by GE.

At 2:30 in the morning, I start to get testy, more mother tiger now than human daughter. I want somebody to make a decision about where in this huge institution my mother belongs and admit her NOW! so she can get into a real bed and, if possible, get some sleep.

A male nurse in blue scrubs comes in with an antibiotic for the urinary tract infection and automatically flicks on the overhead light. I ask him if such a bright light is really necessary to give a pill. He pouts and turns it off. By now, over and over, I am playing the age card in an attempt to move things along. "This woman is 92," I say, "and it's the middle of the night." Etcetera.

It's four in the morning when the door to the Geriatric Psych Ward is unlocked for us, along with all my trepidations about my mother someday being a patient here. She is rolled into a brightly lit room. The woman in the other bed is wide awake. Did I mention that it's four in the morning? Have we gone through all these steps, all these hours, for a brightly lit room at four in the morning?

I leave my mother in the care of a nurse who begins

to undress her and arrange the bed. I follow the administrator into the hallway, her manner and starched white jacket signaling that this is the changing of the guard. At least for now, my mother is no longer mine.

Black Briards

The rest of the night

I drive west on Wilshire Boulevard, looking for a motel to spend the night. With Ginger's guest room promised to out-of-town relatives for the weekend, my plan, until life got in the way, was to drive up the coast and find a place on the water to rest.

I drive all the way to the ocean, but nothing feels as right as being alone in my car, on the move. I swing back along Santa Monica Boulevard to Sawtelle, north on Sawtelle, south on Sepulveda, east on Venice and back to Sepulveda, turning north to follow the 405 all the way out to the Valley. I keep moving.

Eyes starting to close — it's now 6 AM — I pull into a motel no better than any of the others. All preferences gone, I ring the bell. An Indian woman emerges from a side door, followed by her sleepy-eyed daughter. "I'm sorry," she says. "No vacancy."

"I don't understand," I say, turning to the empty parking slots outside most of the rooms. "Where are all the cars?"

Doubling back, I head east on Ventura Boulevard and, remembering a random piece of my ex-husband's philosophy about California real estate — "Buy the least expensive house in an expensive neighborhood." — I turn into a quiet residential street south of the Boulevard in Studio City, a street with well-spaced homes overhung by large shade trees. I pull up in front and slightly to the garage side of a chocolate-brown house with green trim, turn the motor off, lean the driver's seat back as far as it will go, cover myself with my mother's gray fleece jacket which I took with me when I left her at the hospital, sigh, allow my gaze to travel beyond the houses and black branches of tall trees into a sky that's turned a pale and icy blue and give in to the darkness that's been waiting quietly behind closed lids.

I wake with a start to the sound of a man talking to the two large black Briard dogs he's taking on their early morning walk. Jumping to sit up, I bump into the horn, which draws to me the exact attention I was praying to avoid. It's eight in the morning, and I have been sleeping in my car on a Studio City street lined with beautiful homes.

While it's true that I don't have a home of my own in

LA, I wouldn't call myself homeless. Not that I don't fear it could happen. Or haven't felt homeless, on and off, over the course of my life. When I lived in New York in the '60s, well-paid and getting awards for my work on Madison Avenue, I wondered, whenever I saw a particular bag lady on Fifth Avenue just down from Tiffany's, whether that would be my fate, too, someday.

Was it *60 Minutes* that did a feature piece about women who used to live in big Brentwood and Beverly Hills homes and were now sleeping in their cars in the same neighborhoods where they used to live? Homeless through divorce and other catastrophes that can befall women in their middle and late years, they'd managed to hold onto their fancy cars, classy clothes and, I imagined, still had a stash of expensive makeup from Neiman-Marcus in the glove compartment. Just as I feared that one day my mother would be a patient on UCLA's Geriatric Psych Ward, I feared I would one day be living in my car. I didn't think it would all happen on the same day.

Dr. Slouch

September 28

I arrive at the Geriatric Psych Ward at noon and, from the hall, through the chicken-wire-protected glass of the Day Room, I see my mother motioning to me. "Come right away!"

An unseen person buzzes me in through a locked door.

"Get me out of here," Mom says. "Look! Do I belong here?"

She's strapped into a huge blue lounge chair on wheels, wearing the same striped jersey she was wearing when she was admitted; on top of it, a Posey, a short pale-blue apron that covers her chest with ties that go under her arms and around the back of the chair. Even if the wheels hadn't been locked, the chair still would have been too heavy, too hard for her to move it on her own. It's the job of men and women of every imaginable national origin to push these unwieldy chairs around. As adamant as my mother was yesterday about staying alive, she is that adamant now about my getting her out of that blue chair, off this ward and out of this hospital.

I tell her I'll see what I can do, though I know that The Jewish Home is not likely to take her back until she is more manageable, and I don't have a home of my own to take her to.

My mother has indeed become a patient in the Geriatric Psych Ward. Those calls I'd heard back then to "Get me out of here" were not just in my imagination.

As her advocate, a job I didn't realize I had agreed to take on, here I am, doing my best to stand up to institutional forces — nurses armed with white coats, aides and orderlies who, following doctors' orders, secure patients into chairs too clumsy for them to navigate on their own, creating a kind of imprisonment meant for their safety perhaps but, from what I can see in my mother's case, is making her crazy. Craziness I'm still hoping will turn out to be the result of a temporary delirium. Take a 92-year-old woman, add a urinary tract infection to an already there confusion caused by too little sodium in the blood, and craziness might be the absolutely normal response.

I try to look on the bright side. While she's here — this is a hospital, after all — maybe we can gain some understanding of the bladder and bowel problems that have become the bane of her existence, and mine.

Still, I tell the nurse my trepidations were correct, this is not the right place for my mother. As if I am not the first relative of a patient she has heard this from, she ushers me through another locked door into a small office where she introduces me to a very young man, probably an intern. He turns slightly to look my way but doesn't get up from the chair he's slouching in. "Your mother will have to stay," he says, going on to tell me the decision was based on the psychiatric resident in the ER lending her agreement to the 5150 written by the nurse at The Jewish Home.

He shows me the resident's notes. They say nothing of her own appraisal, only that the patient is a 92-year-old woman who is insisting on drinking water and having her stomach massaged. Oh yes, and that she is able to accurately answer questions about date and time and place. Again, pretty normal, if you ask me; certainly nothing that would require someone to be placed on a psychiatric ward behind locked doors. Maybe on a medical floor with some psychiatric input about how better to manage anxiety. And time for the antibiotic to work on the UTI.

What the resident didn't write in her notes is that it was 2 AM, that she herself was exhausted and repeating herself and that an even more exhausted 92-year-old woman on a gurney had the sense to tell her to stop bothering an old lady in the middle of the night.

Dr. Slouch (no one has mentioned his actual name) turns back to his cell phone that has now begun to play the overture to *Peter and The Wolf.* "I'll be home soon, honey," I hear him say. "How's the game going?"

The next doctor, who respectfully includes my mother

in the conversation, explains what I've been hoping to hear, that her condition is probably temporary, associated with the infection and that this is a good place for her to be until things improve. "We'll get to know her," he says. "Chances are this could happen again."

All of this, except maybe the part about it happening again, goes a long way toward calming us both down and, when visiting hours are over, though my mother is still insisting she isn't staying, it isn't with the same vehemence. Later that day, I find her putting the finishing touches on her makeup, no longer begging me to take her home.

To celebrate, I go to The Sushi House, a small restaurant in West Los Angeles where there are always people outside crowding around the door, waiting to get in. The prices are good and the sushi chefs are unusually generous with that pink mountain of sweet ginger that goes next to the foothill of pale green wasabi. Tonight, as if in a dream, I'm able to walk right in. I sit at one of two empty places at the end of the bar. The young man next to me doesn't look up. Farther down, a handsome, middle-aged Japanese man with graying hair is drinking a Sapporo and eating tempura. He and the sushi chef are joking in Japanese. No one seems to notice me.

The Japanese man leaves. A tall Caucasian man takes

his place at the bar, opens a thick book with a black, white and red cover, *The Road to Berlin*, and begins to read. His reading glasses have red frames. The waiter brings me a hot sake. I order a Sukiyaki roll — crabmeat and egg and salmon roe dipped in batter and fried like tempura. I drink my sake. A rock song from the '70s grows louder and faster as I watch the tall man turn pages in his book. The sushi chef, as if in a race with time, piles spicy tuna high on beds of rice, wrapping it all in sheets of seaweed. Slicing each roll into six pieces, he wipes the long blade of his knife with the paper towel he unrolls from its holder above the bar. He and the other sushi chef confer and, as if they are dancing, turn quickly toward each other and, just as quickly, away.

I can barely keep up with how fast everything is moving — how fast the music is playing, how fast the man behind the counter is making spicy tuna rolls, how bright the lighting has become, how handsome is the face of the man in the poster behind the bar.

A smile breaks out over my face. Soft and warm and wide, it has a life of its own. My shoulders drop from where they must have been held up around my ears, and I sit back in the chair, my breathing becoming deeper. The man with red-framed glasses looks up only to order.

I wonder: will I be able to move slowly enough to walk away? Or will I dance?

Outside, I feel part of everything. The cool night air. The traffic light at the corner swinging lightly in the breeze. The sounds of passing cars. The color and busyness I've just left inside. An unendingly empty space opening out in front of me.

I pull into the Tokyo Princess, a motel in Encino I've passed hundreds of times. The room is restfully dark, soft light reflecting off black lacquer — a desk, a bureau, a night table on either side of the large bed. I fall sleep surrounded by hundreds of tiny empty drawers, a stone statue of Buddha sitting in a nook under the window that opens out onto busy Ventura Boulevard.

In the morning, the eyes of the tiny Japanese man at the desk lock onto the charm I'm wearing around my neck — a square of amber, framed in gold. He reads the Chinese character and tells me how auspicious is its message, promising long life to the wearer. I tell him that, many years ago, I'd brought it back from China as a gift for my mother, that she is in the hospital now and I am wearing it for her until she is well again.

"Very good, very good," he says, his eyes returning to the charm as if his own life could be enhanced by it.

I turn it over to show him the character on the other side; he is equally impressed. "This one is for good luck," he says. "Good luck and long life! You should have a charm like this of your own."

I tell him I do, that it's in the shape of a heart, that I don't usually wear it and don't know what it says.

"Love, probably love. You should wear it."

"I'll bring it in so you can read it for me."

By now, his attention has turned to the Star of David I am also wearing. "Are you Jewish?" he asks, as if the answer didn't have to be yes.

"It was a gift when I was fourteen," I tell him. "After September 11th, I dug it out of an old jewelry box, polished the diamond at its center and started wearing it again. With all the anti-Semitism in Europe, I felt it was time for me to make some kind of statement." He says he thinks it's good to be Jewish, doesn't understand why so many people hate Jews.

We're in a world of our own, this tiny Japanese man and I, having fallen into a space where nothing but what is happening right now matters, one of those tiny drawers that surrounded me as I slept, the Buddha sitting faithful and silent between me and the busy boulevard.

Not Even Russian Dressing

September 29

"Wawdah. I need wawdah. NOW!"

The sound of my mother's voice is the first thing I hear as I'm buzzed onto the ward, its guttural harshness enough to erase from my mouth the last remnants of the deliciously bitter taste of my morning coffee. When did her Bronx accent become so pronounced?

There's an interlude of silence as she turns to study the signs hanging on the wall next to her bed. Dentures, check. Hearing aid, check. Sheepskin, check. Attends, check.

"Sheepskin?" she asks. I tell her it's to protect the sore on her back.

"Attends?"

"That's the name of the diapers they use here."

My mother isn't incontinent in the way we imagine when we think about old people. Urge incontinence is the continual feeling that she needs to urinate and, together with the fact that she's — to use her word — fastidious, she's started wearing a diaper, just in case. Add to this, pelvic muscles too weak to hold her uterus from pressing on her bladder, this from two vaginal deliveries: the first, a perfectly formed baby boy, alive in her womb for nine months and, at the last minute, born dead; two years later, a girl baby, me, born very much alive. Five years after me, Bill, who entered the world by Caesarian section, giving her a break.

What if he'd lived, that first boy? I've yearned for that older brother and the rest it might have provided me, not to have had to be the older child.

"After your father died, I was relieved you were old enough to take care of yourself," my mother had told me. "I could devote all my attention to Bill, who needed me." I was all of nine at the time.

I'd left Bill a phone message with the details of Mom's condition, where she was, how to find her. He'd just returned from Hawaii the night before and, when I didn't hear from him, I called his office. I was impatient at having to repeat everything as if my message had never arrived, angry that he offered no appreciation or even acknowledgment for my having spent all of the last week putting out fires.

Still, at evening visiting hours, I'm happy to see him, tan and rested. Smiling. Anger on one side of the brother-sister coin, love on the other. How it's always been with us.

He and Mom are at a table in the Day Room, in front of Mom a plate of barely cooked poultry. I stare at a yellowish wing sitting atop the breast of half a small chicken, its bumpy edge of gristle along the bone, raised pores where feathers had been.

At The Jewish Home, they serve chicken — a Jewish staple, after all — practically every day. Mom had had her fill long ago, asking each time for something else instead. Tuna. Egg salad. Gefilte fish. Anything but chicken. The aide says he can order her a hamburger.

Bill tells me about his own health, that he needs to have a second test to find out more about sugar in his blood. I say maybe this is a wake-up call for both of us to be more careful of what we eat. Tell him that Baba, Daddy's mother, had diabetes and I'd watch as Aunt Esther gave her an injection of insulin every morning. I know things he doesn't about our family.

The hamburger arrives and, before Mom can push it away, I tear open the packet of ketchup and squeeze it out over the lettuce, thinking I'll mix in some mayonnaise. Next to Italian, Mom's favorite dressing is Russian. But seeing the splattering of ketchup on the lettuce, she pushes the plate away, and that's the end of the hamburger. She hadn't eaten lunch either.

Patience gone, I leave, giving Bill a chance to deal on his own with this latest vicissitude of our mother's old age.

Late that night, there's a message from a doctor. "We've decided to keep your mother for another two weeks," he says, his tone cold, the implication being that it's they who own her. I send Bill an e-mail, tell him I'll follow it up in the morning.

Where There's Life, There's ...

October 1

Just inside the entrance to UCLA Medical Center is the Surgery Waiting Room. It's where doctors come to give people life or death information about people they love. Some of the doctors, fresh from operating, will have changed into crisp white coats. Others will still be in their blue scrubs, paper coverings over their shoes.

Some will have that serious look. Some will be smiling. All will be weary.

It's a place of moments. Moments of dread as people, for hours, sit facing into the unknown. Moments of relief. "What we did will give your father more time," a doctor says.

A place of hope. Sorrow. And just plain boredom, with time out for a cigarette. A place of banana peels and apple cores, cups of cold coffee, crinkly packages of tortilla chips, ancient copies of *People* magazine and *Newsweek*.

A place where a man sleeps sitting up, his head hanging back, mouth open, tongue falling to the side. Where three young men in blue jeans, caps worn backward, sit shoulder to shoulder with an elderly man in a conservative suit, a lone matron in powder-blue cashmere and diamond rings. A place where you can hear every language this city speaks.

All of this is what brings me here. The constant coming and going of people at the edge of waiting, at the edge of hope. Akin to life hurrying on in the crosswalk of a busy city street. So different from how things are upstairs in the Day Room of the Geriatric Psych Ward where, right now, my mother is sitting, strapped into a monstrous blue chair, and life as we've known it seems to be over.

I come here, too, because, in a city where I don't often feel at home, I have some history here. Eleven years ago, I was one of these people waiting for a doctor to come and tell me about the surgery he had just performed on someone *I* loved. It was late on an August afternoon. A neurosurgeon had just come to tell me that my then-husband had survived the seven hours of surgery it took to remove the bony tumor in the center of his brain. Though I could see no evidence on Dr. Black's impeccable blue scrubs that anything had gone awry, he went on to say that a scalpel had nicked a small artery, deep down, and it had taken thirteen pints of blood to replace a flow that wouldn't stop.

As Dr. Black was doing what *he* could, upstairs or downstairs or wherever the operating rooms are in this huge hospital, I was doing, out on the patio of the Waiting Room, what *I* could to manage my sense of powerlessness and fear. A gray feather had wafted down through the air, and, hour after hour, I used it to perform the surgery myself, minus the nick, gently scooping shard after shard of bony tumor out of my palm.

I'd worked hard to get myself ready for that day. Met with Dr. Black to study CT scans that showed a white-hard, walnut-sized tumor directly in the center of Matt's brain. There was no way of knowing, the medical team said, how long it had been there. Maybe it had been growing since Matt was a child. No matter. What mattered was that the last micro-millimeter of growth had begun to press on his optic nerve, turning things from steady-as-you-go quiet to a screaming ruckus. Not only was Matt going blind in one eye, his head was literally splitting open. The first surgery, just to relieve the pressure, had taken place directly from the ER four months earlier. Now it was time to finish the job.

Dr. Black shared with me his plans for the actual procedure: the entry, the fiberoptic cable through which an electricity-powered drill would be strung, allowing him, through a microscope, to see what he was doing as he chipped away at the tumor.

At home, I blew three decades of dust off the *Gray's Anatomy* I'd lugged from one end of the UCONN campus to the other, on my way to yet another meeting with the cadaver I and my fellow physical therapy students were getting to know intimately. Dug out the Human Neuroanatomy book I'd studied, backward and forward, working as a PT at Columbia-Presbyterian Medical Center in Upper Manhattan.

I had already saved Matt's life for real at least three times since the tumor had been discovered. One time, putting a stop to what another hospital was about to do for a diagnosis made in the heat of emergency. As he was being wheeled to the OR, I'd suddenly remembered that that wasn't the problem at all and insisted he be transferred to UCLA where they already knew him from when the tumor was first discovered, years before.

I saw him through that first emergency surgery to relieve the pressure on his brain. Weeks later, rushed him to the hospital when he collapsed from a pulmonary embolism that had reduced his blood pressure to the very edge of what it takes to be alive.

All that, and he and I were still fighting over the same old stuff.

Eyes finally open wide enough to let in the truth, I could see the marriage was over. A marriage needs more than love.

After the final surgery, I stayed on until he recovered enough to take care of himself. And five months after that day in the UCLA waiting room, filed for divorce.

Dr. Black went on to become Chief of Neurosurgery at Cedars-Sinai, which I found out one day while waiting in line at the supermarket; there he was on the cover of *TIME*.

Matt went on to marry Alice, an old friend.

And I went on. To go on. Where there's life, there's going on.

Sometime after 11 PM on the night of the final surgery, with the bleeding stopped and Matt coming back to life in the recovery room, I slipped the feather into my pocket and walked to a falafel stand in Westwood for a late supper. There, on an overhead television, I found out the whole world was about to change.

August 19, 1991. The Soviet Union was falling apart.

Give Us A Hug. Give Us A Kiss

Back upstairs

Dr. Rafi, a kind, red-haired Internal Medicine resident, tells me Mom's sodium has increased from 122 to 125. "Good that it's coming up slowly," he says.

Mom's still confused however, can't understand why the cranberry juice is thinner than the cranberry juice she is used to or why the clock isn't the same one she's always known.

She's still wearing the striped wool sweater she came in with, and someone has wrapped a flowered sarong around her as a skirt. She's a sight for sore eyes, as she might say. Thin slipper socks slip off her feet with each step she takes and the walker's wheels run over them. Which, aside from the aesthetics or comfort of the situation, is just plain unsafe. "Please make sure my mother has her shoes on when she's walking," I tell the nurse.

Bill comes in just as lunch arrives. He hovers over Mom, hoping she'll eat the meal he ordered for her last night. But she's as disinterested in the turkey sandwich and french fries as she was in last night's chicken. "What will be the punishment if I don't eat?" she asks.

She's much more interested in watching one of the patients than she is in eating; can't keep her eyes off him.

"He's crazy in the head," she says, pointing toward him with her chin. "I don't belong here."

Hari, an Indian man, is dressed in crisp khakis and a starched beige and white striped shirt. He has already put four sugars in his coffee, asks for two more. He walks up and down the hall, clapping his hands in time with his steps. On a schedule of his own making and, to make sure he's keeping up, he keeps close watch on the clock.

The day before, I happened on him just as he'd won a game of Solitaire. He was ebullient. Lit up even more when I asked if he'd like to play Gin Rummy. Ready with his own rules, he said we'd play with thirteen cards, then dealt us each seven. Whenever it was his turn to draw from the deck, he would slide two cards off the top, then slide the second one back, but not before getting a peek at the one I would be drawing. He won.

"Give us a hug. Give us a kiss," he repeated in ecstasy. Unable to contain his energy sitting down, he began pacing again. "Give us a hug. Give us a kiss."

We played again. This time, against all odds, I won. His head lowered. His chest drew back. It was as if he was collapsing into himself, his world having fallen apart.

He told me he was an accountant (I wasn't surprised!), that all he ever did was work. Just a quick snack for breakfast and off to work, where he'd stay 'til late at night. Tears pool in his eyes as he tells me his wife wants him to be well. Then, just as quickly, the tears are gone.

Today, he shoots me a smile. He and I have made a connection, as tenuous as that might be, interrupted as it is by his intense need to keep moving.

Mom turns her attention to the chicken soup on her tray. Sucks hunks of watermelon. Then, in protest to no one in particular, slaps a slice of tomato on the turkey inside the sandwich and eats most of half of it, open-faced.

Bill leaves, happy at having participated in keeping our mother alive.

I wait until she's been wrapped in a blanket, like a papoose, for the "quiet time" that comes after lunch, assure her that if she has to get up to go to the bathroom, all she has to do is ask. She's responding well to the every-two-hour bathroom schedule they've put her on, a relief perhaps to have someone else taking on the worry about her bladder.

It's People Like You Who Make People Like Me Crazy

October 2

Bill and I arrive for visiting hours just as Mom is asking to be taken to the bathroom again.

"Pretty soon, no one will believe you," I say, reminding her about the story, "Wolf, Wolf." Before the words are even out of my mouth, I feel ashamed, talking to my mother as if she's a child. Mom says she really does have to urinate, and the aides take her into the bathroom, where she sits on the toilet for fifteen minutes. "Just a few drops," they tell me.

As Bill and I wait in the hallway, a week of pent-up fear and frustration tumbles out of me. "We're going to have to talk about me and Mom," I say.

Bill makes a quarter-turn away, everything becoming hard and lifeless in the lower part of his face. He seems to be watching a scene playing out on the inside of his head, the place he goes to take in what I'm saying, the place from which he can prepare his reaction. It's familiar to me, this turning away, this way of cutting off conversation, one of the many things he and our mother have in common.

He's heard it all before. This need of mine to strike

out, create a life of my own. The outpouring of frustration at not feeling able to do it. Sometimes uttered as a plea, sometimes a threat, sometimes just a weary whine. He's even seen me take action toward what I say I want. Until the initial excitement fizzles, and I fall back into the supposed safety of the familiar — Mom. Cultivated, not always but sometimes, by her expert ways of luring me back.

I see wheels begin to turn, his head the insides of a clock where thoughts tick, tick, tick along predetermined pathways whose purpose is to keep things in line and moving along; all the things *he* feels responsible for, his *own* family *mishegas*. The responsibility, the burden *he's* been carrying for our mother's well-being — and, I suppose, for me, too.

I see the toll it's taken on both of us. His insistence on the strictly practical pitted against my tendency to trust that a commitment to what's-happening-right-now will, somehow, provide. Whatever I do, he can't be happy for me. The kind of things that make me happy — adventures where I place myself out on the edge of the unknown — create extra work and worry for him, and he already feels overburdened.

I appreciate his practicality. Thanks to his management of our mother's finances, Mom is able to pay her own way at The Jewish Home, something she's very proud of. I admire, too, how able he's been to put a good life together for himself. How I wish he could appreciate my talents and skills and the sense of responsibility I bring.

Despite what Mom had told me about the need to devote all her attention to him when our father died, she also needed a man to rely on. At five, he became that man. How confusing it must have been for him. On one hand, a young boy being held close by a mother who had already lost one baby boy. On the other hand, man of the family at five.

When Daddy died, we'd lived in California just two years. To recover from the shock, we moved back to Connecticut to live with Aunt Doris and Uncle Joe. Where there'd been the lively, on-the-edge instability of our father, now there was the buttoned-upness of Uncle Joe for Bill to fashion himself after. Uncle Joe was all business.

At eight or nine, Bill began delivering *The Norwalk Hour* to people's front doors. When The Treadway Inn came to town and opened up right across the street from where we now lived in our own apartment on East Avenue — motels were new in Connecticut and a big deal — Bill landed the job of delivering multiple copies of the newspaper for the Inn's guests. In a picture of him on the front page of the paper, he's standing in front of The Inn wearing a hat with ear flaps, a winter jacket with a mouton collar, a serious look on his face, a heavy newsbag over his shoulder; that photograph documenting the beginning of a successful, lifelong career as a businessman.

During his 28 years at General Electric, hundreds of millions of dollars, based on his financial analyses, had been invested in companies whose profits would line the pockets of GE's pension fund. My on-again, off-again work life confounds him. "What makes you think you'd be able to work in Santa Fe?" he asks when I tell I'm thinking of moving there and taking Mom with me.

To tell you the truth, it confounds me, too, though I seem to have little control over it, intent as I am to follow my nature, which has included moving from profession to profession. Given the times and the culture I grew up in — '40s and '50s America — it's likely, too, I was groomed to believe, that as a woman, a Jewish woman, a Jewish woman in my particular family, either Bill *or* I, not both of us, were born to be financially successful. A belief, if true, that's left us, each in our own way, impoverished.

Maybe too, I'd dedicated my own life's work to completing our father's job of finding himself. Not something Bill would understand. He hardly remembers our father. While, for better and worse, I'd had the time, by nine, to find common ground with him.

During the summer after his second year at NYU, Irving hitchhiked to Los Angeles, selling those strung-together wooden puppets that come all folded over until you hold them up, release them, and they begin to dance. He returned to Connecticut, spending the next many years working in the family store. Until finally, married to Hannah and father to two children, it was time to tear himself away from his own mother, return to sunny California and the soil in which he believed he could grow. Two years later, he died. I don't believe the truck in the driveway of our Long Beach home, filled with automobile parts he would sell to gas stations, was the long-time dream he had in mind.

Irving was a romantic who wrote love songs to Mom for her to play on the piano; an excitable man who argued with her over how much money she spent on plasticized paper for the kitchen shelves. Like all the other Bragins, he had grown up working in the family's dry goods store, first in Brooklyn and then in Old Greenwich, where his older sister, Esther, would unroll oilcloth from rolls that hung on the wall and measure it out on a long, low table. Who needs expensive plasticized shelf paper when you had grown up surrounded by unlimited supplies of oilcloth?

"I certainly can't work here," I say. "The only reason I've stayed here, since Mom moved to LA, is to be close to her. She takes up all my time and energy." The two of them had followed me to California from Connecticut a few years after I met Matt and decided to stay. Now that

I no longer had a marriage to hold me in place, I was, at least on paper, free to fly.

"That's not why you don't work," he says. Implying what? That I'm lazy? That I don't like work? That I need to be close to Mom? Well ... maybe.

As much as I may understand what's behind my brother's judgments of me, as much as I've learned, for the most part, to breathe through them, as much as I realize there may be more than a little truth in what he's saying, I feel my teeth clenching, the meaty masseter muscles in my cheeks pulsing, anger breaking through. My voice rises. I'm losing it.

But not so completely that I don't see the dark humor in the situation. Here, outside a large, darkened hospital Day Room, where twenty or thirty people in various states of dress and undress are just waking from a nap, sit the adult son and daughter of an old Jewish woman who can't stay out of the bathroom. He, staring straight ahead, eyes turned to slits; she, almost panting with rage. Brother and sister, having an increasingly loud knock-down, drag-out fight in the hallway of a psychiatric ward.

How do I let him do this to me? How do I let myself get so out of control? Embarrassment fills me, bordering on shame.

And then ...

I wish someone *would* see us. Pay attention to all this

pain. Not ask us to leave, as happened once in another hospital when he and I had gotten into it. It was during one of Mom's bouts with pneumonia. She was in the ICU being kept alive by a breathing tube, when a nurse told us we'd have to go if we couldn't be more quiet.

I wish someone would be sensitive enough to see all the family history, all the cultural chains caked with rust that keep us stuck. Maybe if someone would care enough to help, the love we have always had for each other might find a way to flow.

"Part of it is that you don't ever acknowledge me for what I do with Mom," I say.

"You always want a thank you," he says. As if I'm wrong for wanting it.

"Not even a word when you returned from Hawaii, not even a, 'Wow, Sara, you've certainly been under the gun ...'"

"I would've done the same thing if I'd been here," he shoots back.

"But you weren't here. I was. And when you do things for Mom, you have an office and a job and a salary waiting for you."

I don't say, "And a home. Lynn to cook you dinner." I don't say how hard it is not to have a home of my own, unable to manage the costs, working, as I am, for no money.

I don't say what else I'm thinking. That he *wouldn't*

have done the same thing. Busy at work, he wouldn't have put in full days at The Jewish Home. Wouldn't have been there for the minute-by-minute unfolding of this latest crisis. On Friday night, when Mom was in the Emergency Room doing her best to prove her sanity, he would have been home, sitting down with Lynn to a Sabbath dinner, the lilies he'd stopped to pick up on the way home in a vase on the table.

Yes, he would have met us at the hospital once the situation had developed into full-blown emergency. And, yes, he would have stayed all night — he's a good son. But he wouldn't have managed the chaos in the ER the way I was able to. Wouldn't have said "no" to the contrast CT scan which would have left Mom's kidneys further stressed by injected dye.

To every one of our mother's hospitalizations over the past two years, I've brought my strong medical background, been the one to work with doctors to manage her care. For all this, he's never said thank you.

"Yes," I say. "I do believe in acknowledging people for what they do."

My throat is even tighter now. I'm having trouble breathing. My voice is about as unattractive as a voice can get, thin and loud at the same time. Hot tears begin to spill over the rims of my eyes.

"Keep it up," he says, "and you'll get yourself admitted here."

"*It's people like you who make people like me crazy.*" I want to say it. But I don't.

Mom is wheeled past us into the room where she'll eat — or, more likely, won't eat — her dinner. I stop her in the doorway to get and give a kiss. She gives me that look I'm familiar with that says she can feel the strain in the air around Bill and me.

All of our lives, she has pushed Bill and me to love each other. "It's what I want more than anything," she says. Yet, in some way that I am flailing around to bring into focus, she has played a key role in keeping us apart. Is it the way she removes herself from arguments, claiming that all she wants is to keep peace? Funny how there has always been war around her. Has the tension between Bill and me given her a reason for being? And now, is it this tension, not our ministrations, that's keeping her alive?

"I know you have to leave," she says gently. For the moment, she is the only sane one among us.

I stand in front of the unit's locked door, wait to be buzzed out. Down the elevator and all the way to my car, I am crying. Whimpering really.

Do You Know How To Get To Where You're Going?

October 3

"Do you know how to get to where you're going?" the UCLA parking attendant asked me this morning as I handed him the last seven dollars in my wallet. There hasn't been even one extra minute this week to get to an ATM for a fresh supply of cash.

Driving slowly, I follow a woman walking to her car. "If you can wait, I'm the Jaguar," she calls to me. I remember a Los Angeles before you had to wait for someone to leave a spot so you could pull in. It was the '70s and I'd just come from New York City, looking forward to not having to plan my life around alternate-side-of-the-street parking.

"Where *am* I going?"

I arrive on the ward at the end of a court hearing to determine whether Mom's condition warrants keeping her here longer, even against her will. I stand on the outside of the locked door, looking in through a small, high window, hear my mother talking coherently about wanting to go back to The Jewish Home as soon as there is an opening for her. I bristle when I hear the psychiatric resident refer to my mother, as if she isn't there, as "demented."

Is it because UCLA is a teaching hospital that it's okay to treat a patient in a way you wouldn't want your own mother treated? Is insensitivity to be tolerated as long as a patient is very old?

No matter that this 92-year-old woman is fragile and confused, recovering from the mind-altering effects of a diuretic she was given by her well-meaning physician.

No matter that the diuretic had left her whole body parched and that anxiety over feeling her life being threatened made it impossible for her to stop calling for water. Let's not forget that all that water had diluted her blood, lowering its level of sodium and that low sodium itself can cause confusion, even delirium. Let's not forget either that the psychiatric resident who is calling my mother "demented" has only known her for a few days — and under extreme conditions. Where she's not only medically compromised but having to adjust to life on a psych ward. And the urinary tract infection! I wonder: has this doctor ever had a urinary tract infection and knew, just knew, she had to keep flushing her system with water? Have you?

Can you imagine being an old lady sitting in a locked room surrounded by people the age your grandchildren would be, if you had grandchildren, calling you demented?

I get someone to unlock the door, let me in.

I reassure Mom that yes, it's okay to stay here a few more days until her condition resolves itself. I remind her, too — and I want everyone in the room to hear it — that she is becoming more clear-headed every day.

Court hearing over, I am let off the ward, through a series of three locked doors, to a tiny social work office for a Family Meeting arranged by a social worker named Dara. Bill, who is at his office a few miles away, is patched in by phone.

The resident tells us what I already know (I've been following this hospitalization like a hawk), that they're considering starting Mom on Zyprexa to relieve her long-standing anxiety. "It's a drug we use to treat psychosis," she says. Then quickly, to reassure me, "We're not saying your mother is psychotic." Well, that's a relief!

Mom arrives in a wheelchair. The occupational therapist says how much better Mom's been doing, that she is no longer "combative." What I have been calling "adamant," they call "combative." What ways, I ask you, does an old, frail, confused, even sometimes delirious woman have left to express herself? What would you call the behavior if it was your mother we were talking about?

My mother says the OT is "terrific." She likes the activities she plans. I don't think I've ever before heard my mother use the word "terrific."

Juana, my mother's nurse, is a woman with skin the color of café au lait, who spends a lot of time in the nurses' station doing her lips. Dark liner. Light lipstick. Gloss, lots of gloss. Today, she is wearing a tan spandex jumpsuit, sleeveless, with a low neckline, bell-bottom pants and a wide leather belt with fringes low on the hips. A far cry from what I wore as a physical therapist in the '60s in another teaching hospital: the white uniform that would come back from the hospital laundry with so much starch it could stand up by itself; white oxfords, white support hose.

Juana is quick to offer excuses when I ask why my mother rarely has her shoes on, her dentures or hearing aid in, even by the beginning of evening visiting hours. I didn't think it would be as necessary at UCLA to blow whistles. But there are whistles that need to be blown. Or is the problem how clearly I see things?

Meeting over, I tell the social worker I want to stay and talk with her. It takes only a minute for my tears to start. I tell her how it's been at The Jewish Home. How, if I'm not watching, and even when I am, things often degrade to the level of emergency before they've caught anyone's attention.

I tell her about the past two years of emergency hospitalizations. "'She's always so anxious,' nurses and aides say, shaking their heads side-to-side as if my mother is to blame. They give her medications to sedate her before taking the time to find out what's wrong. Could what's wrong be those very medications? That those very medications are causing the agitation?"

I tell her how painful it is not to be acknowledged by my brother for what I do, not to be understood when I tell him Mom is my work.

I tell her how, at four in the morning, after my mother was finally wheeled from the ER onto the Geriatric Psych Ward, I couldn't find a place to stay, finally sleeping in my car on a residential street in The Valley.

I realize I'm throwing caution to the wind. UCLA's Neuropsychiatric Institute could be the very worst place for me — a licensed psychotherapist — to be so honest about what sounds like, and may actually be, a precarious living situation. But Dara is respectful, says she understands how much has been required of me. Too much, in fact, and for too long. Focusing only on what I said about The Jewish Home, she suggests I look around for other living situations for my mother, says she will call me with a list of possibilities. Though moving from The Jewish Home would hardly solve the problem at its heart, it's a relief to have let down my guard, fall apart, let someone see the chaos inside.

Am I so different from anyone else, I wonder through a haze of shame? Do we ever know what's really going on inside another person, the stresses and strains we cover up with shows of competency? "Be kind," the ancient philosopher Philo of Alexandria is reputed to have said.

"Everyone you meet is fighting a fierce battle."

I leave the hospital and drive to Sycamore Cove, way out beyond Malibu on the Pacific Coast Highway. The ocean laps gently as I sit on sand warmed by the sun. To my left, a large black bird lies dead, ragged in the sand; a cormorant or dark gull. To my right, sits a woman in a red canvas chair, her legs crossed, doing the New York Times Sunday crossword puzzle. Behind us, the edge of a mountain gives form to a clear blue sky. Infused by all I see and feel, I hear again the parking attendant's question. Do you know how to get to where you're going?

What I *do* know is this: I'm doing my best, day by day, to be who and where I am. To be true to the world as it shows up in all its crazy — and sometimes quite wonderful — happenings, its sights and sounds and tastes and smells. To be open to love wherever I find it, offer it wherever it might do some good and, when I get lost in worrisome thoughts, remember to come home to here.

Here, where each hair on my arm is standing up to a cold gust blowing off the ocean. Here, where I can lean back into the steady support of the mountain behind me. Here, where the reality of death presents itself in the decaying bird and the joy of ordinary living in the woman still engrossed in her puzzle. As I have been engrossed in mine.

Here, too, in the growing confidence that, as long as

I continue to muster as much consciousness as I can to what's actually happening, the time I'm spending with Mom is time well spent.

"Do I know how to get to where I'm going?" Ask me something easy!

Zyprexa!

October 4

I'm told that Zyprexa has indeed been ordered. Not knowing what else to say, and as if I have any choice in the matter, I say yes. But who will be watching my mother to see whether its well-known side effects appear? Worse, get out-of-hand?

Dizziness. Sedation. Weight gain. A life-threatening high temperature. Pulling of the head to one side. Hypertonia, as in Parkinson's Disease. The jerky, repetitive movements of tardive dyskinesia often suffered by schizophrenics.

All of these are bad enough in a young schizophrenic. What might they mean in an already fragile old woman?

Overdose can cause tachycardia, agitation, dysarthria, decreased consciousness and coma.

The resident tells me Mom will also be put back on

a low dose of Remeron, the antidepressant Dr. Smith discontinued when he thought it was causing the confusion that got Mom admitted here in the first place. With Mom so on-the-edge, I don't dare to imagine what the effects of a glass of seltzer might be on her body, let alone a mixed drink: Zyprexa mixed with Remeron.

Years later, in the Age of Wikipedia, I read that the half-life of Zyprexa — the time it takes for one-half of its effect to vacate a *young* person's system — is 33 hours; in an elderly person, 51.8. In 2004, the Committee on the Safety of Medicines in the U.K. issued a warning that Zyprexa should not be given to elderly patients with dementia and, in the U.S., it comes with a black-box warning for increased risk of death in the elderly, advice that, according to a BBC investigation four years later, was widely ignored by British doctors. Originally manufactured and marketed by Eli Lilly for treating schizophrenia and bipolar disorder, Zyprexa sales in 2008 were $2.2 billion in the U.S., $4.7 billion worldwide.

I'm tired. The joints in my hands and in the rest of me, too, are stiff, painful. When will I have a bed of my own again? I have no energy, or time, to do the simple things that are on my to-do list — pick up groceries, return a phone call. It's enough to be going to the hospital to keep an eye on Mom, shoring myself up afterward. Then, there's my brother.

I don't anticipate any relief. When Mom returns to The Jewish Home, I will have to oversee what goes on there, too. What does "skilled nursing" mean, anyway? What can you expect for six-thousand dollars a month?

Obsessed with wanting my mother to be well taken care of, I've transferred my long-term need to take care of myself to making sure that Mom's urgent needs are met. Could I have done anything differently? What if I didn't spend so much time attending to her day-to-day needs and only appeared for the more dramatic emergencies? What's more dramatic than staying alert for the effects of Zyprexa?

What would my life be about if I didn't attend to Mom in the moment-to-moment way I feel called to do? But wait! Is this any more than an exaggeration of how it's always been with us?

After graduating from college and moving to New York City to work as a physical therapist, every other weekend I'd take the subway to Grand Central and the train to Connecticut to make sure she was okay. I don't remember exactly what okay meant. It had somehow become my job to keep my mother alive — ward off her depressive ways, anxiety, unresolved grief. Did I apply? Was I recruited? Was I the stand-in for *her* mother, Sarah, for whom I'm named, and who, at the time Hannah was born, was grieving a loss. One day, in the kitchen of their

Bronx apartment, Sarah's young son, Samuel, pulled a pot of boiling water off the gas stove, was scalded over a good part of his body and died.

Was I still in the crib when I was offered the job of breathing life into my mother, my only qualification the fact that I'd been born *alive* two years after she'd given birth to a stillborn boy?

Did I inherit the job? To soothe, with my presence, the nerves of a woman whose husband had died without warning, as she sat in the ambulance next to him, leaving her with two young children to raise alone?

When the coast was otherwise clear, there was always the congenital deformity in her right foot to worry about, how one foot would brush against the other with every step she took.

More than once, after a particularly difficult visit with Mom, I'd leave The Jewish Home, run to my car, make sure the windows were rolled up, and scream.

"When will I be able to live *my* life?"

One day, a window opened. Resentment flew out. Love flew in. And I heard a voice, my own voice, say, "This *is* my life." Daily turmoil had worn down the edges of anger and self-pity the way rough stones are turned into gems in a jeweler's tumbling machine.

If I had continued to believe there was someplace more important to be, something more important to do,

I would have missed the living in my mother's dying. Still, it's hard not to be waiting for the other shoe to drop. A fall. Another pneumonia or urinary tract infection. The on-again, off-again confusion that comes when her body is out of balance. Now, with Zyprexa, a whole closetful of shoes could come tumbling down.

Is this just how it is with old people? Very old people? My mother?

Santa Fe, with its green mountains and red mesas, had been the perfect landscape to play out the fantasy that I was free of the burden of being my mother's caregiver, free of the task of finishing my father's job for him. Free to step out of the noisy world of the Bragins and the too-quiet world of the Wittenbergs into the circle of my own life. "To deconstruct a life and reconstruct it takes everything you've got," I heard someone say.

Under a sky that seemed to go on forever, ideas for creative projects had bubbled up like the Old Faithful I'd seen when I was eight and we'd driven cross country, Daddy's attempt to leave behind the too-close connection he felt with his own mother and find *his* life.

As hard as it is now, while Mom is still alive and the need for taking care of her is greater than ever, I have a funny feeling that I'm finally growing up. That it's time to find a good place to live. Buy a bed of my own.

Nothing To Do But Live Each Moment

October 5

Mom's hand is trembling in a way I haven't seen before. She's having trouble getting the salmon up onto her fork, is bringing empty forkfuls to her mouth. Is this a side effect of the new medication? Has her sodium level dipped lower again, blurring her contact with reality?

She talks to me, eyes closed.

"Mom, your eyes are closed. Are you tired?"

"Very tired," she says, "I want to lie down for a nap. I didn't think I was going to make it to lunch. Take me home so I can sleep in my own bed."

"You're not well enough yet," I say, so softly there's little chance she can hear me.

"I see your hand is shaking."

"My hand is shaking," she says.

"Is that something new?" I ask.

"Of course it's new," she says, energized by indignation. "It's never happened before."

I am enthralled with my mother at times like this, when she knows clearly, and states clearly, something about herself. I'm grateful that, at 92, she is fighting for her own reality. During much of her earlier life when, seemingly, not as much was at stake, she'd often act wishy-washy, unwilling or unable to take a stand. "I don't know," she would sing-song, refusing to offer a definitive "yes" or "no."

I've seen my mother become assertive in her old age. As if feminism, and the understanding that a woman can have an opinion of her own, had just caught up with her. No matter that she'd seen to the raising of two children alone.

Many people don't realize this about her — her power, her presence. When she doesn't appear to be listening, people assume she's not paying attention. I have been guilty of thinking this myself. When her attention is focused on something that's bothering her, something she's working out inside herself, people may wonder whether she's really there. Then, boom, she wows you with a flash of clarity.

In the darkened Day Room, people are watching *The Sound of Music.* It's the part where Baron von Trapp is trying to convince the Nazi functionary to let the family sing one last time. Their escape has been planned and singing is part of it.

Eyes still closed, Mom has somehow seen me arrive. "It's almost over," she says. Is it her life she's talking about? The movie? Julie Andrews looks over to Christopher Plummer as if to say, "Let's get the hell out of here."

The dinners arrive, and a nurse, in a quick one-two punch, turns off the tv, turns on the lights. "It's almost over," my mother says again.

I'm ashamed at how human beings treat other human beings — the nurse, with no warning, turning off the movie just as the von Trapp family is about to escape from the clutches of the Nazi occupation of Austria. I feel rage, even, that she doesn't explain to these patients — psychiatric patients, people who are trying to make sense of their lives — what she is going to do. They have invested their afternoon, after all, and maybe even their daily allotment of real feelings, in the possibility of freedom. Then poof, it's gone.

Before I can drape a towel around her neck, another across her lap, my mother, ravenous, begins to dig into the vegetable soup. I see the spoon heading toward her nose. Which scares me even more than when I would sit and watch, day after day for three weeks in the ICU of another hospital, the coming and going of air in the breathing tube that was keeping her alive.

Now, hunched over more than usual, eyes closed, hand shaking, life has come down to one spoon of vegetable soup after another, most of which ends up on a towel.

I take the spoon out of her hand and slowly feed her the rest of the soup myself. Each swallow takes an inordinate amount of time. She used to talk about "jumping out of her skin." I am jumping out of my skin.

With her fingers, she picks the cheese off a slice of pizza and chews and chews on it. Drinks down the bright yellow Gatorade she's being given to up her sodium.

It's the weekend and no doctors will be here until tomorrow. Even then, they won't be the same doctors who followed her during the week. At The Jewish Home, and even here at UCLA, mistakes get made. I offer the only continuity and I'm worried about what I'm seeing.

In the four years that my mother has been living at The Jewish Home, but especially in the last two when she has needed to be in a skilled nursing area — "sniff," the hospital people call it — I have been fighting an uphill battle to get for my mother the full attention of people whose job it is to take care of her.

It's a daunting task. Is it that new medications and heroic procedures have made it possible for people like my mother to live too long? Does having to look into the face of old, old age make people whose job it is to take care of old people blank out, doze off, go through the motions?

Maria, a kind blonde woman with a Spanish accent, tells Mom she will be taking care of her tonight, getting her ready for bed. Maybe most people here *are* kind; sleepwalkers, the exception. Still, all it takes is one mistake.

"I have to brush my teeth."

"I'll help you brush your teeth," Maria says.

Mom opens her eyes, smiles at Maria.

I slip out, grateful for Maria's kindness. Still with a heavy heart, wondering if I've left my mother thinking that she *will* be sleeping in her own bed tonight, failing her in the way the nurse did who came in and flipped on the lights. I want to help my mother escape from the ravages of old age and the institutions set up to house them, want to help her escape all the way to freedom.

Perhaps there will be another chance for us to see the von Trapps singing, as they walk hand in hand in the Austrian Alps, over lush hillsides dotted with the friendly faces of Edelweiss. Perhaps there will be a moment for each of us, sometime during our life or at the moment of our death, when we will come to the end of whatever dominates *us*. And we, too, will be able to walk happily and surely into freedom.

More Moments

October 6

It's a cool, clear morning. Ginger and I are sitting in her garden. She reads me a poem from Mary Oliver's *New and Selected Poems*, a book I carry with me when I travel.

... *when death comes/like an iceberg between the shoulder blades* ... "I like that line," Ginger says. "This one, too."

... *When it's over, I want to say: all my life/I was a bride married to amazement.*

"It reminds me of you, Sara. You're married to amazement."

I feel deeply seen. Then, suddenly, the sharp, cold edge of an iceberg, as it travels unerringly to that place between my shoulder blades, a sudden sense of knowing that my mother has entered her dying.

I tell Ginger what happened last night. How the nurse, with no warning at all, turned off the tv.

"It's what we do with children," Ginger says. " When it's time for dinner, no matter that the child was in rapt attention to a cartoon." Together, she and her husband, Bob, have raised five children.

Ginger and I talk about how children and old people have no control over their lives. How we, for the few years in between, think we do.

At the same time Mom has been getting better physically, she has also been profoundly depressed, keeping her eyes closed unless I ask her to open them. She has had no appetite except for that time she was ravenous and couldn't tell the difference between her mouth and her nose.

"It's over, Sara," she tells me. "I've been listening to my heart. The beat gets slower, and slower, and slower until it almost disappears."

I tell her I was at Costco, bought her a navy-blue fleece jacket, the kind she's been wanting.

"You wasted your money," she says.

"Mom, I know it feels like you're dying, but I'm pretty sure you're still going to have a chance to wear it."

"I hope you're right," she says.

I bring a spoonful of soup to her mouth, ask her to open her eyes. She strains the soup with her teeth, spitting out kernels of corn and small chunks of meat. Refuses the spaghetti, eats a few bites of garlic bread, drinks two cups of apple juice.

"Look who's here, Mom."

Her eyes light up as she sees Bill and Lynn. Still the gracious hostess, she thanks them for coming, accepts the package of graham crackers Lynn takes out of her purse, and slowly eats one. She is happy to hear the news that Lynn's mother, in Florida, is more able to accept her macular degeneration now that her pain from arthritis has been relieved.

When I leave for the evening, Mom is standing up surprisingly straight, her hands on the bedrails, as Jorge, the extremely handsome aide who has attended to her for a few nights now, applies a protective dressing to the redness at the base of her spine. I'm relieved to see that the pressure sore is healing from the inside out.

Life As A Verb

October 7

This interests me, this idea of healing from the inside out. For Mom, it started with someone paying attention. Which led to a lessening of pressure from the outside, allowing dead and defending tissue to soften, give way to the new.

This morning, Jasmine, a tall, skinny, middle-aged yoga teacher from England, shed the light of *her* attention on a bunching at my hip I was totally unaware of. She saw it. She touched it. I felt the touch. And the bunching let go. Later, she directed my attention to an unevenness in the way my feet were connecting with the ground. Muscles and ligaments and bones had somehow — and at some time in my life — begun to function in a way that was pulling me out of balance, causing me to approach the world in a crooked way. The gift of her attention opened a new door through which I could walk, helping me to see habitual ways of thinking and acting and feeling that have, until now, been so "natural" to me I couldn't see them. Might they fade away in the light, allowing for new possibilities?

Still in my yoga clothes — black t-shirt, black tights worn thin from too many washings, silver Birkenstocks and my usual no-undies— I come to visit Mom.

"*This* is how you walk around one of the world's largest cities," I say to myself, a little more sure of its complimentary meaning than if Mom had said it, giving it the confusing spin I'd grown up with. "This is how you walk around one of the world's largest cities ... ?" Never knowing if the question mark at the end implied a negative judgment or was an exclamation of wonder.

Diana, who was a psychologist in Peru and, here, is an aide, has dark, shining eyes and a sincere smile. "You're getting thin," she tells me.

"It happens whenever I do yoga," I say. "I come away

thinner."

I know what she's trying to say. It's not just that I look thin. After an hour-and-a-half of paying close attention to the insides and outsides of my bodily being, I'm here, really here. People are attracted to that.

If my arms feel like dead-weight, which they often do, a few moments of bringing my attention to them fills them with just the right amount of lightness. If I'm slumping — and I recognize that I'm slumping — breath comes to fill my chest, sitting me up straight. If I can feel the ground under my feet, my walking may not be exactly like a model on the runway, but it is like a 62-year-old woman who appreciates being able to walk.

On my way into the hospital, I saw a man, in a suit, propelling himself in a battery-operated wheelchair. Seeing him gave me a chance to remember how grateful I am for being able to maneuver the sidewalks and curbs of Los Angeles on my two feet. Grateful that I am able to hike in the mountains, slip and slide and hardly ever fall as I find my way down paths made more for goats than humans.

During the last years with Matt and the years recovering from the divorce, I was reluctant to be seen. I collected a closetful of clothes loose and black: slacks with elastic at the waist, tunic-length tops to cover the roll of fat that had developed around my middle.

Now when I wear black, it still sometimes means

I'm in hiding. But when I'm able to climb outside of old thoughts and feel, from the inside, the precise way my body moves, I'm willing to be seen, willing to be known.

Wanting solitude amidst company, I take a break and return to the patio of the Surgery Waiting Room. Feel the sun beating down on my head, sweat dripping down my cheeks. I watch an ant climb the white wall that separates this patio from the hospital building itself. Watch as the ant wanders — to my eye, aimlessly — before disappearing into ivy.

Ants, ivy, sweat — what difference can it possibly make to be paying attention?

A bird doesn't sing because it has an answer. It sings because it has a song.

This is my song — putting into words the simple things I see and hear. Feeling inside the dark of my own body the way green leaves tremble on the lowest branch of the bush that rises up out of the ivy. Feeling the effect on me of the force we call wind.

I feel a burst of gratitude to be able to hear the hum of the conversation behind me; individual words, full sentences if I listen carefully. I think about the hearing aid my mother wears in her right ear, how she is almost totally deaf in her left.

I am grateful, too, for all the teachers who have helped me to know the wonders of the ordinary world. Charlotte Selver who, at 101, sits in a wheelchair at the front of the class where, for seventy years, she has been leading people to the soothing well of the practice she calls Sensory Awareness. Such simple things she asks us to do — come from sitting to lying, lying to standing. "Are you there for it?" she asks. Charlotte claps her hands, we jump to standing. Claps again and we lie down. It takes some of us a long time to respond. Instead of simply living, we go through the motions. As if we need to think about it, listen for some inner voice to tell us what to do. Rather than meeting, with the whole being we are, what's being asked of us this very moment.

What if we *could* be new in each moment — in each encounter with a friend. with the wind, with an ant wandering along the top of a wall.

What if I *could* see each moment with my mother as fresh and new? Precious, no matter how painful. Life as a verb.

"Never a dull moment," Charlotte says.

To Be The Daughter Of A Mother Is Complicated

October 8

Long after the dinner dishes have been cleared, three women sit around a kitchen table in Los Angeles talking about mothers. Ginger, who lives here. Laura, a friend who has been staying in an extra bedroom upstairs. And me.

Laura's mother died over the weekend after being diagnosed two years earlier with small cell lung cancer. The doctors had given her two years to live and the two years were almost over. Laura had flown down from Vancouver a few days earlier with Bert, her small parrot, in a cat carrier. When the flight attendant wasn't looking, Laura took him out, and he flew the rest of the way under her coat, perched warm against her chest.

"Mom died suddenly," Laura says, "after being ravaged for two years by the disease."

"A year ago," says Ginger, "my mother decided not to go through with the surgery that would have replaced, yet again, the shunt that allows for dialysis to happen. I had to hold back the almost unbearable urge to say, 'You can't do this, Mom. You have to live.' Soon, the hospice nurses came in and, day after day, I sat in my mother's bedroom and knit. Knit and tore. Knit and tore. Not knitting anything in particular, just knitting. I'd like to knit again, but I'm not ready. Whatever I was gathering together and tearing apart isn't finished."

Ginger quelled her anxiety by knitting, while her mother, she tells us, said "yes" to all the Ativan she was offered.

I know about Ativan. For many years, my own mother has seen it as an always available friend, today's "phenobarb." Once, it landed her in the hospital where she needed a respirator to bring her back to life. In addition to quelling anxiety, Ativan can suppress breathing.

Ginger's mother, in her last days, would tell Ginger how much she loved her. Unable to believe her mother really knew her, Ginger couldn't bring herself to say the words her mother wanted to hear. Couldn't say, "Mom, I love you, too."

"Mom was the baby of her family," Ginger tells us. "The object of everyone's love. That's how it was in her marriage, too, until, with the help of alcohol, her husband started going crazy over other women. When Mom was dying and began to see Jesus, I wondered if she was seeing herself as a beloved baby again, who would soon be in the arms of a man who loved her for eternity."

I'd dropped my purse and writing notebook on the chair outside the downstairs guest room to join Ginger and Laura at the kitchen table. Set my bag of groceries next to me and showed them what I'd bought: one crisp pickling cucumber; one baking potato wrapped in tight plastic whose instructions promise it will taste like an oven-baked potato after three minutes in the microwave; three Bosc pears; two bananas. And a bag of fancy jelly beans I'd practically finished off, by the handful, in the car — caramel corn, sizzling cinnamon, cappuccino and coconut. My knitting, *my* Ativan, *my* Bert the Parrot.

I tell them that, every year on my birthday, I send my mother a card thanking her for giving birth to me. Tell them about the recording I made for her one Mother's Day, to express my love. And that, after tonight's conversation with them, I feel ready to let her off the hook, ready to accept that, when she tells me she loves me, it's really me she's talking about. That I am, at least, a central vignette in the frame of her love, a frame in which we also find me as a reflection of her; and a substitute, if imperfect, for her own mother, the mother she still yearns for.

My Daughter. Isn't She Beautiful?

October 9

The kitchen has finally gotten it right, Mom's lunch has arrived as ordered. Hungry, she starts on the grapes. Squeezes out the juice between her teeth, spits the skins into her hand and deposits them onto the plate. I cut the cantaloupe and honeydew into small chunks she picks up with hands made shaky by the new medication. She has a few coughing spells, her face turns red. By the end of the meal, she is breathing hard, wheezing. Heaving, to use her word. Deep in her throat, I hear gurgling.

A nurse comes into the Day Room to draw the curtains, turn off the lights for a nap. Mom needs medical attention. I help her walk into the dining room.

One doctor, and then another, listens to her chest. They decide to get her into bed, give her Lasix, intravenously, to quickly draw out the fluid they think has collected in her lungs. I'm wary, Lasix being one of the drugs responsible for getting her here in the first place.

When I hear that her blood pressure is 230 over 113, I sit down and begin to breathe very quietly myself, as if I can translate my own calmness over to her, as if even the slightest move on my part could explode a blood vessel in her brain, setting off a stroke.

Doctors and nurses hover around, hook her up to oxygen, stick leads under and on top of her breasts for an EKG, place a glob of nitroglycerine paste over her heart. An attending physician arrives. I tell the story again of what I saw when she was eating. The doctors decide to move her to a medical floor. I am relieved that she will be leaving the psychiatric ward.

A doctor arrives from the floor where she will be going. Given his interest, I feel safe to tell him about the worrying side effects of the antipsychotic drug: her sudden dark depression, the tremor in her hands; even a tremor in her speaking voice which, I imagine, may also be affecting her swallowing muscles and may have caused her to breathe in the food she was eating.

She coughs; he points to bits of orange in the mucus. Carrots, cantaloupe. He agrees she may have aspirated food at lunch, that what we're seeing could be the start of an aspiration pneumonia.

"Take care of yourself," I hear my mother say. With all this attention she's receiving, my guess is that she imagines she's dying. "Don't worry about me. I'm an old lady. I've lived a good life. I love you."

"I love you, too, Mom."

A few moments of silence and then, "It's no use, Sara."

"I don't think you're dying, Mom. But, if you are, can you think of a better way to go than with love on your lips?"

"You're right," she says.

A few minutes later — she hasn't yet begun to urinate from the Lasix, and her breathing is still labored — she begins to speak again.

"Dahling," she says, in that Bronx accent that seems to be getting more pronounced, "did you eat?"

Alice and another nurse, who have been checking her vital signs as they get her ready to leave for the medical floor, stop what they're doing. The three of us look at each other, look at her. The tension that has been building is broken.

"Can you imagine," I say to them, "if those should prove to be the last words my mother says to me? 'Dahling, did you eat?'"

"Shows what a good mother she is."

"A Jewish mother," I say; then, not very gracefully, try to take my words back. I meant them to be humorous. But Alice has a mother, too; maybe a Protestant or Catholic mother. Wouldn't she also want to make sure, if she was about to die, that her child had eaten? And the other nurse, dark-skinned and dark-eyed, from Thailand or Vietnam, doesn't she also have a mother who would have wanted *her* to eat?

The three of us have been given this delicious moment, amidst high twentieth century, big city, medical center drama, to celebrate mothers, daughters, love.

On 5 West, Mom is placed in the far bed, next to the window. In the other bed lies a woman half of whose head is shaved, post-cranial surgery. Someone comes to draw blood to determine whether Mom had a heart attack. Sent on a journey to the bowels of the medical center, she is passed through the white tunnel of an MRI machine, which will let us know if she had a stroke. A kind doctor whose name on her business card is Sue — a doctor with a business card, I like that, and she's not Susan but Sue — listens carefully to what both my mother and I have to tell her, a refreshing experience from how it's been on the psych ward.

Breathing easily now, Mom, her cheeks pink from oxygen, looks straight at me and says, "You're finding all this very interesting, aren't you?" She means all the medical stuff. There is admiration in her voice for a daughter she is just now coming to know — or is finally able to know. A daughter she is, at last, willing to depend on, trust with her life.

"I know you," she says.

During my senior year in high school, I'd announced that I wanted to be a doctor. "Be a nurse," said Uncle Joe. We were all indebted to Uncle Joe. Uncle Joe and Aunt

Doris who, with no children of their own, had been willing to take us in after Daddy died, until Mom could find a way to support us.

"No," I said, asserting my independence as much as I felt I could in those days — the year was 1957 — "I won't be a nurse." I didn't become a doctor. I became a physical therapist, and, though I only worked at it for six years, I've made good use my whole life of the medical knowledge and experience physical therapy offered. Ten years earlier, there'd been Matt's two brain surgeries and, in between, his near dying from a pulmonary embolism. Over the last two years, Mom's close calls and hospitalizations.

I didn't know she'd been watching. Didn't know she knew.

That evening, Mom says she'd like some ice cream. Though there are orders that she not be given food until tomorrow, when a speech therapist can come to assess her ability to swallow, I ask Sue, who is still in the nurses' station writing notes, for her okay. I tell her I'll be very careful. I feed Mom small spoonfuls of strawberry and vanilla ice cream, waiting each time for it to melt on her tongue and slip down as easily as cream. When she is thirsty, I feed her ice chips, a few at a time.

"What would today have been like if you hadn't been here?" Mom says, shaking her head back and forth, that gesture again. Amazement? Appreciation? Who is this stranger who says she belongs to me? Can it be that this competent woman is my daughter?

"This is my daughter," my mother says to Rashmi, the Indian woman who will sit with her through the night. "Just look at her, isn't she beautiful?"

Rashmi isn't paying attention. She's involved in the conversation she is having with another aide about second jobs available at UCLA. I have to ask her, twice, to come closer and take over the feeding of ice chips.

"Rashmi," I say, standing directly in front of her, making sure our eyes meet. "I'm leaving my mother in your hands tonight. STARTING NOW."

She begins to feed Mom the ice chips. Fast.

"Slow," I say, "and only what's absolutely necessary. She's on restricted fluids." Even Mom, who has come to love water as her savior, finally tells her, "That's enough!" And then repeats, more a demand than a statement, "Just look at her, my daughter. She's so beautiful!"

I sleep well for the first time since I've been back in LA.

Daydream

October 10

In the whirring of a Mixmaster, there is the coming together of separate ingredients. When it's time for the switch finally to be shut to the off position, there will be no chance of finding myself as I was, as who I was, before.

Listen To Her

October 11

I wake up early, vibrating at low speed — heart, belly, nerves. Something is changing in me from the core out. There's nothing I can do to stop it.

I fall back to sleep and, at eight, call the hospital. The nurse who answers has just come on shift, says she doesn't know much in the way of details.

"Did she make it through the night?"

"Oh, yes," the nurse says as if it were impossible for it to be any other way.

Yesterday, all Mom could talk about was dying. "It's no use, Sara. We have to face it," she said over and over.

"I'm an old lady. My time has come."

Blood tests had shown no sign of a heart attack, the MRI no evidence of a stroke.

She wasn't in congestive heart failure.

Her blood pressure had come down to its usual high.

And the echocardiogram showed nothing new — a heart enlarged from years of beating into vessels that resisted the push of blood, but beating nonetheless. Beating strongly.

Still, she *could* know something no one else is privy to. "I'm no longer able to control it," she tells me. "I wish I could, but I can't."

It? Death? Is her constant talk about death her way of making peace with its inevitability? She does seem more willing for it to come than I've ever known her to be.

Over and over, she tells me she loves me.

"Don't hold me back," she says, as I rub worry lines from her forehead.

"If this is your time to die, Mom, you'll die. But as long as you're alive, I'm going to treat you like a living person. Do you want Cream of Wheat for breakfast or 'fluffy scrambled eggs'"? I'm reading to her from tomorrow morning's menu of possibilities, the speech therapist having given the go-ahead for her to return to regular food.

Maybe I *am* holding her back. Encouraging — you

could call it cheerleading — her to eat, get out of bed into a chair, open her eyes when she talks to me.

Am I ready to let her go? Again, that sense of vibrating.

I think about Mom's decision, four years ago, to move to The Jewish Home. Suddenly, I understand a statistic I'd heard. That, on average, people don't live more than five years in nursing homes. Mom's unraveling started two years in when the urinary tract infections began. With the UTIs came confusion, weakness, the pneumonias, the falls. If I still had a home to take her to, I'd scoop her up and take her there.

During the month I was away — I see it clearly now — she'd taken a further turn on the path of decline she was already walking. Heightened confusion, anxiety and an electrolyte imbalance in a class by itself, leaving The Jewish Home not knowing how to take care of her. Followed by these two weeks of hell.

Just today, the UCLA doctors finally came into agreement with her own Dr. Smith as to what caused the drama in the first place. The diuretic meant to drain fluid from a weakening heart had been too much for her body to handle, causing her to become dehydrated. Parched, she drank so much water that her blood became diluted, lowering its sodium content, causing not just confusion but delirium. Add to that a urinary tract infection which, in an old, frail person can cause delirium all by itself and, as anyone who has ever had a UTI knows, a burning need to get urine out along with the inability to do so. Who wouldn't be glued to the toilet? Who wouldn't be anxious?

Again and again, I've learned that if I can quell my own anxiety and wait, I will come to see the logic in my mother's seemingly strange behavior. Can the medical establishment afford to wait? Can doctors and nurses quell their own anxiety in the face of seemingly strange behavior in an old, old woman without rushing to judgment with the only thing they have in their quiver — ever more powerful drugs?

"How can you be so sure she needs a drug developed to treat psychosis when her anxiety can be explained by a temporary medical condition?" I'd asked. "For 92, she's taking pretty good care of herself, don't you think? Aren't we the ones who are calling it inappropriate for her to be so adamant about the need to drink water and stay on the toilet until the urine comes?"

Finally, tired in the presence of so many white coats and locked doors, I'd agreed to the Zyprexa. After all, hasn't my mother been anxious as long as I can remember? And doesn't she now have more to be anxious about than ever?

The Zyprexa had been started on Thursday. By Saturday, she was profoundly depressed, eyes closed even when

I was with her. A tremor had developed in her arms and hands; even her voice trembled. The one time she agreed to eat, she downed a bowl of soup like a ravenous animal. I was worried sick each time I saw the spoon heading toward her nose. She played with her food, brought empty forkfuls to her mouth.

By the following Monday, she was less depressed, though still refusing to open her eyes. On Tuesday, I noticed that someone had made up her face, her eyebrows perfectly done. The next day, at lunch, I'd cut cantaloupe and honeydew slices into small chunks which she chewed on for their juice, spitting out whatever was left. The same with a large bunch of red grapes. She drank a bowl of soup, too fast. I kept asking her to open her eyes. A couple of times, she stopped eating to cough, her face turning red. Her breathing became labored. She was wheezing and gurgling. By then, her blood pressure was death-defyingly high. A doctor, considering these to be signs of congestive heart failure, had ordered an even bigger dose of the diuretic and, fearing the worst, transferred her to this medical floor.

It turns out my impulse to say no to Zyprexa had been correct. The smallest dose had been enough to oversedate her, and, eating while half asleep, it's likely she aspirated food and may be on the way to another pneumonia.

Why do I fight so hard to keep my mother alive? For

me, it's simple. She's alive!

Why do I fight so hard against what others are quick to call dementia, when all signs are that dementia could well be a factor? Her MRI shows atrophy of the cortex and the white matter around the ventricles, those wide open spaces in the center of our brains. There are small areas of ischemia, too, deep in the brain — cell death from lack of blood supply associated with years of high blood pressure.

I'm not arguing for the brain of a twenty-year-old. But wouldn't it be more useful, instead of slapping on a label that comes with heavy baggage, to understand how atrophy and ischemia and the very real tendency to become brittle with age can explain why even a minor medical change, let's say a UTI, might be enough to send someone over the brink of normal reaction into confusion and anxiety? What if, instead of a label, we were willing to see behaviors that look strange to us as appropriate, if exaggerated, reactions to bodily changes?

Maybe there's a fine line between what happens in an old woman's body and, just on its other side, dementia. It's a line I choose to walk. I consult the dictionary and see that the origin of 'dementia' is Latin for 'out of one's mind.' And isn't it mind that makes us human?

When Mom is well, she is very much 'in her mind,' mentally sharp and socially gracious; annoying, too, in her good old ways of being annoying. There's too much normality still there for her to be reduced, especially by medical people who don't really know her, to a diagnosis that is literally dehumanizing.

A little more about diagnosis and vibration. I've been thinking a lot about psychiatric diagnosis, my mother having landed in a psychiatric hospital after a lifetime of simply being "nervous" and "blue." I can only imagine the diagnostic categories that must appear in her chart, categories she has fallen into or been squeezed into by medical students and interns on their psychiatric rounds, residents, nurses, internists, psychiatrists, all these people in white to whom she's been shuffled back and forth.

I hear a child psychiatrist interviewed on the radio. "What a terrible thing," he says, "to let children fall through the cracks of today's diagnostic criteria when they could be diagnosed with ADHD, anxiety, bipolar disease."

Did I hear him say that?

If all those experts who are constantly rewriting the DSM, psychiatry's bible, would just add a few more symptoms to the already long lists that make up a diagnostic category, fill those cracks, there'd be no room for any of us to fall through — we who now get our stimulants at Starbucks, our calming agents at the liquor store or Ben and Jerry's.

Widen the categories enough and there'll be room for all of us inside! Men who love men had their own category until the zeitgeist changed. Suddenly, they weren't sick anymore, just gay.

A caller asks about the root of anxiety; the doctor says it's like having a motor inside that's always running. Uh oh.

Deep in the silence of the last several nights, I have felt a vibration, long and narrow, extending down through the middle of my chest, from under my breastbone down to my pubis. Something is moving in me. Energy that's been stuck for years is firing up.

A yoga teacher talks about channels that, according to Hindu philosophy, extend between energy centers, or chakras. She asks us to pay attention to our torsos, to stabilize and strengthen what is below the waist so that what is above can rise easily up and out.

Elements of what it actually takes to be a good and faithful daughter to my nervous, sometimes blue, mother are finally out on the table where I can see them, name them, move them around into fresh constellations.

Can I be good to her without losing myself?

Until three months ago, I was living in her house, dying in her house really — the way a plant slowly dies when all the minerals in its soil have been used up. I was losing my ability even to orient toward the sun, my leaves turning light into sustenance. Now, I am asking questions that include the possibility of a future. If I were to move to Santa Fe, would my mother's 92-year-old heart be able to beat, lungs be able to breathe at high altitude? If I do move and she chooses to stay in Los Angeles, is the cord that extends between us flexible enough for life to flow through it, sustaining us both?

The vibration says "yes."

And then ...

Living in a world of psychiatric savvy, I have been trained to say "anxious" instead of just plain "nervous." "Depressed" instead of just plain "blue." When the doctor on the radio says that anxiety appears as the whir of an internal motor, I feel my confidence shake. My belief that the vibration I'd been welcoming as a sign of life begins to waver. Fade. I'm falling.

This time, I catch myself.

Falling turns into a slow and gentle tumbling and I'm free. Not bound by a diagnosis. Not even bound to my own happier belief about what the vibration might mean.

I'm simply here.

Here.

Here on the patio of the Surgery Waiting Room, where a man with a big teddy bear, its black button of a nose sticking out of a soft canvas bag, its padded arms reaching to the sky, has just phoned someone I imagine to be his wife, their child's mother. "The surgery went well," he tells her. "He's in the recovery room."

I turn my attention away, their conversation too intimate for eavesdropping.

Back upstairs, Jack, the aide, greets me by motioning with his head to the toilet door. "She's been sitting there for half-an-hour," he says.

Mom looks up, out of concentrating on her task, to greet me. "A lot of urine has come, Sara, but I know there's still a little more and no, I won't get up before the last drop comes." Her smile tells me she is remembering the relief she feels when she's squeezed the last drop through, the satisfaction of a job well done. As much as I don't want to see my mother spending so much of her life on the toilet, who am I to judge what soothes her nerves at 92, turns nervous and blue into whatever color happiness is?

Is She Dying?

Later the same day

Mom's dinner arrives in small plastic cups — cottage cheese, custard, thickened nectar, two different puréed fruits only one degree apart on the color chart. Both taste like apple. She refuses it all except for the cream of tomato soup. I feed it to her, spoonful by spoonful, remembering the red and white Campbell's Soup can of so many childhood dinners.

Bill comes in, stays an hour and is gone.

"He's good as gold," Mom tells me. "But you spend more time with me. You're the woman."

Which brings me back to something else I'd heard on the radio. How women are putting off their own careers to take care of their parents, losing time often impossible to re-capture. While the work they are doing goes unappreciated, unpaid.

Though it's true no son has been more devoted to his mother; that the eagle eye Bill has kept on Mom's finances has made it possible for her to pay her way at The Jewish Home; and though Bill and I have come together to see our mother through emergency after emergency; still, the everydayness of caring for this woman whose physical and emotional needs are great has fallen to me.

Though I often feel burdened, see myself as a victim of the situation and of Bill, who unwittingly represents the culture that fosters it, I am committed to seeing it through: our mother to her dying. In this way, paying myself with wages more valuable than money — the chance to feel satisfaction for a job well done; compassion for the conditions women, almost always women, struggle under; compassion for caregivers and the old people they advocate for.

"Take care of him when I die," Mom tells me. With all his worldly success, she still sees him as her baby, depending on me, God help us, for emotional stability.

"Tell him it had to be. I hope you can find love for each other — you're family."

Enough!

There's something fishy here. Too dramatic. And I've heard it way too many times. She's as lost in the craziness of our decades-old threesome as Bill and I are, the challenge of still trying to manage it. I see it: craziness can keep people alive.

"I do love him," I say, "It's just that we're so different."

But are we?

Bill, rising the corporate ladder with his MBA in hand, lived with Mom in his boyhood room in Connecticut well into his 30s; still her man at a time when his energies might have gone instead into marrying and raising a family.

And me? Even after I moved away to New York City, I took the train up to Connecticut every other weekend all the way through my twenties to make sure Mom was okay; not too unhappy or, god forbid, bored.

Can it be that Bill and I are simply playing out different parts in the same family drama? Bill, on stage at a time when, for whatever his reasons, he needed to be there with her. The same stage I'm on now, for reasons of my own. He didn't ask for my thanks then — and I didn't give it. He's not offering me his thanks now.

Mom asks me to sit by the side of her bed and hold her hand. I do. I tell her I've reached my limit of how many times I can stand to hear her say she's dying.

I say I'm going to leave, that I'm hungry, hoping my need for food will loosen her mother's grip on me. It only tightens it. "Okay, I'll die alone," she says, closing her eyes. If I weren't so knowing of her ways, I'd be screaming again.

Before getting into bed, I call the hospital.

"Your mother is agitated," the aide, who is sitting with Mom tonight, says. They'd woken her up to change an IV, now they're trying to catheterize her to get urine for a test. "Who wouldn't be agitated?" I say.

I ask to speak with her. She wants to know where she lives and is stuck on trying to spell Connecticut. I give the aide the address of The Jewish Home, ask her to write it down and give it to Mom to hold.

I hang up in turmoil, wondering if I have abandoned my mother just as she really is about to die. The shock of suddenly losing my father when I was nine left me shying away from death. I'd turned away from Aunt Fritzi and Aunt Theresa, two of the most important women to me, as they were dying. I'd promised myself I'd never do that again.

E-G-G. P-E-A-C-H. C-O-F-F-E-Y

October 12

"Do you happen to know what month it is?" asks a man who introduces himself as David. Just David. Psychiatry's latest envoy wears an Oxford-cloth button-down shirt, pale blue. After facing into and up to so many white-coated men, David seems strangely and freshly casual.

He sits opposite my mother on her side of the curtain. Mom is doing her best to sit up straight, but, each time she adjusts herself, the scuffs on her feet slip on the polished floor and she ends up where she was, practically out of the chair.

She's spent the morning spelling every word that

comes into her mind, every last food on her tray. "E-G-G. P-E-A-C-H. C-O-F-F-E-Y." Writing them down as if she's required to do it, as if this is what is going to make the difference.

"Give me my clothes," she writes in block letters in the wide margin of a two-day-old newspaper. And, turning to me, asks, "What else do I have to do to pass?"

"Are you an intern?" I ask this man in jeans. I want him to know that I'm not about to let my mother go through the same drill she's been put through so many times before.

"I'm the chief resident," he says.

"Sorry."

Mom tells him to stop asking her foolish questions. He tells her he doesn't think she's crazy.

"Mom, this man is a psychiatrist," I say.

"Oh, wonderful," she says, narrowing her eyes to stare him down.

"I'm telling you this because if a psychiatrist says he doesn't think you're crazy, that really means something."

"Very good," she says, voice flat, expression angry. "I think you're writing bad things about me," she says, pointing to the papers in his lap.

"Here's what I've written." He shows her two perfectly blank sheets.

"Then let *me* write something."

At first, he's protective of his paper, then gives her a sheet — and his pen.

Pressing extra-hard with his ballpoint, she writes: Get me out of here! Today! "Today underlined twenty times!" she says, showing him, with his pen, what she means.

Oh, how I love this woman!

Bill has come into the room.

I tell David, bit by pernicious bit, what Mom has been going through over the past two weeks. He's increasingly impressed with the seriousness of what he's seeing.

"I think she's showing a post-infectious delirium," he says.

"It's just nerves," she says, insisting there is absolutely nothing wrong with her.

He tells us she is going to have to tough it out — the confusion, the frustration, the disintegration. "It may take a while, and she may never get fully back to her baseline." He's talking specifically now about the effects of withdrawal from Klonopin, the psychiatric drug she'd been given at the beginning of her stay here. He'd shown surprise when I told him how quickly she had been taken off it. All in one day, as I remember.

I tell him about the urinary tract infection. The antibiotics. The stress of being kept awake all night in the Emergency Room. The craziness she was seeing all around her on the Geriatric Psych Ward. The SIADH, this latest set of letters that have been bandied about by various doctors. Syndrome of Insufficient Anti-Diuretic Hormone. Her bad reaction to Zyprexa and the possibility of another pneumonia having been brought on by aspirating food.

I hear him, about how she may never recover fully. Feel myself sink at the possibility of her experiencing the rest of her life as a test she has to pass, a test she believes she's failing.

"Get her a new battery for her hearing aid. Right away," David says before any of us can fall into despair. "If she hears only bits and snatches of conversation from the other side of the curtain, that in itself could be disorienting."

"There have been at least ten different people in the other bed since she was admitted to this room," I tell him. "It's enough to make anyone nuts."

"And get her walking," he says. "The more she can see normal life around her, the better."

Now we're talking!

Mom is wearing her own striped sweater over the hospital's pajama bottoms. A few minutes before David came in, she had insisted on getting dressed as part of her ready-to-go-home project.

Chancy, the aide, and I get her out of the pjs, into a

pair or her own black slacks, shoes and socks. I hand her her makeup case; she brushes on blush and powder, does her lipstick perfectly without a mirror. I help her with her eyebrow pencil and blue shadow.

She reaches for her walker and, stopping at the threshold of her room, looks into the hallway, left and right, seeing beyond the confines of locked doors for the first time since she has been in the hospital.

"Look! A baby!" she says, thrilled at the sight of a baby in its mother's arms. Heading for a chair in the hallway outside the elevators, she says she wants a tuna sandwich.

I leave her with Bill who, out of nowhere, has found a new hearing aid battery. I go downstairs to pull myself together, celebrate over a cup of coffee.

Outside, it's cold and gray. Inside, there's the warmth and familiarity of the Surgery Waiting Room.

A woman on a cell phone is spelling — everyone is spelling today! — a diagnosis. Her husband's? Her brother's? Her sister's? Her child's?

"G-L-I-O," I hear her say.

"Oh, no," I whisper to myself, remembering the worst kind of brain cancer anyone can have.

" ... B-L-A-S-T-O-M-A," she continues. " ... M-U-L-T-I-F-O-R-M-E." She's speaking in Spanish and sounds amazingly business-like until her voice breaks. She is having trouble breathing.

Bill passes by on his way out. "I'll be here tomorrow," he says, without stopping. He's all business. "She looks good, she ate the sandwich," I hear him say as he disappears out the glass door.

I find Mom back in her room. "Coffee and sleep? Coffee and ... sleep?" she asks me when I return. "What else? What else am I supposed to do?"

"Let's take a walk," I say, remembering what David said about the importance of re-establishing some semblance of normal life. We walk back out to the elevators.

Choncy wants to take home with her the two pages my mother had written while I was downstairs. Her face drops when I tell her I've already put them away.

"I didn't realize it was a letter to you," I say, handing the letter back to her. "Would you be willing to make me a copy?" She hands me the original, keeping the copy for herself.

What Mom wrote is more understandable to Choncy than it is to me, but I get the gist of it. Thinking she's about to be discharged for home, she's thanking Choncy and the other nurses, telling them to take care of themselves so they can keep helping people.

Dressed and walking, Mom's showing newfound confidence. "I can do everything there I can do here," she tells me.

Would the confusion clear, I wonder, if she were back in familiar surroundings?

To get outside the box, you have to see the box.

This lifelong commitment I've had to ward off Mom's sadness and, now, her dying; the knowing, deeply felt, that to keep my own heart beating, I would have to keep hers beating, too.

During that month in Santa Fe, I'd entrusted my mother's well-being to Bill and the staff at The Jewish Home; good people, but none as finely attuned as I have learned to be. When I came back, she was falling apart.

Is it grandiose to think I could have held her together? I suppose so.

Do I think, deep down, I can keep her alive forever? It's a real question.

Though she is still alive and may pull through this crisis, too, something is beginning to change.

The Craziness Of Insecurity

October 13

Mom says she's waiting for Dr. Smith, her doctor at The Jewish Home, to arrive. Says he called to ask her to come to work on Sunday, which she thought was very unusual. Why should he want her to come to work on Sunday?

At least, she knows it's Sunday. And that there's something unusual going on.

The aide and I get her into her striped shirt again and black pants. "Let's walk out to the elevator," I say. Is it possible that taking a walk might be enough to derail the train of thought she's riding, the destination a visit from Dr. Smith?

Sierra, nine months old, with braids that start close to her scalp and end in tiny multi-colored barrettes, is the baby she saw in the hallway yesterday. She's sitting on her mother, Crystal's, lap.

Mom has backed up to the chair next to them and is still too far away to sit. "Mom, don't sit down yet." I must have said this, or something like it, a thousand times over the course of these last few years. "Back up all the way," I say. "Make sure you can feel the chair behind you." "Reach back. "Put your hand on the arm of the chair."

Her usual way of sitting is to fall back into the chair, hands still on the walker. She did this even before she used a walker, in her own living room. Flopping back into her television chair, the pale blue velvet, swiveling rocker. She's been lucky. So far, a chair has always magically appeared behind her.

Two-year-old Marisa is in the chair on the other side of Crystal and Sierra; next to Marisa, a boy, three-year-old RJ.

Since my mother has been in the hospital, I've seen prejudices rise to the surface I didn't know were there. One afternoon, in the psych ward, Mom pointed to the woman who shared the room with her. "Get me out of that room," she said. "It's not right. Look at her." What she meant was that the woman was black.

Earlier today, she'd pointed to Toni, the aide who'd helped me get her dressed. "I won't let her do anything. She's not the Dr. Smith I know. My Dr. Smith is white."

Toni understands, tells me she has an epileptic son and knows about the mental deterioration that can happen from drugs.

What's going to happen out here in the hallway? I wonder.

Mom reaches her hand out to the baby, who looks on with interest, but hardly enthusiasm for taking this old woman's hand, black and blue from so many IVs.

Crystal tells us that the name Sierra is to honor the land; Marisa, to honor the sea. "And RJ?" I ask. "He's just Reginald J," she laughs. "After his grandfather."

They're waiting to see Crystal's mother who, in her early 40s, is in the process of rejecting her third kidney transplant. Crystal's grandmother, a stately woman with thick gray hair pulled into a bun, travels back and forth between her daughter's hospital room and the rest of the family waiting in the hall. Crystal is in her 20s; her grandmother could be my age, 63.

A man appears and disappears. A big man. "Maybe he's Crystal's husband," I say to Mom. Crystal and the man laugh. "That's what everybody thinks," she says. "He's my stepfather."

It's Sunday afternoon, and I've got the Surgery Waiting Room to myself. Even surgery, unless it's an emergency, is a Monday through Friday kind of business.

I walk out onto the patio, where a family, eating from take-out containers, is just being told that their little boy, who broke a leg for, no reason at all, or so it seemed, had a benign cyst in his thigh bone. "Some people just have them," the surgeon says, "and you don't find out 'til the bone breaks, or you see it in a routine X-ray."

"It was basically a hole in the bone," he continues.

"We filled it with some bone we took from his hip and covered it over with a plate. Luckily, it won't get in the way of his growing."

One of the women needs to hear — four times — that it isn't cancer.

"So, it's not a tumor," she says, part-statement, part-question.

"So, it's benign?"

"So, it's not going to grow back?"

"You got it all?"

She reminds me of me.

"So, you don't think it's malignant?" I'd asked Dr. Black on this same patio, eleven years ago, about the bony tumor that had been discovered in the dead center of my husband's brain.

"I don't think so," he'd said, "but it isn't something you can be sure of immediately."

"So, it isn't malignant?" I ask again, when the tissue comes back from pathology.

"Might other parts of it you didn't see be malignant?"

"It's not going to grow back?"

I don't remember if he said, for sure, that it wouldn't. But Matt was 66, the tumor had probably been growing since he was a teenager and, until now, hadn't caused any trouble.

Still, my insecurity had needed breathing space. A

refuge, no matter how temporary, that the life of someone I loved wasn't going to be snatched out from under me.

Mom greets my return by telling me she is having trouble seeing. She directs me to look at the newspaper picture the nurse, on my mother's instruction, has taped to the wall.

"What do you see?" she asks.

"A woman in a strapless dress ... "

"No, the words," she says. "I can't read them and I recently had my eyes examined."

"I wouldn't be able to read them either from where you're sitting," I say.

"Come here," she orders. "Tell me what you can read."

Bill shakes his head at our mother's latest preoccupation. Yesterday, it was spelling. Today, it's seeing. She's doing whatever she can to assure herself that her brain is still working. What is it about this life that makes it so precious? That makes most of us willing to go to any lengths not to lose it?

"Her eyes look fine," my brother says. "The nurse said she'd flush them out."

"It's not how her eyes look," I say, an edge to my voice. "It's what's going on in her brain that she's worried about."

"I know," he shoots back.

"I wish I had my artificial tears with me," I hear myself say.

His head-shaking is now directed at me. "The *nurse* is going to flush out her eyes," he says.

"Don't talk to me like that," I say.

He gets up to leave.

"We don't have enough to be upset about, do we?" I say.

"No, we don't have enough to be upset about."

The Possibility Of Fresh Air

October 19

Mom has been transferred back to the Geriatric Psych Ward. She is quiet, smiling, says she feels better.

"Physically better? Your mood? Your thinking?"

"Just better," she says. "Mood ... maybe my thinking."

Mildred, a light-skinned black woman, very beautiful, very heavy, reaches over from her own blue reclining chair to touch my mother's arm. "We like each other very much," Mildred says. "We're roommates."

Mom smiles.

"Maybe by tomorrow, Mom, I can get permission to take you outside. You haven't felt fresh air on your skin for three weeks."

She's surprised to hear me say she's been in the hospital for three weeks. I wonder how much of all this, how much of any of this, she is going to remember.

A Room From Which There's No Returning

October 20

"And then?" she asks when I tell her it's time for dinner. "What then?"

After dinner, she asks me to tell her what she ate. "Say it clearly," she demands.

"Tu-na," I say, pronouncing each syllable as if it were a word. "Jel-lo. Po-tay-to. Cake. Caw-fee."

She tries to repeat the list but doesn't make it past tuna. "I have to know, otherwise I won't sleep."

"I'll write it down for you." I write the list in capital letters, on a sheet of blank paper, one food to a line.

"JELLO."

"TUNA"

"CAKE."

"COFFEE."

She reads the list. "Bread," she says, remembering

there was bread.

I rewrite the list to include BREAD, throw away the old list so she won't be confused about which one is correct, fold it and slip it into the pocket of her fleece jacket.

"What will I do with it there?" she asks.

"You can check it whenever you want," I tell her. "I want you to have a good night's sleep."

My mother isn't the only one being tested. When I can roll with the punches of her life, I can roll with the punches of mine. Unless I'm thrown by some dramatic change which leaves me carrying close her latest mood or jiggled thinking, I can feel myself as separate from her.

An old friend, tells me how her mother was before she died, how her thinking was mostly disconnected from the world she formerly knew. "Maybe it's preparing us for how it will be when we die," my friend says. "I heard someone describe dying like this: that it's like a mysterious dream where we walk through doorways into increasingly deep and unknown rooms. Usually, we turn around and come back out. One time, we enter a room from which there is no returning. Having seen it in our mothers, maybe we'll be able to be with the mystery of it when it's our turn."

All I know for sure is this: I'm doing my best to be with it now — the dying process as it seems to be working its way through my mother.

Another Shoe Getting Ready To Drop

October 21

"I'm waiting for him," she says, pointing with her chin to Michael, a nurse with a blond crew cut. I've noticed him. He sits in the Day Room, watching patients but rarely interacting with them. "He's in my group," Mom tells me. "I'm waiting for my group. Then, I'll eat."

It's useless to explain that everyone has already eaten and the trays have been sent back to the kitchen. I ask my mother's nurse if Michael could sit with her while she eats a snack — pudding or toast or ice cream.

"I asked him already, he says he's too busy."

"Mom, am I in your group?"

She says yes, but then, when I try to make hay with it — when I say, "Well, then, will you eat with me?" — she says, "No, you're not in my group."

Michael leaves for his break. Mom thinks she will be eating with him and the rest of her group when he returns. We've reached an impasse. We sit, quietly facing each other.

I catch my mother looking quickly to her right side and then down. It takes several beats for me to recognize this as something out of the ordinary.

"What just happened?" I ask.

She shakes her head no, as if to say I don't want to talk about it.

"Did you just see something over there?" I ask. "Or hear something?"

"I won't tell you," she says. "I can't." I see that arguing or cajoling will get me nowhere.

"Mom, let me just tell you this. If you did see or hear something, I can imagine it was scary, and I want you to know it won't last. It's either from one of those medications you were taking or some medical condition the doctors are trying to clear up."

Earlier in the afternoon, I was convinced she was on her way to going home. She'd put on her make-up, was neatly dressed in khaki slacks and a khaki and white striped knit top, there was no food decorating the front of her blouse.

She'd given me a big smile, unlike so many times when my arrival has been a chance to move from high anxiety, sure that I had died, to only moderate anxiety, recovering from being sure I had died.

She hadn't said one thing that didn't make sense. Hadn't insisted she had to go to the bathroom. She didn't look away from me as she has done, to one extent or another, our entire life together, as if it is too much for her, too demanding, too intimate to look directly at me as we speak.

I'd begun to fantasize that she was going to return to The Jewish Home better than ever. Her whole life would no longer be about having to go to the bathroom. She would play the piano again, would have real conversations with people who live there. The staff won't avoid her because they don't know what to do with her anxiety. When I'm not with her, I won't feel as if I should be. She'll like the food. She'll eat chicken again. She won't die.

But there are two visiting hours every day and, each one, she's different. No way of knowing, from one minute to the next, how things are going to be.

Better to return to reality, to the fact that she is on a psych ward again. She may have been re-started on antipsychotic medication. Another shoe may be getting ready to drop.

A Bit Of Heaven, Here In The Middle Of Hell

October 22

I find Mom in a pink, short-sleeved robe, looking silly. It's after lunch, which she didn't eat after not eating dinner last night either. Is not eating one of those mysterious steps that makes it possible to move through the inner doorways?

"Why isn't my mother dressed?" I ask an aide walking by.

"She doesn't have any pants," the aide tells me, without stopping. "Only blouses."

"But I washed her clothes and brought them back," I say. "They're in her closet — whole outfits on hangers. Look under the blouses; you'll find the pants."

I remove the blanket from my mother's lap. In the spaces between the snaps that keep the robe partially closed, the blue plastic of a diaper calls out; the white, white skin of young-looking legs reaching down to ankle-high socks and black SAS oxfords.

I get her walker, lead her out of the Day Room into the dining room. I ask the aide to bring a snack. Eyes closed, my mother lets me feed her yogurt and toast.

I tell a nurse, who is writing notes at another table, that I think my mother is oversedated again and I don't like the way her aide dismissed me. "If you can't be treated with kindness on a geriatric psych ward — at UCLA, no less — where can you be?"

"You *can* be treated with kindness here," she says, leaving it there.

I'm halfway through feeding Mom a container of peach yogurt when Alice, the nurse who has been with my mother more than any other, returns from lunch. She sits down with us a little behind my mother and to her right. I face them both. Mom's eyes are still closed. So is her mouth as she refuses the rest of the toast.

I settle a little deeper into the chair. Alice's eyes are hazel, like mine, and her hair is the soft brown mine was when I was younger. She is probably in her 40s and has a depth to her I don't see much here.

"I hear you're a therapist," she says. "So am I."

I tell her I'm worried that the longer my mother is here, the more psychiatric symptoms I'm seeing in her: misperceptions, thinking that appears to be attached to a different reality, what looked to me like a hallucination last night.

"Overall, she's improving," Alice says, without going into detail.

"They talk about dementia here and memory loss," I say. "But all they know is what they've seen since she's been in the hospital. As long as she is 'compliant,' they say she's better. They aren't concerned, as I am, that she's talking as if she's crazy. It's my mother who is becoming lost to me, not theirs."

She listens. I realize I've been addressing her as if she is not one of *them*.

I tell her about the hard life my mother has led. About all the deaths in the family between the time she married my father and when I was born. The stillborn baby boy before me. "She has a lot of unresolved grief," I say, reverting to therapist language.

Mom opens her eyes. She's been listening carefully.

"My father died when they were both 40," I say. "She went back to school to find a way to support us. Had a bad second marriage to a man who was *certifiably* crazy." I feel anger rising in me at Joe Epstein for those years of aggravation.

"I should have never married him," Mom says.

"You didn't listen to me."

"I was afraid of being lonely."

"It was probably a clinical depression with psychosis," I tell Alice. "He thought there were people in the bushes outside our front door who were coming to get him. And he was finally right. For years, he was in and out of the state hospital, where they gave him several courses of shock treatment."

I wonder if my mother has equated being on this psychiatric ward herself with what she saw when she visited Joe in Newtown. Does she equate her own sometimes disordered thinking with what she saw and heard in him?

"I've always been devoted to my mother," I say, by now talking through tears.

Changing the subject — is she uncomfortable with

my tears? — Alice says she has just a small private practice. Most of her energy is devoted to being here.

"My mother is my work," I say. "I sometimes wonder whether I'm too connected to her, but I'm coming to accept it as my fate."

"There are things you haven't done with your life because of me," Mom says, looking straight into my eyes.

"No, Mom, not because of you. Whatever I've done, I've chosen to do. You chose whatever you did with us, and with Joe, too, didn't you?"

Her head cocked to the side, she slowly nods. Seeing, maybe for the first time, the marriage to Joe — something she has always considered to be a mistake — in a way that includes respect for herself.

"There's something else I'm coming to understand," I say to Alice. "Because of all the attention I've paid to my mother, I've learned to be very attentive. Not just to her, but to everything around me. It's been a gift."

"I like your mother," Alice assures me. "She says what she means."

"More than ever," I say.

In the dining room of a geriatric psych ward, sitting between two women who are showing her their respect, my mother is showing herself to be as intelligent and as elegant as they come — the best in her shining through, silly pink robe and all.

Down the elevator and all the way to my car, I cry deep sobs of relief.

My Mother's Daughter

October 23

Yesterday's angel tells me she refuses to hear any more complaints from me and that, if I have anything more to say, I'll have to say it to the doctor. Then turns on her heel, leaving me to stare at her back.

When I'd arrived this afternoon and saw that once again — how many days straight has it been? — Mom had tuna salad in front of her, I was upset and said so. Was it this that pushed Alice over the edge? Was it something about yesterday's conversation?

It won't be the first time I've been accused of pushing someone over the edge. ("Do you have to be so intense, Sara?") But we are on a psych ward. And I wonder: have they diagnosed me as paranoid? And, uh oh, what might it mean that I'm even wondering!

Yes, I've complained. If everyone visited as often as I do, wouldn't they see the glitches? No, I'm not used to living in a world in which a man wearing the power of a white coat casually attributes my mother's behavior to dementia. "All demented people do that," a psychiatric resident had said, right in front of Mom.

Okay, I'm picky. I do think that, before an aide says there are no clothes in my mother's closet, she should look more carefully. I do think that, when I say I know they're there, the aide shouldn't insist they aren't and keep walking. I do think that good nursing care on a psychiatric ward should include making sure menus are filled out according to the foods a patient says she likes and that those menus actually find their way to the kitchen instead of the patient having to face confusion at every meal, expecting one thing and getting another and, by that time, the only alternative is tuna — again. I do think that when I ask to see my mother's doctor and I'm told the doctor has been paged and I say I'm going to wait outside the unit and the secretary who paged the doctor passes me half-an-hour later on her way to a break, it would be respectful of her not to just walk by but to tell me what the status of the page is. I do think staff members, when working with confused patients, should say goodbye when they're going off duty, not just disappear; and the person who comes on next should introduce themselves.

With all of this, the shock of Alice turning her back on me is the most upsetting thing of all.

For my own good and maybe even my mother's, I will

have to find a better way to deal with what I see. Even if it means letting go of thinking I really can control the quality of what could be the last days of my mother's life.

When I was five, maybe even younger, my mother would take me to the Old Greenwich Library and leave me with Mrs. Black, the librarian in the Children's Room. It was there, in the deep quiet of a library, surrounded by books, I'd learned there was a place in the world where I was respected and could rest. If not in control of everything, at least safe, knowing there was something that could be depended on.

That evening, I take myself to Barnes & Noble, where I feel myself filled with the colors and shapes of books carefully lined up on shelves, a sight as orderly and confidence-producing as the produce department at Gelson's, with its green and red and yellow and chocolate-brown peppers, all wet and shiny under carefully thought-out lighting.

I pick up *The Crazed*, a new novel by Ha Jin. Just as I will see any new movie by Woody Allen, listen to any new CD by Keith Jarrett, I'll read any new book by Ha Jin. The dust jacket says it's about a Chinese professor of literature who, after a stroke, raves and rages, suddenly able to say what no one in China, whose brain is still thought to be coherent, is allowed to say: the truth. His young protégé fears for his own safety, that *he* will be condemned, Tiananmen-style, for associating with this truth-telling old man.

When my mother says, "If you want me to live, get me out of here now," I know she is speaking not only *her* truth, but *the* truth. "I don't belong here," she says, looking clear-eyed from one of her fellow patients to the next. My mother is the only one here able to fill in the words of the crossword puzzle the occupational therapist has put up on the wall. Who, when Mildred her roommate, is being discharged, would think to get up to play something for her on the piano. I remember what David, the psychiatrist, said about the importance of normal experiences.

After a month in this most abnormal environment, this morning there's a meeting in preparation for my mother's discharge. I'm told how much better she is doing. Which doesn't stop the newest young psychiatrist, who has known my mother exactly five days, from offering "dementia" in answer to every question I ask. When I do acknowledge that I've noticed some disordered thinking in my mother late in the day, the social worker is quick to call it "sundowning," says she can give me some booklets that will explain it. The booklets she gives me are from the Alzheimer's Foundation. If I should call and ask why she gave me booklets on Alzheimer's Disease, when my mother has never been diagnosed with Alzheimer's Disease, it will only add fuel to the fire of my reputation.

With all the efforts to quiet me, all the diagnoses and drugs to quiet my mother, Mom and I can still be counted on to say what the crazed Chinese professor could only say after his stroke. The truth. At least as we see it.

And what about Alice's strange behavior toward me just a day after she'd said how much she appreciates my mother, how Mom always says what she means? Had she seen something she wasn't quite ready to see about truth in the face of power? Am I crazed to even think that's what it might be?

Not Just The Door I'd Been Looking For The Key To Get In

October 24

How does it work, this opening of a book to the perfect page at the exact moment when you're ready to hear what you need to hear? When someone else's story has the power to help you see clearly how your own life has been proceeding? And you're led to a widening in your road, the possibility of turning in a new direction that could mean everything.

A book has just arrived from the library. *The Lives*

of the Muses, Nine Women & The Artists They Inspired, by Francine Prose. I open to a random page and read about Lee Miller, who, after devoting herself to supporting the more well known Man Ray, became an artist in her own right. "It happened," she says, "when I moved from needing to be seen to needing to see."

This is the very turnaround I've been waiting for.

From the time I was a child, my attention has been directed to knowing what was needed to keep Mom from losing herself in depression and anxiety. With Matt, even after it was clear that the marriage was over, during his brain surgeries I turned all my energy toward keeping him safe. Now, it's Mom again.

I'm understanding more each day that much of this good-doing, much of this seeing myself as savior, has come with its own kind of payment. The securing of my survival, yes; also a sense of my value, my power. Now that Mom actually needs me and is too weak to turn away, I've shifted into high gear. If I can get her to see me, I'll know I'm real. And if I'm real, I can be me.

I am seen, therefore I exist. And that's the starting point.

It's strange and wonderful to consider the possibility that this was something she needed, too. That coming to really see her daughter could help her to become more whole and alive herself, give her a starting point of her own. Is this a paradox? Is love a prerequisite for both living, and for letting go of living; for being willing to die?

If this is true, maybe I can forgive myself for all those times I've forced the issue to get Mom to see me, all those times I've resisted her tendencies to give up and fade away.

Interestingly, new physical challenges have arisen in Mom's literally being able to see me. Osteoporosis in her upper spine points her face downward. The anxiety medication, too, draws her head down, her attention to the ground.

I kneel at the side of her chair and she lights up. Not the cold light of, "Oh, Sara, thank god you're here, if you only knew what a terrible time I've been having, you're the only one who can save me ..."

No. The warmth of, "It does my heart good to lay my eyes on you, my daughter. I see you, and the world is right."

"You're happy to see me," I say.

"How could I not be," she answers. Not a question, but the truth.

She's actually *kvelling*. If there were no other reason to put a high priority on preserving the Yiddish language, the word *kvell* would be enough.

kvell verb, from the Yiddish 1. to gaze upon a person in such a way that you can barely contain your appreciation, not just for their human qualities but for their beauty; you know you are partly responsible for what you see and, so, the overflowing you feel speaks not just about the object of your gaze but of the relationship between you; 2. bursting with pride.

It seems that *all* of living, at its best, takes place in this kind of give and take.

Gravity, as it pulls me down, invites vitality to lift me up.

My need for oxygen is answered by trees breathing out, those same trees that rely on my out-breath to give them what *they* need.

In the way the tree is rooted, I feel my own stability.

In response to the rush or meander of a mountain stream, I come to know my own possibility for purposeful or restful movement.

A tomato appearing from behind a flower shows me life's mystery.

Showering my mother with love allows me to know the love that brought me into this world, the same love that will keep me alive after she's gone; the same love that will provide her with the heart she needs to die.

The Last Drop

October 27 and 28

"I'm scared to be alone," Mom says. "I don't know anyone here. What if I have to go to the bathroom? Who will help me? How will I get their attention? Shout?"

It's Mom's first night back at The Jewish Home. She begs me not to leave her. As I had begged her friend Ruby not to leave me on the playground of Franklin Street Elementary School my first day of kindergarten. Mom, pregnant with Bill, had stayed home. Clusters of little kids, people we called Negroes in those days, were standing around in ragged groups. There was nobody who looked like me.

I find a copy of *The Snow Goose* in the drawer of Mom's nightstand. A small, hardcover classic about a bird saved by a kind lighthouse keeper who, in turn, saves him. "This can soothe you," I say. When she has been able to read nothing else, she has been able to read *The Snow Goose*.

"Not even that," she says. You can't leave me. I can't be left alone here."

I ask a nurse to watch over her.

"She'll be fine," the nurse, who doesn't know my mother, says. "She'll be fine."

"I'm not so sure," I say. "She's just gotten back from a

month in a psych ward, where there was more staff than you have here and other patients to divert her attention away from herself. Some who moved their limbs in wild and unexpected ways, others who called out to family members not there. One woman, who had come from another nursing home in the Valley, was sure she was on a cruise.

"She feels all alone here," I say.

But it's late. And I need some soothing of my own.

I take myself out for a bowl of ramen topped with a mountain of crispy bean sprouts and rounds of fresh scallions. A few drops of oil, red from hot peppers, splatter onto my blouse. It's a skill I learned from Mom.

When I call in the morning, the charge nurse says he doesn't know my mother, holds the phone receiver to his chest as I hear him ask several people if they can "talk to the family of Hannah Epstein."

"I don't know her," I hear one after another say. After a few minutes, I hang up, unable to bear how sad I feel for my mother's aloneness.

As is so often the case, what my mother tells me — even when it is the voice of anxiety speaking — turns out to be true. I am learning to listen more carefully to the plight of an old woman in its many creative expressions.

In a few minutes, I call back. The nurse has walked the few steps to Mom's room. Through the phone, I hear that my mother is sitting on the toilet.

"Let me speak to her."

"Sara, my stomach ... there's just the tiniest little piece that still has to come out."

I've heard it all before. "Sara, the last drop of urine has to come out. I won't get up until the last drop comes out." The very words, exactly one month ago, that set in motion the drama that got her admitted to the Geriatric Psych Ward.

"Mom, your body will take care of it. You've got to get up and have breakfast. Yes, it's okay to have breakfast in your room."

"My daughter says I should get up and have breakfast in my room," I hear her tell the nurse.

I shake my head in grateful amazement. My mother is willing to trust me.

The next day, I find her sitting on a low couch in the tv room. She looks up at me, her face breaking into a smile. "It did me good," she says, about the nap from which she's just awakened.

Standing up is a challenge. Reaching for the walker, she tries to pull herself up rather than remembering that to stand up you have to push down. It's always struck me how little interest and skill my mother has shown in physical activity. Everywhere but at the piano.

She veers drunkenly to the right, dropping me into sober wariness. Bumps her walker into the medicine cart. In the dining room, she begins to sit before there's a chair behind her.

Still, she's smiling, seems relaxed. That's good enough for me, I think, kidding myself.

At 7:30, she's ready for bed. On the way to her room, she's pulling to the right again. "My legs feel like lead," she says as she flops into the chair next to her bed. "I've never felt like this."

Remembering that stiffness can be a side effect of Risperdal, the antipsychotic medication she was switched to just before leaving UCLA, I test her arms for mobility.

"I don't think I'll be able to get out of bed in the morning," she says.

Lulled over the years into turning away from the inordinate amount of attention she has seemed to require of me, I am now learning discernment: which passing disgruntlement I can allow myself simply to hear and what to do with the chunks of truth that need attending to.

Yet Another Crisis

October 29 and 30

I sit next to Mom's bed, my chin supported by hands that seem to be praying. When her breathing is quiet and regular, I rest easy, tighten up when I hear gurgling in her throat. I know she needs to cough and also that she is too lethargic to expel the phlegm that's caught there. I don't dare to turn away, a plug of mucus could cut off the passage of air.

The next day, too, I pray to find her well. But she's nowhere to be seen through the windows into the dining room. I'm afraid my prayer is not going to be answered

In her room, a nurse is standing next to her bed, trying to get her to eat. As the nurse turns to see me, she continues to move pasta shells toward my mother's mouth.

I'm shocked to see how puffy Mom's face is. "I've never seen her like this," I say to the nurse. "Look!"

The nurse, too, is shocked. There is no expression on Mom's face, only soft flesh and dull eyes.

I ask the nurse to stop feeding her, tell her it was only a couple of weeks ago that, oversedated, Mom had aspirated food and ended up with another pneumonia. I say I'm afraid it may have happened again.

"How are you feeling, Mom?"

"Fine," she says, offering a sweet, watery smile.

"Do you feel drunk?"

"Yes," she says, her blue eyes seeing something far away. Or maybe it's that each eye is looking in a different direction. I can't quite make contact with the person behind the eyes. I try to grab hold of an old, old feeling of wanting to reach my mother and not being able to. At least today she knows I'm here.

"Mom, I love you," I say, kissing her forehead, warm, but not feverish. "Can you give me a kiss?"

She nods but, when I offer my cheek, nothing happens.

"Mom, can you give me a kiss?" I ask again.

She brushes my cheek on her way into a deep sleep, pulling to the right as she always does. Today, without the strength it would take to roll all the way over, it is only her head that moves.

A man in jeans rolls a small machine into her room. We are waiting for a chest X-ray, can this be it? The machine could just as easily be a floor polisher. He places a metal plate behind her rounded back, asks me to step out. I stand at the doorway, looking in. He has raised the head of the bed so she is sitting. Her head is so heavy I am afraid that it will suddenly catapult her forward and, with the rest of her body following, she'll tumble to the floor.

"You have to be careful!" I call to him.

A young man in blue scrubs comes to draw blood. I am relieved to see the vials fill with beautiful dark red liquid. Mom's blood is flowing! She's alive!

The on-call doctor who was notified wants to send Mom to the hospital.

"No," I say. "I'll sit with her as long as it takes for the drug to wear off." I'll stay as long as it takes for her to wake up, open her eyes, eyes I can depend on to see me when they point in my direction.

I am angry that at this home, where hundreds of old Jewish people live, a nurse had been feeding my mother without even watching her. Angry, too, that the on-call doctor, who isn't aware of everything that's been happening over the last month, and even acknowledges how hard it is to know what to do without seeing the patient, has decided to manage the situation by phone.

"She fell," the doctor tells me. "There might be something going on intracranially." Sometime during the afternoon, Mom had tried to get up on her own, slipped off the bed and was found sitting on the floor, her head resting against the metal bed frame.

"What would they do in the hospital if there was something going on intracranially?" I ask.

"Not much," the doctor admits. She agrees to keep her here. She orders an antibiotic in case there is another pneumonia.

Something else had happened that afternoon. A workman had come in and emptied, into the drawers of Mom's bureau and closet, contents of boxes that had been in storage for the past year while Mom was in the Transitional Care Unit. Every drawer of the bureau is bulging. A stack of framed photos sticks out of the closet, making it impossible to close the door. An unplugged TV sits on top of a white, under-the-counter refrigerator, a good idea when Mom was living in residential care, now useless. Was it the chaos in which the workman had left her room that had Mom trying to get out of bed on her own?

As the evening wears on, I go back and forth between watching Mom breathe and using this quiet time to sift through piles of stuff. Sweaters and scarves and half-used, year-old bottles of cosmetics and lotions; the instruction booklet for a special phone on which you can turn up the volume in the handset; hearing aid batteries, some loose and some in unopened containers, many past their expiration date; perfectly good bras that will now be too tight around her curving back; birthday cards and Mother's Day cards from me and Bill from all four years she has lived here; three pieces I wrote and gave her to read, carefully put away in a well-used, see-through plastic bag; cellophane-wrapped hard candies turned white with age; two different wrist splints meant to relieve carpal tunnel syndrome, neither of which I could ever convince her to wear; two pairs of gloves she took to wearing even when she was inside; at least a hundred Poise pads — her favorite brand — that she used to wear in case she couldn't get to the bathroom in time; myriad styles and sizes of panty girdles to hold the pads in place. Only recently has my mother opted for the greater security of a diaper, so she can stay asleep rather than have to get out of bed and onto a commode three or four times during the night.

I fold the pink down comforter, a birthday gift I'd ordered for her from the LL Bean catalog many years ago; the blue and beige afghan crocheted by an Hispanic woman I'd bought at an artist's sale in Dixon, NM. I stuff them into a drawer, together with her favorite down pillow that had been part of her trousseau, HANNAH EPSTEIN printed by me in pink marker on its zippered cover when she moved here.

Into the wastebasket goes the plastic bag full of knee-high stockings I'd once taken the time to sort and knot into pairs; I decide, for the moment, to hold onto the thigh-highs, though I doubt if she will wear them again now that she has gotten used to wearing white socks with her SAS oxfords.

Oh, those SAS oxfords. The black pair, the brown pair, the beige. Each right shoe stretched at its inner side, thanks to her downwardly rounded arch. How the instep of each right shoe became deformed where that damned displaced bone protrudes. I remember how each time we'd go to Nordstrom's, shopping for yet another pair, she'd stop to gaze longingly at the kind of strappy sandals this Cinderella used to squeeze her deformed foot into, leaving me with my heart in my throat, afraid she would twist her ankle and fall. How I'd worry and how, too, I loved the fact that she never lost her desire to be attractive.

When I've managed to bring her half of the shared room into some degree of order, I break the seal on a deck of cards Bill must have brought back from a Las Vegas casino. I play game after game of Solitaire, first on her nightstand and then on the edge of her bed, whose leg portion is raised to allow for a bend in her knees. Which means the cards — already slippery — keep sliding off their piles. I play for five straight hours, stopping only when the nurse asks me to leave so she can insert an IV; or for ongoing phone discussions with the doctor about whether or not to send Mom to the hospital; or to munch on the egg salad sandwich on white bread that Angie has brought me. Angie, who is as shocked as I am about Mom's room being left in such disarray and the dead-sleep my mother is lost in. Five hours of Solitaire and I win just once.

Who won all those other hands? I ask you. In life, who is the House?

I talk with Erwell, the aide who will be watching my

mother during the night. His enthusiasm is irrepressible, intent on recounting the idiosyncrasies he had noticed in Mom the few times he worked with her when she was living in the Transitional Care Unit. He says she fell at least four times in the bathroom, that she always insisted on going there herself.

While he and I are talking, I see Mom trying to reach her hand, the one with the IV, up to her nose. Something about the oxygen tube has caught her sleeping attention. She soon tires of this, intent now on scratching a place in her right nostril, then blowing her nose into an empty hand.

When she finally seems to be waking up, I decide to go home and get some sleep.

The next morning, Vickie, who knows my mother well and appreciates her, sounds upset. "She's so lethargic," Vickie says. "I can't wake her up."

"Has the doctor seen her yet?" I ask.

Halloween In The ER

October 31

I drive to Encino Hospital as fast as I can, hurry into the ER just as the paramedics are wheeling the gurney out that carried Mom in. A young woman with long, curly, dark brown hair reaches out to shake my hand. "I'm Dr. Bauer."

I fill her in on my mother's medical history — two miraculous recoveries from pneumonia, followed by the recent month in UCLA with its oversedation on anti-psychotic medication that may have led to yet another pneumonia. She listens so carefully I begin to cry.

"Last time she had pneumonia and her carbon dioxide levels went through the roof, I'd agreed to have her put on life support. She wasn't ready to die. Now, there's a Do Not Resuscitate order."

"That's good," the doctor says. "I know what I'm talking about. I've been there."

"What makes it all so hard is that in between being sick, she's completely here. Clear-headed. And I love her."

"That's how it *should* be. Better to have her go like that than save her for too long, in the last year of her life, lying there like a vegetable. I'm not saying that's what's going to happen, I'm talking in general. Anyway, I've seen some things. My fiancé was in a terrible accident. But people don't really die. He's not really gone."

She hands me a tissue and takes one for herself, her tears on the verge of spilling over, too. Her face is a patchwork of healed scars. This young woman has seen more than the death of a fiancé.

It's Halloween and the ER staff has just been told they won first place in the hospital pumpkin-carving contest. The nurse who was about to start my mother on an IV removes her uniform smock to go and collect their prize. She returns with a pumpkin pie decorated with whipped cream, cuts it into slices, and everyone on the staff takes a piece. She comes to the rest of us with a plastic pumpkin filled with miniature candy bars. I dig out a Butterfingers. Bill, who has arrived, ends up with a Snickers. "You got the good one," he says, eyeing my Butterfingers. I pocket it. Later, as I'm crunching into the sweet honey of the Butterfingers bar, I find myself wishing I'd offered it to him, my baby brother.

Mom's eyes are, by now, wide open. I've never been so aware of how blue they are — the Pacific Ocean off the beach at Honolulu on a sunny day. I ask Dr. Bauer to come in behind the curtain so that she and my mother can get a sense of each other.

"Mom, this is Dr. Bauer. She's been taking care of you here in the ER I like her."

The doctor has gotten into costume, her hair rearranged into two braids; brown reeds woven in that stick out the top of her head. "Do I look like Pocahontas?" the doctor asks Mom.

"What is it, Halloween?" my mother asks. "October thirtieth?"

Not bad, I think, only one day off. I never remember which day Halloween is either.

"I want to go home," my mother says, "I don't want to miss the party."

Seeing Double

November 1

"Double, I'm seeing double," Mom says.

After being back in the relative normalcy of The Jewish Home for six days, Mom's now a patient in Encino Hospital with pneumonia again, caused by aspirating food while she was oversedated.

In the ER, she'd come out of the deep sleep she'd been in since the night before. Suddenly aware there was a great big world to see, her eyes were so clear and blue it was as if I were seeing them for the first time.

Now, she's seeing double.

I cover one of her eyes. "Double?" I ask.

"Double."

I cover the other eye. "Double?"

"Double."

She's looking out the door of her room toward the nurses' station. A woman in a red sweater walks by. "I see two," she says.

Two of a woman in a print blouse with magenta flowers sitting at a desk.

Two of a nurse wearing blue.

I hold a finger close to her face.

"One," she says. I wonder, is this happening just with distant vision?

I try again. "Two."

A nurse comes in to check the IV. "My mother is seeing double," I say. The nurse leaves the room without saying a word.

I tell another nurse who says she'll tell the doctor when he comes in to make rounds tonight. It's now two in the afternoon.

Has she had a stroke? I check my mother's grip. Stronger on the side without the IV, but that's to be expected. Nothing on her face looks out of kilter, she can move both feet up and down. Is a tiny blood vessel leaking, the one that supplies the optic nerves near where they cross? Is it a TIA, a transient ischemic – what does the A stand for? Attack? Accident?

"I'm seeing double," she says again, shrugging her shoulders and shaking her head as if it's a fact of life. Like: "Can you believe it, I'm seeing double. What's next?"

I suggest she close her eyes, rest them.

"It's not my eyes," she says.

"I know. Still, maybe it'd be good to give yourself a rest from so much testing."

But why? What am I trying to save her from? Why wouldn't someone, to the very end, want to hold onto every last drop of awareness? If I think, and I do, that being aware is of the essence, why hide from ourselves, or someone we say we love, the inevitable deteriorating that takes place as we come closer to dying?

I think about the book I was reading yesterday — how thought leads us to identify with our physical bodies as if that's all we are. But what if we're awareness itself? And our bodies are gifts we're given to help us love this human life, know the fullness of who we are?

Why not be there as a witness to the deconstruction of this vehicle in which we have been navigating through the world? Why not be there right up to the last moment, the last breath? Life, good to the last drop.

Love And Fear

November 2

The salad bar at Gelson's Market can be counted on to offer the latest in what the Beautiful People of Los Angeles crave. Steamed edamame, black bean salad, couscous, chunks of broiled tofu, these last a nod to the fact that Whole Foods is starting to give Gelson's a run for its money.

I gather the foundation for my salad from things green — spinach leaves, assorted baby lettuces, green peas. Add a layer of white — mushrooms, hearts of palm, hard-boiled egg. Reds — red onion, beets, pearl tomatoes (cherry tomatoes are out, it seems, pearl tomatoes in). A mound of crab salad — who cares if it's fake, it's yummy. At the very top, a scattering of sliced scallions like the maraschino cherry on the mountain of whipped cream at the top of a banana split. Neither Mom nor I have deigned to let go of "scallions" — what a beautiful word — for the "green onions" preferred by Angelenos. I forego the prepared dressings for a sprinkling of olive oil, balsamic vinegar, red wine vinegar, a turn of black pepper.

"Mom, here's a math puzzle for you," I say, having arrived back at the hospital. "If the salad bar salad costs $5.29 a pound and this salad weighs 1.4 pounds, how much did it cost?"

"Whatever it came to, it's worth it," she says. Smart answer!

"But how can I eat a salad in front of you?"

Mom hasn't had one of her beloved salads, drenched in bottled Italian dressing, for weeks, her ability to swallow having become untrustworthy. She gazes on my extravaganza with aesthetic appreciation.

"Go ahead," she says. "You eat."

"You won't be envious?"

"Maybe you *could* give me a little," she says. "Maybe a tomato ..."

I pop a tomato into her mouth. She juices it and spits out the skin. A slice of mushroom. A crinkle-cut beet. A thick slice of palm heart. A round of egg white. A circle of red onion.

"I'm sorry I came," she says, spitting out what she can't chew.

"You didn't have much choice," I say, thinking she means the hospital.

"I should have stayed where I was. Does he have a spare room?"

"Who?" I ask.

"Bill."

"Why?"

"Maybe I could stay with him tonight."

Half There

November 4

Mom's eyes are half closed. She knows I've come into the room but doesn't look up from the lunch she's eating on a way-too-high tray table. To my surprise, her lunch includes a salad.

She holds the fork limply, her hand puffy and decorated with patches of color, a lighter black-and-blue than the steel-gray of her forearms, colors I hardly notice anymore as unusual.

Since she has been taking the drug Plavix to prevent the clotting that could occur from longstanding atrial fibrillation, she bruises easily. Atrial fibrillation is an arrhythmia in the upper chamber of the heart that can cause tiny clots to form and travel, closing off a small vessel in the brain, causing a stroke. But what if the drug, instead of preventing stoppage in a vessel, is causing blood to leak into my mother's brain, the way it's leaking into the tissues under the skin of her forearms?

The way she holds the fork, its tines pointing halfway between up and down, I am surprised she is actually able to get pieces of lettuce up onto it, from the bowl to her mouth. That she keeps trying says how much she still treasures the chance to eat salad.

The lettuce is sodden with French dressing, reminding me of the curvy bottle of Kraft French that sat on our kitchen table in Connecticut, next to the off-center, hand-turned wooden bowl full of the salad she would prepare for our dinner each night — quartered tomatoes, cucumbers scored with the tines of a fork, radishes cut into flowers, the standard iceberg lettuce. She was the first mother, of all my friends, to step out and experiment with Romaine.

She swallows the lettuce, unlike the turkey which she chews and spits out, leaving little mounds lying next to the still-to-be-eaten chunks, lightly glazed with gravy. Strange how many hospital meals resemble Thanksgiving dinner — turkey, stuffing, a green vegetable, mashed potatoes, gravy. Even cranberry sauce.

The day I'd brought the salad for my own lunch back from Gelson's, we'd had a peaceful time together. Mother and daughter, she still definitely the mother, I still definitely the daughter, though I'd fed her, morsel by morsel, like a mother bird feeds her young, attending to their nourishment and pleasure. We'd talked a little that day — she was wide awake — mostly about what she would like to have in her mouth next.

The next day, she was restarted on Risperdal. Once a day, rather than the three times the doctors at UCLA thought she could handle.

Today, Mom is falling asleep in her chair. As two people try to get her into bed, her feet slide out from under her as if she is totally unaware of the ground with its possibility of ever-present support. She rolls toward her right side; they prop a pillow under her to return her slightly to the left, which she doesn't like one bit but quickly falls back to sleep, anyway. A fitful sleep, as she struggles against something she is seeing behind closed eyes, bad dreams passing over her face like clouds.

I wait for the doctor, who has been in the nurses' station writing notes. Dr. Lando is the internist who follows Jewish Home residents when they are in the hospital. For better and worse, he knows my mother well. She remembers him, too, though she has forgotten everything else about all the other hospitalizations.

Mom always talked about the healthy life she lived. "Never sick, never in the hospital," she'd been fond of saying. And it was true. She'd never been seriously sick until well into old age.

One day, home on vacation from college, I noticed a lump under the wide white elastic of her brassiere, the kind of brassiere that came to her waist. Didn't everyone's mother wear that kind of brassiere? And didn't we call them brassieres? I begged her to ask Dr. Corwin, our family doctor, about the lump. She was worried it was cancer, nobody ever said the word cancer in those days.

I was in physical therapy school then and pretty sure it wasn't anything serious.

It took months, maybe it was even years, before she would have it removed, no longer able to live with the worry of what it might actually be. It was a fatty tumor, benign. Now that she's in and out of hospitals, in and out of hospital gowns, I see the long white scar on her back and feel my own scar from those days of inherited worry.

When Dr. Lando comes in, I don't speak, wanting him to see for himself how hard it is for Mom to be roused.

"How long has she been like this?" he asks.

"Since restarting the Risperdal," I say. "I'm so discouraged — that month of hell at UCLA — and we're right back where we started, even worse."

"I know," he says, "we have to stop the Risperdal and take it from there."

He returns to the nurses' station to change the order. I lean over the side railing of Mom's bed, kiss her forehead. She opens her eyes partway. "You're so beautiful," she says.

"And you're so beautiful," I say, putting my cheek next to her mouth for a kiss. It's a weak kiss, reminiscent of the way she was lifting the lettuce to her mouth.

Returning To Some Kind Of Normal

November 5

Not ready to be alone yet, to sleep in my newly rented room where I'll be housemates with Lily and Bonnie, two women I don't know, I call Ginger.

"Can I come to sleep in your house one more night?" I ask. "I feel like a baby."

"Come home to mama," Ginger says.

Bill is sitting next to Mom, not knowing what to do, an almost full dinner tray in front of them. Mom is in bed, head leaning hard to the right, eyes closed.

I lean in close to her and say, almost singing it, "Mom, I'm here." She mimics me and smiles.

"She's better," I say to Bill.

"I know," he says. "I'm just discouraged."

Yesterday, I was down. Today, it's his turn.

Mom seems extremely tired but, whenever she wakes up enough to say something, it's coherent and comes with a soft smile.

I plant my cheek next to her lips. She gives me a whole flurry of kisses.

Getting up to leave, Bill reports she ate all the vegetable soup Lynn made for her, half of the Ensure, a little of the cut-up chicken, one or two pieces of potato and half the Jello. When he and I are good with each other, we are very good — attentive to our mother and accurate reporters to each other about her condition.

Dr. Lando comes in and wakes Mom. She gives him a big smile, tells him she feels fine.

"The nurses say she was more agitated," he tells me. "Maybe we're beginning to see how she's going to be off the Risperdal. We'll have to decide what to do about the anxiety once she's totally out from under the drug."

"I worry when I see her smile," I say.

He shoots me a critical glance. I hurry to explain. "When her carbon dioxide is high, she smiles a lot. Acts drunk."

"Ah," he says, respect returning.

He leaves, and I ask Mom if she'd like me to stop bothering her, stop asking her to wake up. "Would you like me to leave?"

"Maybe that'd be good," she says.

"I'll say goodnight, sit next to your bed for a while and write."

In the next breath, she begins to snore.

Worlds Colliding

November 10

I'd planned to drive down to the hospital between sessions of a weekend Sensory Awareness workshop in Santa Barbara. Relieved to hear Mom sounding so coherent when I call, I remind her I am with Charlotte Selver. She suggests I stay, says she'll be fine.

Over the years, I've spoken to each of them about the other. Mom knows that Charlotte is a hundred-and-one and enjoys hearing about her. Charlotte always sends Mom her best wishes.

Workshop over, I find Mom in bed, eyes wide, pupils large and black. She's insisting to Bill that something bad is going to happen to Lynn, Bill's wife — maybe a car accident. "Somebody's going to be killed," she says. Adamant that something terrible is going to happen or has already happened, the need to tell her story keeps her from hearing what Bill has to say — that Lynn is at home, making dinner.

Her gaze keeps returning to the television that's attached by a mechanical arm to the wall above the foot of her bed. When I came in, the screen, now black, had been tuned to CNN. When Bill is here, the tv is likely to be on. Mom must have seen some violent incident, it might have been an accident, maybe she heard someone say something that sounded to her like "Lynn." I remember what David, the UCLA psychiatrist, said about how easy it is to become disoriented by disembodied sounds.

Bill calls Lynn, hands Mom the phone.

"You're okay?" Mom wants to know. It takes some time but she is finally reassured.

Ninety-Three

November 11

I wake up tired. Tired of all the hospitalizations. Tired of aides who roll my mother back and forth between them like a log as they change her diaper, change the bedding, talking all the while to each other about their own lives, in their own languages. Accents that make it hard for me, let alone my hard-of-hearing 93-year-old mother, to understand them. Tired of the mistakes that get made. Tired of all the people who don't accept that my mother is very old, that very old people act differently than people who are just plain old. It's something I'm learning myself.

"This is Sara, Hannah Epstein's daughter," I say when I call. "How's my mother this morning?"

"She's sitting in the chair, screaming," the nurse berates. I can almost hear her tongue as it tsks against the roof of her mouth.

"What do you do when she screams?" I ask.

"Nothing. We can't give her medication. She has to be awake enough to eat." Do I hear anger in the nurse's voice, petulance? Is she annoyed they can no longer depend on Risperdal to keep her quiet?

"Don't you go in and talk to her?" I ask. "If she's screaming, she must be scared, or need help."

"Oh, yes. We talk to her," the nurse says, bored. Evidently, medication is everything. Talk, nothing.

One day, I walked out of my mother's room, Room 209 in Encino Hospital, to go to the cafeteria in the basement where they have complimentary coffee. It's not Peet's, but it's the hospital's way of reaching out, and there's real milk to go with it. I'm grateful for the gift it provides of a few minutes' respite. I was almost at the elevator when I heard my mother's unmistakable voice. "It's coming. It's coming NOW," she shouted, suddenly aware that urine was on its way. Or a bowel movement.

I rushed back. There was that look in her eye that says, "I'm supposed to do something but I don't know what and even if I knew what I wouldn't be able to do it."

I asked a nurse to come in and "clean her up," words I'd heard myself say more than once, each time hating to hear myself talk about my mother as if she's a thing, an object, milk spilled on the floor by a baby, a car with mud splattered on its fenders, some thing that has to be "cleaned up."

Sometimes, when I find Mom lying in bed with that wild look in her eyes that speaks of fear more than I've ever heard words speak of fear, and I take the time to talk to her in a soothing voice, I discover I have the power to change that look. Lids come slightly down, pupils get smaller, and, rather than stare — not exactly into the distance but also not at anything close-up — she begins to make contact. With a person. With me. And, at least for the moment, fear dissipates, dissolves.

Over the weekend, I had the chance to see how, at a hundred-and-one, Charlotte's energy waxes and wanes — Charlotte, who has always been, literally, a fount of energy. Sometimes now, she comes to class and sits in a wheelchair, tiny and attentive, as an assistant leads the class in her place. Sometimes, she stays in her room.

I saw how willing I was for Charlotte to be just the way she is. How I don't require of her anything other than what she is able to give. I felt the contrast to how I am with my mother, still wanting her to be — what? —- young? I think about how I am still cheerleading her to feed herself, cooperate with the physical therapist who comes to get her out of bed, let go of the stubbornness she's lived by and show the true strength I've always known her to have.

I saw that continuing to force those issues might be depriving Mom of whatever dignity she has left and I determined I would bring a more accepting attitude back with me. To let Mom, like Charlotte, be old.

She's given clues that this is what she wants. In hospital rooms, I've heard her tell me to leave for a while, that she doesn't want me watching over every bite of food she takes. I've heard her tell Bill, whom she dearly loves, to leave altogether.

Of course, she does scream. How would I react to being dependent on a constantly changing parade of people to remember to bring me my hearing aid, help me turn over when my skin is burning from too much pressure, soothe me when I hear something on the tv that makes me think my daughter-in-law has been in a car accident? How would *I* react if urine suddenly streamed from my body with no warning? If, for weeks, I didn't feel the wind, see a tree, watch clouds move across the sky, hear the sounds of traffic? How will I be when I know the end of my life is just around a corner I know is there but I can't quite see?

It poured the whole weekend I was away. I saw rain fall in sheets, heard it pummel pavement, felt it cold on my skin. I saw San Ysidro Creek, crackling dry until the rains came, swell into powerful action.

Several inches fell. Old trees came down. The Los Angeles River actually flowed. And I'll bet that Mom, in her hospital room, didn't even know it was wet outside.

I don't know what grace, or punishing Fate, has seen to it that my mother has lived this long. Ten years ago, unable to imagine her as not just old, but old old, I wouldn't have guessed it or even wanted it. For her, or for me. I wouldn't have guessed there could be something new for us, trying, as I was, to stand upright under what felt like the lifelong burden of our relationship. I'm still not able to articulate exactly what it was that allowed frustration to turn into willingness, annoyance into appreciation, resentment into respect. But I know this: the fact that she has lived so long has been a great, even necessary, gift — definitely for me and, I think, for her, too — a gift wrapped not in red grosgrain, but in Depends and sterile gauze, held together with the plastic tubing of an IV.

For her birthday, I bring Mom the gift of a carefully composed salad-bar salad which, it turns out, she doesn't want. A card, which she does.

An adult elephant and a baby elephant are standing in a small pond. The baby elephant is spraying water as the adult looks on with those white plastic eyes with black beads in them that roll around. Mom gazes at the artwork then feels around to discover how the eyes are attached to the paper.

I ask her if she remembers reading me the stories of Babar, the Elephant. She doesn't.

I watch as she opens the card, reads slowly what I've written, resting on each word and phrase, as if carefully chewing the tomatoes and mushrooms and crinkly-cut beets of the still untouched salad that sits next to the card on the tray table. I acknowledge what a long and full life she's lived. Tell her how happy I am we've had all this time to be together. Say that she and I just keep getting better and not every mother and daughter can say that. "Yay for us," I write and end up wishing her "good health, stimulating days and peace."

She finishes reading and looks at me, shaking her head slowly from side to side. I know what she is going to say and, though I've resisted it my whole life, held it against her for what felt to me like ambivalence and ambiguity, today I look forward to hearing what I am finally ready to accept as a high compliment. "You're something else," she says with a smile.

I take the card from her and read it slowly, out loud. I ask her if she thinks it's true, what I said about us getting better.

She shakes her head yes. "I'm willing to let things

pass," she says.

"And I stick to my guns," I say. "Maybe we've both come toward each other, more to the middle."

She shakes her head again.

I read the part about wishing her peace, afraid it sounds too much like rest-in-peace. "Would it be better if it said 'peace of mind'?" I ask.

"Peace of mind," she says.

I'd found her sitting in a chair behind a piled-up tray table. She had already eaten as much of the soup and jello of the hospital lunch as she wanted and was picking at the soft center of a grilled cheese sandwich. Even before saying hello, she'd told me she is worried about something having to do with her stomach.

I see that what I always thought was true is true. That my mother's worries immediately get translated to whether or not she has recently had, or will ever have again, a bowel movement. "Stomach," in my mother's lexicon, has always meant bowels. Now it includes whether she will make it to the toilet to pee.

I suggest to her that she may be nervous about being discharged from the hospital and feeling that nervousness as concern about her bowels. "Could be," she says.

Ninety-Three And Counting

November 12

Mom's getting ready to be discharged back to The Jewish Home. She asks me to help her put on her face. I get her makeup out of the blue mesh bag that hangs on the side of the aluminum walker with its yellow tennis balls over the front feet to keep them from screeching on bare floors.

"I like this lavender shadow," I say. "With your eyes, it's more subtle than the blue." I brush some rouge over her cheeks and run the brush lightly, playfully, down over her forehead, her nose, her chin. Dab lipstick on her upper lip and ask her to bring her lips together to finish the job. The eyebrows aren't easy, hairs so white they're almost impossible to see. I give it a try, short strokes to form an arch. I lean away, see that the right brow needs to be re-drawn. Put a little soap on a washcloth, create a clean slate, begin again.

Finished, I step back, amazed at how beautiful an old woman can be in a hospital gown, a cotton blanket over her lap littered with soft shards of red Jello.

A Brighter Pink

November 13

Back at The Jewish Home, Mom tells me Dr. Smith came to see her. "He told me I have to stay calm. I'm trying."

Whatever he actually said, she believes that what he meant is that she's dying. She's taken it to heart. "My time is up," she says, closing her eyes.

I tell her I have another thought: that medications she'd been given to blunt her nervousness have been too strong and, by asking her to stay calm, he's asking her to take over some of the responsibility for her mental state.

"Could be. Could be," she says, closing her eyes.

"Hold me. HOLD ME," she shouts. I'd been getting ready to leave.

She's falling through space — or slipping on an icy sidewalk — and needs to feel the weight of a body, my body, against hers, to ease the fear, soften the pain (this is my guess) of leaving this life, alone.

It's a winter's day in Connecticut and my mother and I — I am a little girl, about five — are walking together on the path that winds around the small lake in Binney Park. It's a narrow, icy path. We are bundled up. I am wearing woolen leggings that make me feel clumsy, brown rubbers over my sturdy oxfords. Mommy is wearing galoshes over her pumps with Cuban heels and there's a furry animal around the collar of her coat. Her left hand grips my right; she holds onto me to keep herself steady. Through my mitten, I can feel that she is afraid, afraid she will lose her footing and slip on the ice. I follow her fear from my hand all the way up her arm and into her body. I follow it down, too, into me, into my arm, my shoulder, my back. To the iceberg that's made its way to that space between my shoulder blades and behind my heart.

Until I met Matt, whose hand I got to hold for a while and feel how different it could be to walk on snow and ice with someone who isn't afraid, I was afraid of falling, too. When Matt's foot would slip, it didn't seem to bother him. He'd welcome it, playfully finding his balance again.

Whenever I saw my mother walk, no matter the conditions — winter day, spring day, on a sidewalk, at home in the kitchen — I would be afraid for her. Afraid she would trip over her own foot, as I watched the heel of one foot hit the side of the instep of the other; that way she walked, one foot splayed out, the other straight.

A few days ago, I asked my mother if she was ready to die. "No," she answered emphatically, angry that I would even mention it as a possibility.

"You love life too much to leave?" I asked.

I'd always thought it was *my* love of living that set me apart from the rest of the family. That that was why my mother would say, "Sara, you're something else," whenever she would see me doing something outside the bounds of her own, more careful nature. What if I were to discover, after all these years, that it wasn't only my life she had passed on to me but my love for living? No matter her nervousness and complaining, her resistance to anything that looked like exercise, her telling me to be careful every time I'd walk out the door. What if it was her love for living, despite all the difficulties life had dealt her, that had been my greatest gift from her, the gift I was being given the chance to witness now? The love for living that makes it so hard to die, and maybe, ultimately, easy.

I used to say that my exciting, excitable father, who died, was the alive one. And that Mom, who lived, carried the darkness I felt I had to protect myself against, heaviness that always seemed like death itself. How easy it had been to glorify my father, whose dealings with life were cut short; and to denigrate my mother for her very human faults, faults I had come to know so well. Mom is being put to the test of a long life, a test she is worried about passing, as she tries to hold onto her independence. It's up to me to help her know she's finishing with flying colors.

It's not as if Mom and I haven't had our fun. In the hospital, I showed her a full-page ad for the Clinique gift days. It had been our mother-daughter tradition to make our yearly pilgrimage to the Clinique counter. First, in Connecticut, when Bloomingdale's moved up from New York City to open a store in Stamford. Later, after Mom moved to California, we'd go to the Bullocks in Westwood, when there still was a Bullocks; most recently, to Nordstrom's in Thousand Oaks. I'd help her up onto the high stool, where a young woman in a white jacket would test, with a cotton ball, different shades of powder on my mother's fair skin. We could never quite remember the name of her shade and there would always be the discussion about whether to buy loose powder this time, or pressed. She would go home with a fresh bottle of Dramatically Different Moisturizing Lotion, a new lipstick, and we'd share the treasures in the gift pouch — the little pots of rouge, the hard-to-open plastic cases filled with the never-quite-right-for-anyone shades of eyeshadow. Our only bone of contention being the lipstick — she was always attracted to a brighter shade than I thought was right for her fair skin. Finally, I can smile when I think about the lifelong disagreement we had the chance to play out every Clinique gift season. I may be something else. But she is something else, too.

A Good Enough Mother

November 14 and 15

"This isn't the hospital," Mom says. "I have to get to the hospital."

"Why do you need to get to the hospital? You're getting better."

"Well, then, give me some water."

"Okay, but just a little."

"No, not just a little," she demands, pointing to the pink plastic water pitcher. "Give me the whole thing."

I hand her a Styrofoam cup, filled halfway.

"This isn't where I live," she says, more question than statement.

"It is," I say. "Look around, this is your room." For the moment, she is satisfied.

"You're wearing your new sweater, I wasn't sure you were going to keep it."

"I didn't even notice," she says, looking down at a brown bouclé cardigan with beige collar and cuffs.

"It looks nice. It's really good quality. It's for your birthday."

"How much was it?"

"Fifteen dollars at Ross," I say. "A bargain."

Georgina arrives for her second visit of the day. Mom

tells me that Georgina found the sweater in the closet and helped her into it. Whenever I buy something for Mom, I figure she'll try it on the next day, when she's fresh. Only then will I take the price tags off, hang it back in the closet to be worn on another day. It's a different story when Georgina comes. It's off with the price tags, on with the new blouse or pants or sweater. No thinking about it. No waiting for another day.

Georgina is a sturdy woman, with a huge smile. Her teeth are very white and there is a wide gap between her front teeth. Every time she looks in the mirror, she tells me, she sees the gap as a sign of her own mother's lack of attention to her when she was a child in El Salvador. I tell her I see the gap as part of her beauty.

Georgina and my mother met six years ago when Mom was still living in her own home. Georgina would come in for a few hours every couple of days to help with the driving, the cooking and shopping. They'd go to Vons together, to Dr. Stokols' office, to Roundtable for pizza. Sometimes, Georgina would bring Helena with her, the youngest of her four daughters, just a toddler then, who dubbed Mom "Hannah Banana." When Mom would play for her, she was "Hannah Banana at the Piana."

After Mom moved to The Jewish Home, Georgina and Helena would come to visit and Mom would invite them to join her in the dining room for lunch. After one of their visits, I was surprised to hear Mom say Georgina's voice was too loud. I wondered, was she trying to keep up appearances in this new home of hers, didn't want people to think she needed a caregiver? Now, each time Georgina leaves, Mom shakes her head in wonderment. "No one ever had such a good friend," she says.

A few years ago, Mom started stumbling over Georgina's name; now, it almost always comes out Regina. It's curious to me. Even more curious that Bill stumbles over her name in the same way.

"Mom, who was the first president?" I ask.

"George Washington," she answers. "Oh ... Georgina," she says.

At Encino Hospital, Dr. Lando is her doctor. No matter how many times I remind them — Mom and Bill — both of them pronounce his name as if it had an au at the end: Landau.

Now that Georgina has gotten a job taking care of Anne, a woman in the Alzheimer's building next door, she stops in to visit Mom every day before and after work.

"We should make Georgina part of the family," I say.

"She already is," Mom says. Mom is like a second mother to Georgina, and I'm starting to feel like she and I are sisters.

Mom is lying in bed, her upper body wrapped in the new sweater, the rest of her in a lap robe crocheted by her older sister, Doris. Doris, who died at 85 of Alzheimer's disease in a nursing home in Florida, was an artist who knew how to put colors together, the little afghan an improvisational design made from leftover yarn — one earth tone taking over where the last length of another leaves off. It's been in storage. Mom says she doesn't remember having seen it before.

I don't know what to say about my mother's memory. It comes and goes. Maybe it's better not to remember every little thing that happened yesterday or an hour ago, even everything that happened in the good old, bad old days. I don't know what to say about her judgment either. She tells me again that the breathing machine that sits on her night table is a gift from Dr. Smith.

"Would you like to go to the dining room for dinner?" I ask. Since returning from the hospital, she's been eating her meals in bed. "You could go in the wheelchair," I say. I'm happy to hear her say yes.

As we talk, she becomes less agitated, more coherent. "You're feeling better," I say.

"Since you came," she says.

Arlene comes in to give my mother a breathing treatment.

Angie, who Mom tells me saved her life with some water, comes back to change her diaper.

"It's coming," my mother says, announcing her urine

as much to herself as to anyone else.

I have a cold and am sitting several feet away. "Take care of yourself," she tells me.

"I miss being able to hug you," I say, imagining how it will be when she will no longer be here for me to hug.

The next day, a friend reads to me from her journal about feeling an ancient longing for connection, something her mother hadn't been able to fill, and that even to feel the longing has been an arduous journey. Will a deep pool of unmet needs arise in me when my own mother is gone? Or is my need for a "good enough mother" being filled right now? Conditions have thrown us into a kind of closeness that may not have been possible when I was a baby or any time after. I can no longer disappear, physically or mentally. Can't stomp out in anger. The ravages of an aging body and brain make it impossible for Mom to turn her head away in stubbornness. She hasn't said, "Let's drop it," the mantra I grew up hearing for a very long time.

Mom and Krishnamurti

November 16

I imagine a young girl running to her mother to show her a shell she has found at the edge of the sea. A stick of dried dog poop. A red button. *This* mother is interested.

These days, my mother, formerly too preoccupied with her troubles to pay attention, is interested, too, in what I bring to her. Yesterday, I told her I'd been reading the Indian teacher Krishnamurti and thought about her. Over the years, she's heard me talk about Krishnamurti. Came with me to an evening of meditation with another favorite teacher, Catherine Ingram. Whenever I mention Charlotte Selver, Mom smiles in recognition, appreciation. Years ago, Mom agreed, under duress, to participate in the *est* training. It was in the '70s and the West Coast phenomenon had found its way to Connecticut.

"Mom, Krishnamurti says that if we keep worrying, by the time we are old, even sixty, our minds, our brains are so heavy and full there's little room for freshness. Instead, he says, 'we can let the past and the future go and be right here, for what is *actually* happening.'" Knowing how suggestive she is, I don't tell her that he calls this process dying, dying to each moment.

"Without worrying, Mom, we can make the most of our time together while you and I are still, both, very much alive."

Hot!

November 20

"Can you believe how hot it is!" a woman says.

"I can't," a man answers.

The three of us are standing in the checkout line at B&B Hardware. I lean my head back and squeeze drops of liquid tears into my eyes, feel the wetness pool just above my lower lid, run down my face; temporary relief from air that crackles with dryness. It gives me comfort to hear these strangers speaking out on a day too hot for me to speak for myself.

I've moved into a big, old white house on top of a hill in the middle of Los Angeles. My room has three doors, an inner door that opens into the dining room at the heart of the house; an outer door that opens onto a side walkway, its tired screen door hanging cockeyed on its hinges.

I've come to B&B Hardware to pick up a handle, a

hook and eye, so I can pull the screen door closed as much as possible. It needs to be re-hung, or the bottom shaved, so it can be pulled all the way, not scrape so hard against the stairs that lead down to the walkway. Last night, with all the doors closed, the heat in my room was so oppressive it was four in the morning before I could sleep. My goal for tonight is to be able to leave the outer door open for cross ventilation, the door into the dining room, too. Where Blanca, the Australian Shepherd who lives with us, will settle into her favorite place, sleeping with one eye open for each of us, well-herded, safe through the night.

"How long do you think the heat'll last?" the woman continues.

Yes, how long can this hot spell last, I think. This weather that has straightened my hair and crinkled the skin on the palm sides of my fingers into hills and valleys, rubbed my nerves raw?

"Isn't it great!" the woman says. "Don't you just love the heat?"

Clunk.

Culture shock.

I forget that people in LA actually come here for the heat. The more sun, the better.

"Too damn much light," I've said more than once since I moved here thirty years ago. My heart sinks when spring starts popping up in February, wildflowers along Santa Monica Mountain trails raising their yellow and purple faces to the sun. Back East girl that I am, winter should be in all its glory now, giving us the dark time, the downtime we need to be inside one's home and one's self.

Fall in LA is crazy, too, bringing winds that blow the wrong way. Not up from the ocean but across the caked dirt of the flat central valley, down through dusty canyons to the sea. In the process, turning everything that's electric in us, or magnetic, around, leaving us aswim in positive ions. The only tradeoff for our edginess and the smog-buried horizon is that you can finally see the mountains to the east.

Tempers get short. People are so in love with sun and heat, they don't notice. I fantasize about escaping to a place where mist hangs in the air and gray light softens the edges of mountains. Softens the edges of people.

I love it when it rains and it's okay to do nothing. A reprieve from having to accomplish things. I remember one winter in the '70s when it rained so hard that Canoga Avenue in the San Fernando Valley, near where we lived when Matt and I were first together, became a river and people paddled down it in canoes.

I tell Mom about how hot it was in my room last night, too hot to sleep. She opens her eyes and looks out the window, as if into another world where weather is part of life. She is lying in bed, on her usual right side. "I dreamed that I was dying," she says. "I needed water. I couldn't get it, so I was dying."

"You're alive now," I say. But she'd rather stay with the dream, how upset she was that she was dying.

"It's not just a dream," she says. "It's reality. When the oxygen stops flowing, I'll die."

I readjust the clear tubing that runs from the oxygen supply into two cannulas, one for each nostril. "The oxygen will flow as long as you need it," I say. "I'm not even sure you still need it."

I tell her I'll be back later.

"I may not be here," she says.

"Just in case, is there anything you have to say to me you haven't said? I know you love me. You know I love you."

"Nothing else," she says.

Last night, as I was struggling to sleep, kicking off the comforter, getting up to open the closet door so that air could come in through the closet's open window — this is a strange house, there's a window in the closet — my mind wandered to whether Mom was still alive.

The emptiness I felt was shocking. I was standing at the edge of a cliff, one more step and suddenly there would be no ground beneath me where, just a moment before, there was.

One day, the call will come and there will be no getting around it, Mom having managed to do whatever she needed to do to leave her life behind. About to drop off into sleep, I saw myself sailing into a full moon, throwing an anchor into the light.

Touching Down

November 21

"LA's fine but it ain't home. New York's home but it ain't mine no more." It's been thirty years since I flew into LA and I haven't landed yet. It's especially hard to claim LA as my own in times like this. So hot it's hard to move, even against air.

Just when I imagine LA being brought to its knees by the heat, the image is destroyed by a woman walking by, a lavender yoga mat under her arm, happy determination on her face, the keys to a shiny new Volvo dangling from her hand.

What do you want from LA anyway, Sara?

How 'bout to stop and say hello, recognize I'm here?

In Manhattan, I felt known. By the woman in a hurry to catch the downtown bus. The community of browsers at Doubleday Books. My fellow sugar-donut eaters squeezed together at the Chock Full o'Nuts counter. By the doorman at 14 Horatio Street in the West Village, where I lived in the high-rise Van Gogh. Before that, by Leroy, the super of my fifth-floor walkup on the other side of Eighth Avenue at 34 Horatio. The bag lady who'd hang out in front of Tiffany's until the evening rush hour, when she would pack up her things, return to her own doorway. The man who brushed by me on Fifth Avenue one wintry day in a calf-length mink coat.

In LA, you don't touch people. It's too dangerous, too expensive. Years of increased insurance premiums if you get a little too close on the 405, make even the smallest dent in their carefully waxed armor.

In New York, people run around like chickens without their heads. In LA, everybody looks like they know where they're going.

Does anybody — anybody here at The Rose Café know any more about how to get through this life than I do? Even you, you, in your perfect knee-length black Lycra shorts and fluorescent green t-shirt, latest Ray-Bans, perfect water bottle? Do *you* know where you're going?

Appearances!

A would-be writer might see *me* sitting at this small table, words flowing onto the page, and long to be "committed to writing the way *she* is."

Now, *there's* some ground I can stand on. My commitment to find the right words for each step of this constantly changing journey.

Last night, I found Mom sitting next to her bed. It was after dinner and she seemed to be asleep, though these days it's hard to tell, being awake doesn't look much different.

"Mom, can you open your eyes?"

She gazes around and asks me about the children in the photograph on top of her bureau.

"Alana and Jon," I say, "Joanna's children."

"Joanna ... " She's reaching into memory.

"Joanna, Matt's daughter. And you know Jon, he came to your house, you served him chicken. He always tells me he remembers that you served him chicken."

"I don't remember him," says my half-sleeping mother.

"You could think of Joanna as your granddaughter, Alana and Jon as your great-grandchildren." I say it, maybe for the twentieth time, still trying to give Mom the family I think she wants. She's never bought it.

I tell her that Jon and his girlfriend, Brianna, are having a baby. "You could be a great-great-grandmother!" I say, to which she manages a weak smile.

The truth is that Joanna has always seen me as more

of a friend than a stepmother and Jon and Alana can't quite figure out *who* I am, it's been so long since their grandfather and I have been together.

When I was 39, I missed a period. It was the only time Matt and I had had sex in months, and I got pregnant. I told him and, right away, made plans for an abortion. I don't remember us ever talking about it, then or later. A friend went with me to a women's clinic on Pico Boulevard and, when it was over, brought me home. All I remember is the cramping high up where my vagina meets my belly. That night, I stood in front of 250 people in a hotel ballroom in Universal City and led an *est* graduate seminar. It was called "Be Here Now." It was about upsets in people's lives.

Matt and I had been living together for seven years, had finally gotten married in hopes that that would make a difference. But our home was a tinderbox that could be set aflame by the rubbing together of almost any two words. We fought and not just in words but by restraining each other's physical moves, even hitting each other. I was on shaky ground at work, too, and felt dependent on Matt. Not a safe or stable situation for me to be in, let alone any kind of atmosphere to bring a baby into.

Still, if I'd been more awake to myself in those days,

I might not have made the decision alone. Talking with Matt about it might have been the blessing that was needed to lead to an earlier divorce. I might have given the spark that, for a moment, was lighting up my insides at least the respect of some say in the matter. Some understanding of what was going on.

For the next six years, I fought for the possibility of Matt and me staying married and having a child together. One night, when I was 45 (he was 60 then), he agreed to have a baby with me. We were having dinner at The Good Earth in the Marina. Later, over cups of that sweet, spicy tea we both liked, I went on to say I wanted to get my master's degree and was about to register for classes in the Clinical Psych program at Antioch University. Without missing a beat, he reneged, said he saw himself being left at home with the baby while I was out starting a new career. What was I up to that night? It still confuses me.

Maybe he was right. Maybe I was looking for an out. Or maybe reneging was his way of punishing his first wife, Joanna's mother, who *had* gone back to graduate school in psychology when *their* children were young, leading to the end of their marriage.

I didn't have the baby. I did get my master's degree. And it would take six more years for us to even start the divorce.

The crackle of cellophane and the sound of women singing mariachi songs over the loudspeaker returns me to the world of right here, where, when I'm at my best, I can be how I would have wanted to be with a baby. The way I needed my mother to be with me. The way, more and more each day, I can be with my mother.

I close my eyes and, here at The Rose, enjoy a soup of sounds and sights all mixed up together like the carrots and celery and lentils I puréed last night in a blender.

Life. Nourishing. Delicious.

Dying Isn't Easy

November 22 and 23

The volunteer leading the Shabbat celebration asks who would like to read the blessing over the bread. A wicker basket filled with chunks of challah is making its way around the circle.

Lauretta, a little more dressed up than usual in what we used to call a duster, says, "Let *her* read," pointing at me.

Mom, in her new brown and beige sweater — no dentures, no makeup — raises her hand and reads the prayer, slowly and with feeling, each word enunciated to perfection. I shake my head in wonder. Dementia? We tell her how beautiful her reading was. There is something about this mother of mine that leads people to be amazed.

One day after Mom had had moved to The Jewish Home and I was still living in her house, two friends came to visit. "Is that your mother?" one of them asked, pointing to the photograph on the piano from Mom's 80th birthday party. "She's radiant."

"Glowing," said the other woman.

Months later, at a meeting to review Mom's progress after the second pneumonia, Mom sat at the head of a long table. Chita, the head nurse, was on her left, I on her right. Christine, the dietician, was there; Gayla, the social worker; Howard, the activities director; June, the male Filipino nurse whose job it was to make sure Mom got in a daily walk; the team of Gladys and Elba, who would help Mom get dressed every morning and, I realize now, I didn't appreciate enough.

Mom took over the meeting, thanking each person in detail for the specific contribution he or she was making to her getting well. She was The Little Engine that Could, transporting each one of us on this journey with her to a destination she had clearly in mind.

She called Gladys and Elba "the girls" and thanked Howard — he had always been Howie to her, somehow now he was Howard — for encouraging her to play the piano again.

When she was finished, the room was quiet and peaceful, not much left for anyone else to say. A meeting that had been called for twenty minutes had lasted almost an hour.

"This is my daughter," she added as if everyone at the table didn't know me inside and out. "She keeps pushing me, thinks I should be doing more for myself."

Amidst all the praise she'd been offering to others, this felt like a slap. Tears of wonder and admiration began to sting. Still swept away by this woman's graciousness and command of the situation, I felt hurt not to be included as a member of her team. Or was I?

Today, the Shabbat celebration over, I run into Dr. Smith. It's the first time I've seen him since the day, two months ago, when I'd begged him not to send her to UCLA.

"The problem is this," he tells me. "Hannah's oxygen is low, her carbon dioxide high. She's always at the point where something could push her over the edge. We have to see what we can do to keep her well."

I tell him what an awful experience the psych ward had been — for her, for me. That my intuition had been right, that the antipsychotic medications they were so bent on giving her were too strong.

"We know that now," he says.

"What you told her about staying calm seems to be working."

He laughs. "Maybe I did tell her that. Her memory's better than mine!"

I tell him I'm reinforcing it, the possibility that she can keep herself calm enough for anxiety not to take over, render her out of control. Pluck weeds as you see them growing and they won't choke off the flowers. I tell him I've talked to her about meditation, taught her how to pay attention to her breathing.

He's skeptical about the calm, given her physical condition. I, too, have seen how even a small change can make her wild with anxiety. Still, he says he's willing to keep reminding her of the part she can play.

I return later to find out that a chest X-ray, taken to see what might be causing a high white cell count, shows a problem at the base of both lungs. Another pneumonia? My heart sinks.

Dinner over, Mom turns away from me, orders me to get the aide so she can be put to bed.

"I know you're tired, Mom, but I need something else from you than the side of your face and a harsh tone."

She turns toward me, a broad smile suddenly lighting her face. Even at the end of a long day, even at 93, even in a wheelchair, even with what looks to be the beginning of a new pneumonia, my mother has some ability to manage her behavior and some of this ability has to do with giving me what I want.

In *The New Yorker,* I read an article about the genetic basis of anxiety. How innately anxious people develop all kinds of strategies for overcoming, disguising, avoiding, repressing, and, sometimes, exploiting their tendency to nervousness. "Exploiting" rang true. Thoughts jumped to how hard it's been to be my mother's daughter. The energy I've spent trying to make her happy. How it seems to have taken more than one person to live her life.

I'm suddenly aware that since the last pneumonia (the fourth? the fifth?), I've been expecting very little from Mom. As if I've moved from hoping she will get well to waiting for her to die. Monitoring the tiny in and out movements of her chest, I walk the line between acceptance, resignation, exhaustion.

But wait! Didn't I hear Dr. Smith say, "We have to see what we can do to keep her well."

It's Not Over 'Til It's Over

November 24

The black and white of Mom's jacket accentuates how pale she is. Thin, white hair, combed back and held in place with water, shouts how much she needs a good haircut. We'd bought the jacket a year ago, the day I took her to lunch at Chin Chin, on the second floor of an outside mall on Ventura Boulevard in Encino. She'd been able to maneuver getting on and off the escalator, while I rode behind her carrying the walker. It would take a miracle for us to do that today.

I pull a chair up close, so I can talk directly into her right ear. Her hearing aid is being repaired. For an extra hundred dollars, the audiologist said, we could get an extended guarantee. After a rather long pause, I said yes, opting for Mom to make it through another year. At 93, decisions like this take on a whole new meaning.

I tell Mom I've been thinking about her breathing. Show her, as if I am holding a closed accordion, what I mean. How, when her arms are held tight against her sides, inside the arms of the wheelchair, there's no room for her lungs to expand. I say that whenever I'm here I'm going to suggest she take deep breaths. Invite her to take short walks with me, which will also encourage deeper breathing.

"I breathe," she says, that flat-lipped expression I'm so familiar with around her mouth.

"More," I say.

She yawns.

"What if you made believe you were yawning? That would bring a lot of air in."

In a yoga class this morning, I felt my diaphragm being exercised by powerful out-breaths, how that led to stronger in-breaths. "Remember the story about the wolf who huffed and puffed and blew the house down?" I say. I blow out three times; show her how, if she brings her hand to the front of her face, she'll be able to feel gusts of air against her palm. I blow again and her hair flies.

"Enough," she says. "Get my walker. I want to play Bingo."

At dinner, Shirley wheels over to report that, earlier, Mom had been screaming, that she hadn't expected me to be gone as long as I was and was sure some disaster had struck me down. Shirley is the self-appointed "teller" here.

Mom looks away.

"Next time, Mom, I'll make sure you have enough information so you don't have to worry. Can you look at me?"

"It takes time to recover," she pouts.

Dinner over, she says she's ready to go to bed. I bring her the walker, say I'll follow behind with the wheelchair. Every few steps, she stops and looks back toward the chair, finally losing her temper, refusing to take another step. She leans back ready to sit, as if there's no question a chair is going to appear. Somehow, I'm fast enough to catch her.

I tell Angie how important it is to lock the wheelchair's brakes before letting someone sit down, how the person should reach back with one hand so they know the chair is there, that it hasn't slid away.

"Always something new to learn," says Angie.

Forty years ago, when I was a physical therapist in New York, part of my job was to lead an in-service training every Friday afternoon for new employees. "It's important to lock the brakes on the wheelchair," I would say. "And don't let anyone sit down without reaching back to make sure there's actually a chair behind them."

Has anyone been listening? Has anyone heard?

Needs Of The Soul

November 25 and 26

"Now that you're here, maybe we could go in together," Mom says, having removed herself earlier from the Bingo game. Though the game has broken up, the women are still sitting at the long table, silent as lemons and pears in a still life painting.

"What's going on?" I ask.

Suddenly, everything gets set into motion again, as if these women had fallen into some kind of trance, my attention being the kiss they needed to wake up.

Mom asks her roommate her name. "My memory's bad," she apologizes.

"Miriam," the bright-eyed redhead answers. "And whose memory is good?"

"I'm sorry about last night," my mother offers.

"Nothing to be sorry about," says Miriam. "You need me; I need you."

"I couldn't help it. I thought I was dying."

During the night, Mom must have yelled out as she is getting a reputation for doing, and Miriam, who doesn't mince words, or feelings, must have told her to shut up. That's how she would have said it. "Shut up!"

"You need me to tell you to stop," Miriam tells my

mother.

"What do you need my mother for?" I ask.

"To love me," she says. "We all need love."

Miriam's hair is the dark red that younger women opt for these days. Her scalp is pink, the hair so thin you can see where each individual hair emerges. At the top of her forehead, at the hairline, there is a deep scar. A not-so-good job of hair implantation? Facelift? Can it be that she's had brain surgery?

She's dressed in a cotton housecoat in a bright floral print. The night I was at my mother's bedside 'til very late, putting off, as long as possible, sending her to the hospital with what turned out to be the latest pneumonia, Miriam's bed was empty. It was one in the morning and I wondered where she was. Her radio was playing what it is set to play all night — waves lapping the shore. I found her in the dining room, alone, watching tv.

Miriam and my mother are an unlikely pair. If my mother was asked to choose one word to describe herself, it wouldn't take her long to say, "refined." I would bet that Miriam, over the course of her life, has stayed as far away from "refined" as she could get. "In your face" would be more like it. Maybe they do need each other.

Across the table sits Elsie, her chest even smaller than my mother's, a hard little barrel. She fights for each breath and is never without a canister of oxygen. Elsie and Mom know each other from their time together in the Transitional Care Unit, and, whenever they pass in the hallway or in the dining room, they reach a hand toward the other. Sometimes, blow a kiss.

"I love your mother," Elsie tells me. "I'm tired of fighting. I've lived too long. You get to a point when you're too old. It's time to go."

I ask her how her family feels about it. "I only have nieces," she says, "I never married."

"What work did you do?"

"RN," she says.

Ida, who sits next to Mom's bad ear at the dining table and leaves meal after meal untouched, not even going so far as to pick at her food, joins in. "My back pain never lets up," she tells me. "I'm ready to pass on. I can't talk to my children about it. It's good to say it to someone. I've had enough."

The next day, Ida is out of her wheelchair, walking. I ask about the pain. She shrugs her shoulders, opens her eyes wide, lips opening into a mechanical smile as if to say, "Today it's better, who knows why?" Is it possible that getting it off her chest about wanting to die — off her back — made the difference?

"Might this be a day for makeup?" I ask Mom. Max Factor, for whom this Factor building is named, would be tickled pink to know how often this mother of mine, at 93, is still interested in making up her face. I go to her room, bring back her trusty old blue-flowered makeup case, the zipper torn away from one side, remove the oxygen from her nose, take off her glasses and give the tube of Clinique Almost Makeup a little squeeze onto the tip of her index finger. She dots it onto her cheeks, upper lip, chin. She keeps saying there's nothing left in the tube, but I keep squeezing, and it keeps coming. "Don't worry, Mom. I'll get you more when you need it."

I open the pale green compact of rosy blush, hand her the brush, hold the mirror up. She moves her head to center her face in it. I move the mirror to follow her. It's a jerky dance we're doing. Either I'm not good enough at following, or she isn't leading decisively. Probably, both.

I show her the makeup trick my haircutter, Ginger, showed me, to play the brush lightly from forehead to top of nose to chin for an overall glow.

Tight shoulders make it hard for her to lift the eyeshadow brush to her lid. Lavender powder sifts onto the delicate, white puff of skin under her eye.

I make soft, short strokes along the line of her brow with her red Maybelline pencil, hold the mirror so she can see the finished product. "I didn't realize how homely I am," she says.

I remember better times when she would sit on a chair in front of the mirrored closet doors in her bedroom and gaze at herself after putting the finishing touches on her face, a private, silent conversation going on between good friends. Today, her heart isn't in it.

At dinner, she pushes away the plate of chicken cut into tiny squares. "I'm going to have to talk about this to someone," she says. "They treat me like a baby."

In the two weeks since she's been back from the hospital, they've been serving her a regular diet. Now, all of a sudden, it's back to everything cut up into small pieces, nothing that requires too much chewing. It's hard to find the rhyme or reason for changes that show up; worse, no one explains them and she's left in the dark.

I take the long walk to the main kitchen, bring back a regular meal. She asks me to cut up the chicken breast into small pieces, and she eats.

People die in nursing homes not just because they're old but because little things that could be done to keep them well go unnoticed — chest free to breathe; informed about changes in their diet so they don't get confused and agitated; making sure their companion at the dining table is sitting next to their good ear, not their bad.

I hear myself starting to call The Jewish Home a nursing home. Even the day when I heard Dr. Smith say that almost everyone in nursing homes has a urinary tract infection, I didn't give in. But I'm tired of keeping up the pretense that this place is in another category.

It's true that when you walk in you're not hit with the smell of urine. It's true that Mom is dressed and out of bed every day. It's true there are activities geared to keep people's minds active. With all that, there's a cultural divide that's hard to bridge. People most responsible for the residents' daily lives are more comfortable in languages other than English. Many have accents that make what they say incomprehensible to old Jewish ladies — old Jewish hard-of-hearing ladies.

Even more important, many of the helpers seem to be asleep. Good people, asleep. Too much work for too little money? Too upsetting, day after day, to be around old people? Or is it the kind of unconsciousness that's affecting us all as we try to meet the needs of a world spinning faster each day?

A Precious Moment

November 27

"Wawdah, get me wawdah," Mom says. It's mid-afternoon and she's in bed with the call light on.

"Hold on, Mom," I say, my voice thin and high-pitched. "You're not dying."

"It feels like I am," she says.

I hand her the Styrofoam cup that's been sitting on her night table and she sips eagerly from it. Even if she hadn't been too weak to sit up, the cup would have still been too far away to reach. I realize how dependent she really is.

"Bill called me on my cell phone," I say. "He's on his way over." A couple of days before, I had shown her my phone and tried to explain "wireless." She shook her head, something else in the world passing her by.

"Get me up, I don't want him to see me like this." She actually looks better than she's looked in days, even weeks, her eyes alert to the room, to me, to how she wants to look for her son. "And get me my hearing aid."

Vickie, the nurse, told me that, rather than play Bingo, Mom had asked to take a nap. "Rest a little," I say.

I feel for the bottle of nail polish in my pocket. Mom's been giving me trouble over the look of my nails. My plan is to polish them here. I make sure the oxygen coming in through the wall is turned off, also the valve on the green metal tank on the back of her wheelchair. Mom and I are not past sparks flying.

"Regina was here," she tells me. "She took me outside."

I tell her the traffic was heavy.

"Because of the holiday," she says. "Tomorrow's

Thanksgiving."

I ask you again. Dementia?

Bill arrives, takes his turn sitting in the wheelchair. "I'm officially retired now," he tells Mom.

"We were just talking about you," I say. "How you were the one in the family who got the money gene. You're retired. I'm still waiting for my work to begin."

I show him how to lower the rails on the bed, ask if he'd mind trying to find Mom's hearing aid. "My nails are drying."

He finds the hearing aid rolling around loose in the night-table drawer, battery door closed, not open the way it should be to preserve the charge.

"You wouldn't believe it," I tell him, meaning all the things, big and small, that go wrong.

"I believe it," he says.

"But you don't see it every day the way I do." I'm still pushing for recognition and this time he doesn't fight me. Working together, we get Mom out of bed, into the wheelchair.

Bill wheels Mom out to the lobby. I bring her walker and, with one of us on either side, we walk out the front door to a bench. We help her on with the gray sweater decorated with blue and black sequins I'd found in her stored-away clothes. Except for the moth hole near the right shoulder, it's new to her. "I've gotten compliments on it," she says. "Take me inside, I'm cold."

Is she really cold, or is she anxious about being in fresh air, an environment unfamiliar by now? We ask her to stay for a few minutes more. She agrees, never losing the faraway look that has her inside again.

We arrive for the last Bingo card. Bill sits next to Mom, prompting her to cover her numbers when they're called. She doesn't need prompting. It's *his* anxiety speaking.

Elizavetta sits on my right. She kids with Michael, the man calling out numbers, that she never wins. This hand, she does. Tells me it's because I was sitting next to her. She shoos away the prize Michael offers, reminding him she only plays for books. Romance novels in Russian.

"My Trader Joe's is near a Russian bookstore," he tells her. "I'll see what they have."

She puts in her order for Danielle Steele. "In Russian!"

Rachel waits patiently at the entrance to the tv room for Dr. Phil to come on. Her white hair, parted on the side, falls straight to her shoulders. She wears a dark green turtleneck. I tell her she looks beautiful in green.

You never know which language Rachel is going to greet you with — English or Yiddish. "Are you merried?" she asks with a Yiddish accent, telling me I look beautiful, too.

"Vy not?" she asks when I tell her no.

"I'm divorced."

"Oy." She frowns, nodding up and down as if trying to take in something beyond her comprehension.

"I'd like to be married," I say. "Keep your eyes open for a good man for me."

Her blue eyes go up toward Heaven. I feel comforted by this, even hopeful. If anyone here has a private line to God, it's Rachel.

I leave Mom sitting on the sofa at least facing toward, if not actually watching, Dr. Phil. Bill has his arm around her.

I get his attention, point back to the two of them, so sweet together. A few minutes before, I'd told him I've been wanting to buy a video camera but I keep putting it off, thinking it's too late, that the most precious moments with Mom have passed. And then, there's a moment like this.

I'd asked him if he wanted to contribute; he'd said he wasn't sure.

"I see what you mean about the camera," he says.

Rude!

November 28

Eileen closes her eyes and opens her mouth at the same time her right arm comes up and around as if she is on the mound, winding up for a life-or-death pitch. At 81, she's one of the younger women here on the first floor of the Factor Building. It's angry words she's pitching, her arm, extended out as long as it can go by an index finger that has "pointer" written all over it. Which ensures there will be no confusion about where her rage is directed. It is directed at me.

"Your mother is RUDE," Eileen shouts. "And so are you."

Sylvia, the enthusiastic Armenian volunteer who plans activities for these thirty-or-so Jewish women, has wheeled Eileen to a table where she can sit with her and try to calm her down, the table directly behind where I am sitting with Mom. I feel the heat of Eileen's rage burning into my back.

Since her stroke, she can rarely find the word she's looking for. Which is part of her rage. Other days, she shines a beautiful smile on me and asks how my father is, meaning my mother. As upsetting as it is to hear her hurl "RUDE" at me and Mom, I am thrilled for her that she has found the right word to express outside what her insides want to say.

Mom is pushing away a plate of turkey, tiny pieces in a bed of thickened gravy, a small ball of stuffing, half a yam. The laminated sign on her tray still reads, Soft Mechanical, the kitchen not having caught up with what the nurse and I determined the day before — that Mom is now safe eating regular food.

I find Mom a new meal, one that looks more like Thanksgiving dinner. On top of the piano, find a bowl of cranberry sauce and spoon some onto her plate.

"I'm wet," she says.

"What do you want to do?" I ask.

"I'm not hungry anyway," she answers.

"Mom, let's get you clean and dry. There's no reason why you shouldn't be comfortable for Thanksgiving dinner."

"It'll get cold," she says.

I ask Sylvia if there's a way to warm it up.

"RUDE!" Eileen hurls another pitch.

I tell Tessie that my mother's diaper needs to be changed. Tessie is a kind Filipina aide. When she is here, I breathe easy. Even Angie, Mom's favorite, often seems preoccupied — Mom's hearing aid, just back from being fixed at a cost of $600, thrown into the drawer; yesterday's clothes, thrown into the bottom of the closet.

Tessie brings Mom back to the dining room. Sylvia brings yet another Thanksgiving dinner, the third now, and Mom hasn't had a bite of food yet. I rescue the cranberry sauce from plate #2, transfer it to #3.

Anna, who sits across from my mother, is deaf. "Cold. The turkey is cold," she says, pushing it away with her fork. "And not even cranberry sauce."

"Anna, here, here's cranberry sauce," I say.

It's true, before I arrived no one had brought the bowl of cranberry sauce to their table.

"We had restaurants," Anna says. "Never served cold food. It's not right." She tells me she is a hundred-and-one and that her husband just died. "He was a hundred and one and ten months," she says. "We would have been married seventy-five years. In all those years, we never ate a meal out, not one." She accepts the cranberry sauce I offer.

My mother is picking at the food, finally pushing the plate away in favor of dessert, a small wedge of pumpkin pie, before going back to finish up the cranberry sauce.

I go over to Eileen, looking for a chance to make peace. She glares at me. I pull back, as if from a hot stove.

Until the Twelfth of Never

November 29

To get into the dining room, we've got to pass by a woman who has stationed herself as door guard. I have yet to remember her name, always so taken with those four teeth that rise up out of her protruding lower jaw on the left, as if they are floating in space. "Don't let her sit there," the woman barks, as we are still moving. "People have to pass by."

"I'll take care of it," I say, wishing my voice didn't sound so harsh.

In the process of getting Mom settled, we cross in front of the big-screen tv where Johnny Mathis is crooning. I move Elizavetta's chair a couple of inches forward, so her view won't be blocked by my mother. Even she, my friend who credited me with bringing her the luck she needed to finally win a round of Bingo, is snippy. "I can see," she says.

Fran, a redhead who dresses well and walks on hugely swollen legs, warns, "Don't push her in front of me."

"I see you," I say, narrowing my eyes down and staring directly into hers. She shuts up.

"I'm cold," Mom says. She's wearing a green cotton sweater and has the lap robe draped over her legs. "I want the gray sweater with the embroidery," she tells me.

I go to her room and bring back the gray sweater that's hanging over the back of the commode.

"Not that one."

I go back to her room and look everywhere for the sweater she means, the one with sequins, but it's nowhere to be found. I bring her gray fleece vest and insist she give it a try.

"It won't zip up," she tells me. "It doesn't zip up."

"Be quiet," I say, trying hard not to shout.

"Rela-a-a-x, Sara," Sylvia, the Armenian volunteer says. "Re-l-a-a-a-a-a-a-x."

I take a deep breath, get Mom's arms into the vest, pull the sleeves of the green sweater down and through, zip up the vest and leave her smiling, finally smiling.

Johnny Mathis has just finished singing "That Certain Smile" and is moving into his finish. As I walk away from my now smiling mother, as I move quickly past Fran so I won't block her view, brush Elizavetta's shoulder as I pass by and, as I tread lightly past the door guard with those four teeth that seem to float in space, I hear, "Until the Twelfth of Never, I'll still be loving you."

Risking

December 3

In 1994, two years after Matt and I divorced, I moved out of the last home of my own, a cozy two-story guest house in Malibu, in search of a home inside. After a couple of years roaming around in Northern New Mexico, I came back to LA and stayed with Mom. In 1998, when she decided to move to The Jewish Home, I stayed on in her house in Camarillo.

With everybody gaga over the stock market, I took the $265,000 that was in my portfolio, money I had carefully saved from my work life in New York, together with an inheritance from Aunt Doris, and moved it from being conservatively invested in mutual funds and gold coins into individual stocks. Brilliantly, or so I thought, over the next two years, I ran the principal up to almost a million dollars. Those were heady times, "the internet bubble."

I worked hard, sitting eight or ten or twelve hours a day at Mom's kitchen table and, with a tv screen between me and the kitchen sink, came to know the quirks of all the CNBC anchorpeople. I read analysts' reports. Took a technology newsletter and an underlining pen to bed with me each night. Bought shares in companies that were taking over the world as we knew it. God had a new name — telecommunications, and this time I had a seat in the congregation. One day, as I watched the computer screen, I saw the worth of my portfolio increase by more than $50,000.

I didn't trade in my old car for a new one. I hardly bought any clothes. Did someone sitting all day at a kitchen table need new clothes? And I didn't buy a house. It wasn't about providing myself with a more secure future — everything I had was invested in risky technology stocks.

It was about making money. And watching it grow — on paper. The most spendthrift I ever got was to place an order at amazon.com for more than a hundred dollars' worth of books. Books on investing.

For the first time in my life, I felt rich. I was being creatively productive, and I wasn't worrying about money.

When the bottom started falling out, I didn't feel it. Fear and greed and giddiness can keep you from feeling. And seeing. With my eyes on the trees, I couldn't see the forest.

When my portfolio had worked its way down from that almost-million to $650,000, I told my Jungian analyst that I felt I should get out, sell. An investor himself — wasn't everybody? — he cautioned me that what I was referring to as my intuition sounded to him like an example of the black and white, either/or thinking we had discovered I do.

At $350,000, I said to Bill, "I think I should get out, sell." He cautioned me against making a rash move.

I'm not blaming them. I needed some real help in finding my own ground to stand on and, caught up in fear and greed themselves, they were in no position to help me find it. They were as shell-shocked as I was. I didn't know what I was doing and why. Only that I was playing in a big game and, for once, winning.

When the game was finally called, the house had won. How different is the stock market from gambling? Or from buying into — or being one of the people who sell — pyramid schemes? When the market is on its way up, it seems as if everybody is winning. When it turns around, the field of winners narrows to those who bought low enough that they are still able to sell higher. If you're not trading, if you're one of the people who still thinks you can buy and hold, you find yourself, as the saying goes, catching a falling knife.

November of 2000, right when the market was in the definitive phase of its crash, Mom was transferred to the hospital with her first case of pneumonia. Suddenly, I was spending all day, every day, at her bedside in the ICU, all my attention now directed to advocating for her. I conferred with doctors, read lab reports, watched monitors, and held her hand, careful not to disturb the IVs. I made sure that Ganesh, the tiny bronze Indian god who guards against obstacles, and who usually sits on the dashboard of my car, was always taped securely to her pillow.

As I walked with both feet into this new fire, I fell out-of-step with the market. Nothing mattered but keeping Mom alive. On March 28, 2001, my 61st birthday, I finally sold whatever remained of my portfolio.

Sometimes I wonder if I'm being as short-sighted now as I was when I was lost in the market. If, by this near-obsession with my mother's well-being, I am still being moved by greed and fear. Still avoiding what I need to do to take care of myself. Still missing the forest for the trees.

Mom is on a downward spiral; this job will soon be over. Can it be that if I continue with a whole heart to do what is right in front of me, the future will take care of itself? And I will find ground I can call my own?

It's late afternoon and, instead of going to visit, I call. Someone hands Mom the phone. She can hear me, a good sign. More often than not, we have to deal with the screeching of her hearing aid as the phone receiver comes close to it, and it's downhill from there. Today, it's "How are you, darling," pronounced in her own special New York way. "How wah you, dolling?"

I say I won't be coming in today. She tells me everything is fine, tells me to have fun. I pause to let it sink in. "Have fun," my mother said.

Have Fun, My Mother Said

December 4

The next afternoon, I drive out to La Piedra, a beach on the Malibu coast. Huge boulders, usually underwater, sport mussels and barnacles, doors and windows closed as they wait for the tide to return. Anemones — animal flowers with translucent petals — rest in shallow tide pools, surprised, I imagine, by so much light. Here and there, a hermit crab ambles by, sideways. I pick up and study the reddish shell of a large, dead crab, amazed at the complexity of its articulations, place it gently back down in the wet sand. Pick up a plastic grocery bag heavy with sea water, the top of a yogurt container, an old t-shirt wrapped around a rock by the currents, and take them all with me.

It's 1976. The man leading the *est* training suggests we make it our business always to leave wherever we are in better condition than we found it. On a mission to create a bit of peace in the world, on freeways and city streets, I begin to leave plenty of space between me and the car in front. For two-and-a-half decades, I have wiped dry the pools of water that collect on the tops of sinks in public restrooms; picked up stray towels that have tumbled over the edge of wastebaskets and pushed down, with the heel of my hand, those mountains of towels that overflow their baskets; when no one is watching, I use my foot. Today, it's the sea bottom I'm tidying up!

One day, when Mom was a patient at UCLA, I stepped into an elevator and noticed a scattering of napkins on the floor. Quickly, there came a flurry of thoughts: there are napkins on the floor and there's something I can do about it. Then, just as quickly: is it my job, dammit, to keep the whole world clean? Even after all these years, the impetus to do good doesn't always come automatically.

Bending, again and again, I moved from one napkin to the next as the other person in the elevator — a black man in starched white pants and jacket, a laminated badge attached to his chest pocket — looked on.

"That was nice," he said.

"It's just something I do."

"It was nice," he said again, wanting me to hear.

Today's seascape is something you might find on the edge of a dream. The near-shore made up of boulders dislodged and tumbled down by storms from sides of mountains. I've learned to watch the tide calendar carefully for just this. The chance to walk the beach on a minus-tide day when so much life and beauty, usually hidden, is there to be seen.

My attention lights on a rock in the shape of a wide face with a smile carved into it, the indentation of a nose, one eye winking. I pass it by, am drawn back to pick it up. I take it home with me. A rock that smiles!

I stay until the light is almost gone, climb the steep path back up the hill to the parking lot.

By the time I get to The Jewish Home, Mom is watching the tail end of *Jeopardy*. She greets me with a smile. I say I'm surprised she's up so late. She shrugs. "Late?"

I tell her where I've been, about all the beautiful things you can see at low tide. I remember what low tide means to her and what it used to mean to me growing up on the Long Island Sound in Connecticut. How we'd turn our noses up at the smell, have to gingerly make our way across sharp rocks to reach water deep enough for a swim.

For two days, my mother has been feeling well, her mind clear as a tide pool. It's a window of opportunity through which to see again her many shapes and colors. At the same time, a tide calendar within tells me murky waters are on their way.

If It's Not One Thing, It's Another. And Another.

December 5

The first thing I see is the inside of my mother's lower lip, red and fleshy and loose. Even before hello, she wants to tell me what a hard day she's had. She doesn't remember the details, except that during the night she had to yell for water. "Or was it during the day?" she asks. "I'm serious, Sara, I was this far away from dying." Her fingers are an inch apart. "What else can I do if I think I'm dying? So, I yell."

I'm impatient, just plain tired of hearing again how close she was to dying. I say what I have said before — that she is old, and one of these days she *is* going to die, and, besides, we are *all* going to die, but do we want to spend every minute of our lives thinking about it?

It's all wasted breath, of course, except that by the time I'm ready to leave, her anxiety has pinned itself to something else: whether she's breathing right.

The nurse comes in and clips what looks like a clothespin to my mother's index finger to check her blood, how saturated it is with oxygen. If it is over 90, she is doing fine on her own.

It's over 90. I disconnect her from the oxygen canister

attached to the wall.

Miriam, the roommate, has been listening to our conversation and shows my mother what *she's* been taught about breathing. "You have to lift your arms h-i-g-h up in the air," Miriam says, demonstrating.

Before Mom moved to The Jewish Home, she had started falling. One time, she broke her wrist. Then, it was her thumb. After she broke her shoulder, she'd go to the office of the local physical therapist who would show her how to keep the shoulder mobile by crawling her fingers up the wall and swinging her arm like a pendulum. When I would remind her how important it was to do the exercises, she'd say, "You're right, Sara, you're right." Which is what she continued to say whenever I'd remind her again. But that didn't mean she would do them. There was no way I could convince her that what she did once a week in the physical therapist's office wasn't enough.

She complains now about how tight her shoulders are, that she can't reach to get clothes out of her closet or even off a shelf that's shoulder height. And here's Miriam, telling her that to breathe deeply all she has to do is lift her arms w-a-a-a-y up. My mother is staring at her, her worry now firmly attached to breathing rather than getting water or something down from a closet.

"Is this right?" she asks me. She holds her jaw tight as she takes a breath, the way some young kids hold their jaws when they're working hard, learning to print. She's intent on breathing in the particular way she has in mind. Her chest is barely moving.

"Mom, your breathing is fine," I say. "You don't have to control it, just like you don't have to control your heartbeat; it just happens." I lift her right arm out from where I usually find it, stuck between the side of her body and the side of the chair. "Just try to keep your arm on the arm of the chair, not locked in next to your chest. It'll give your lungs more room to expand."

But she's far away, her eyes looking in, not out. Jaw still set as she tries to breathe some way she thinks she's supposed to.

Miriam is watching my mother as if she is a good tv show. "You have a good daughter," I hear her say, as I leave their room to see if I can find my composure somewhere down the hall.

When I come back, Mom's arm is tight against her side again. With a touch less than gentle, I lift it out. She hardly notices. She is still trying to get it right, this special way of breathing.

I put my face in front of hers and up close. "Stop!" I say. "Stop!" Hoping I will be able to wake her out of the trance she has fallen into. For a moment, her eyes clear, and I have my mother back.

I'm sure of it. This is how it had to be when I was a

baby. There she is in a chair in front of a sunny window, and there I am in my crib, my little head turning side to side and up and down, tilting as I try to find myself in my mother's eyes. Trying to find something alive behind the blue. Waiting for that moment — would it ever be there? — when she would come back and I would have her, when I would have *me* again.

Mom and I walk to the dining room. We pass Elsie, who is struggling for breath. "I don't hear, so people think I'm stupid," Elsie says. I go over and hug her, feeling the bony barrel of her chest under my arms. "How could anyone ever think you're stupid?" I say. "All they'd have to do is look into your eyes." Elsie maneuvers her wheelchair around to where Ida has been sitting by herself behind a pillar, with only a partial view of the tv screen.

Though Mom gives me the kiss I ask for as I'm getting ready to leave, she has that look that says she will be returning to her new worry about breathing as soon as she is free of me. Behind us, I feel a deep quiet. Elsie, with her own thin arm, has reached out to hold Ida's arm. Neither of them is speaking. They're simply sitting together in silent contact, touching.

"What do you think of it here?" Ida asks me. I'm not sure what she means, and she doesn't go on to make it any clearer.

"All I can tell you is how I feel right this minute," I

say. One of my arms is around Elsie's shoulder, my other hand rests on Ida's arm. "Right now, right here, I think this is a pretty special place."

I rest for a few moments in their silence. Stand up, walk past Mom, into the cold.

Not Again!

December 6

I see Mom, she and I separated by the tinted glass windows of the Factor Building. For a moment, I imagine walking on. If she does catch a glimpse of me, it will be as if I am in another world. We will nod to each other. I'll wave and move on.

My reverie clunks to the ground as I see her responding to my actual wave. Not with a wave of her own, oh no, just a slight turning of her head to the right and down, all the acknowledgment she can muster.

Where *did* I learn my enthusiasm? And how is it that, over our years together, it didn't get unlearned? Is enthusiasm something that comes with us from wherever we were before we were born?

Mom is sitting alone at the table where she eats, a

thin, pink blanket wrapped around her shoulders. She is facing the window, away from the other women who are talking or watching tv.

"I don't know what I'm waiting for," she says. "Bed maybe."

I pull my chair up close, circle my arm around her, feel her bony shoulder blades, the roundness of her upper spine.

"They've already eaten," she tells me, looking toward the other women.

"No, Mom, it's almost dinnertime, but not yet."

"Then, what was the other meal called?"

"Do you mean lunch?"

She shrugs.

This is the second day of Mom's increasing confusion, my increasing annoyance. On my way here, I stopped by at a convenience store to pick up some small bottles of water. Is it possible that Mom's yelling for help in the night might be relieved if she has a bottle of water in bed with her? Her bottle.

I show her the bottle, tell her what it's for. I crack the seal on the cap, twist it all the way open, then screw it closed again, showing her what she will have to do.

"It's so you can wet your whistle during the night," I tell her. "But don't drink it all down. This bottle should last for two nights."

She gives me that "Don't treat me like a child" look.

She tries to open the bottle. The cap doesn't budge. I take it back, open it again, re-close it but not all the way. Turn it over to make sure it won't leak, give it back to her. She still can't open it. My patience is growing thin.

Ida sits down next to Mom at the table. I've finally arranged things so that Ida sits on the side of my mother's good ear.

"She's pushing it down, not twisting it," Ida says.

Mom is using her hand with the broken thumb. Can it be she doesn't have enough strength to open a water bottle? The cap finally gives.

Now I have something else to keep me awake. No longer whether she has water to quell her anxiety, but whether she is able to unscrew the cap. And let's say she is able to open it. I see water spilling into the bed as she searches for the lost cap in the dark.

I explain to the nurse, Arlene, about the water bottle. Ask her to figure out how to help Mom use it while making sure it doesn't lead to her drinking copious quantities again.

"The increase in confusion...," I say. "Can you order a urinalysis? I'll bet she has an infection again." It takes only two days now of my own anxious reactions to seeing Mom confused before I remember about the connection between confusion and urinary tract infections. Or, god forbid, another pneumonia.

A phone message is waiting for me when I get home. A chest X-ray shows the beginning of pneumonia in my mother's right lung. She's been put on Levaquin again, an antibiotic she's been on more times than I can remember.

Red

December 7

Bill is coming toward me in that crooked way he walks when his back hurts. He runs every morning. The physical therapist in me thinks about the damage all that pounding may be doing to a back already unstable.

His face is soft, friendly. "Mom's good today," he says.

He's surprised when I tell him the last two days have been hell, that Mom is being treated for pneumonia again.

"How do you like being retired?" I ask.

He laughs. "I went into the office three days this week."

"I know some things you could do with your free time," I say. "All the beautiful tide pools you can see at the ocean when there's a minus tide."

"I'll call you," he says.

I find Mom in the dining room, her hands resting on

a tray table covered with a white towel. It's her turn for a manicure.

She and Sylvia sit peacefully together, not talking.

"This used to be *my* job," I tell Sylvia. I ask Mom if she remembers how we would sit on her patio, how I would polish her fingernails, lift her legs, one at a time, onto my lap for a pedicure. "Vaguely," she says.

Mom chooses a color from the bottles of many shapes and sizes Sylvia keeps in a square, zippered case.

I remind her to keep her hands on the towel until her nails have a chance to dry. All those years of manicures, more often than not she'd forget and at least one nail would get smudged. We'd laughed about it, still I would keep watching her hands as if my watching could keep them still. Doing whatever I could to ward off disappointment when something to which I'd given so much care would get ruined by a moment's lack of attention.

"Is it like that red?" Mom points to the brick wall outside the dining room window. "Is it like that woman over there?" she asks, pointing to a woman wearing a dark red pants suit.

There's some task she's given herself, something about matching the color she's chosen for her nails to some other red, and it's important to her that she get it right. "I'm just trying to see if I know," she says.

I sit back to gaze at her.

She looks over at me, a question on her face.

"I don't know what to say, Mom. I'm not sure what you're talking about."

"I'm not sure either," she says, shaking her head. "I'm so confused."

"It's good that you know you're confused," I tell her. "Some people don't even know."

She starts talking about reds again. "What would you call this red?" she asks.

"Magenta?" I offer.

"I don't know magenta," she says.

"What about plum?"

"Maybe plum. Red with purple in it."

But then, "It's like that one, over there." She's drifted away again from the world in front of us, where we are both seeing the same thing and can talk about how best to describe it, to something else, some test that she alone is taking that I can't help her pass, no matter how much I would like to. She is trying to hold onto her mind, that much seems clear.

I ask her how it worked last night, having the bottle of water.

"I don't know," she says. "I didn't need it."

I find out that the nurses put a straw in the bottle, put the bottle in the mesh bag on the side of her walker, and put the walker right next to the rail of her bed. Maybe just having it there was enough.

Her nails are dry! Without a smudge!

I've brought a new water bottle. This one with a sports cap. I open it. Oh, no. This one, for sure, will be too hard for her to manage. She tries once. I take it back, leaving well enough alone.

There *Is* A God

December 8

I ask her again how it worked, having a water bottle by her bed. "Wonderful," she says. "If I didn't have it, I don't think I would have made it through the night."

"Did you have to drink?" I ask.

"No," she says. "I slept right through."

A Fate Of Her Own

December 13

Rachel is sitting opposite the nurses' station, wearing her dark green turtleneck sweater. Not sure whether her greeting should be in Yiddish or English, her head is tilted to the side as she waits for the right language to come from me.

"Rachel, you're wearing that beautiful sweater again."

"Green. From Sveeden."

"Did you buy it there?"

"Tventy years ago," she says, each of us, in turn, feeling the wool between thumb and first two fingers. "It's still good," she says.

Mom is sitting at her usual table in the dining room with Ida and Anna, quiet and calm, her makeup on, the bagel still in its paper bag; one day I must ask why the bagel always comes in a paper bag. The lox, cream cheese, slices of tomato and cucumber and red onion lie untouched on her plate. She tells me she can't eat it, that food gets stuck in her teeth. She begins to pull air noisily through them. "I drank," she says, pointing to the container of Strawberry Resource. "That's enough."

I try to change her mind, but it is made up. I spread cream cheese on the bagel, fold the lox over it, top it off with the tomato and onion and begin to eat it myself.

"Good. You have it," she says calmly.

"I feel guilty," I say, "eating my mother's food."

"I didn't want to tell you about my teeth," she says. She's told me many times, but this way she has of drawing air through them, and not eating because of them, is something new.

"Goodnight, girls," Mom says, turning her wheelchair away from the table. But Anna is deaf and Ida doesn't hear her. I get Ida's attention and tell my mother that now Ida will be able to hear her. "See you tomorrow," Mom says.

Ida gets up, walks over to the next table where Shirley, the troublemaker, sits. Shirley, the handsome woman whose self-appointed job is to watch what goes on with everyone and come up with her own opinions about what needs to be done. More than once, when she started telling me about my mother's behavior and what has to be done about it, I've told her thank you, but no thanks.

"Tomorrow, just come and sit at my table," the troublemaker says to Ida.

"I didn't want to say anything in front of her daughter," I hear Ida say.

I want to wrap my arms around my mother, protect her from knowing how her world sometimes turns away from her. It must be the way a mother feels when her child is snubbed by a friend at school.

I follow Mom as she makes her way down the hall to her room, maneuvering the wheelchair with her feet. By the time she gets there, she is dark with anxiety, thinking ahead to everything that has to do with nighttime. What will happen when the diaper has to be changed? If I need water, how will I get it? What if I can't find the call bell? And, especially, what about the oxygen? If I think I'm dying, will someone come quickly enough to save me?

Is she thinking these things, or am I?

She stops the chair in the narrow passageway between the foot of her bed and the closet, leaving me standing behind her, no place to move. I feel my nerves getting frayed, feel myself getting slightly claustrophobic. "Mom, if I'm going to stay, we'll have to go back out into the hallway where there's room for both of us."

She brings her worries with her out into the hall. We sit together near the nurses' station. The troublemaker places herself nearby, her back to us, her ears on fire.

For a few days, Mom and I have been in a power struggle over oxygen. Using it keeps her tied to the wheelchair and I've wondered if too much oxygen could be causing the increased confusion. On NPR, I heard a story about a deadly smog that enveloped London in 1952. A nurse remembered how the hospital ward she'd worked on was so dark with soot, she had to feel around for the patients. How everyone, in order to breathe, had to get under an oxygen tent. "People were suddenly confused," she said. "Some people kept smoking, We could have all gone up in flames!"

My mother is convinced that if she doesn't have the tubes in her nose at night, she will die. "I don't want to tell you this," she says to me, "but I was about to die. It was getting quieter and quieter. If someone hadn't come in to give me the oxygen at just that moment, I wouldn't be here now."

"And so?" I ask.

"I don't want to die."

"Why?" I ask.

"I'd like to live a little longer."

"Why?" I persist. "So we can have conversations like this?"

I feel cruel. I am also tired and frustrated. I don't know how to respond to her fear of dying, she so quickly transmutes it into something she thinks is going to save her. Not getting up from the toilet because if she does, she will die. Her preoccupation with oxygen. Having water available at night. And the latest: food between her teeth; this, on its way to becoming something really big — refusing to eat.

I think back to her lifetime preoccupation with her "stomach." See it now as an early warning sign of what was to come.

I ask Arlene to show her, with the clothespin that gets clipped to her finger, that her oxygen saturation is fine. "But what about during the night?" she asks.

"Mom, it's not oxygen you need. Anxious thoughts make you hyperventilate, and that's why you can't breathe. When you finally tire yourself out, you calm down. It's your thoughts you have to get a handle on. You just think it's the oxygen ..."

I think about how I could never divert her attention away from worrying. The years when she'd reach for an Ativan instead of trying to calm herself, herself. And all the years when she'd shake salt on her food or cook salt-laden knockwurst for supper, leaving it to medication to deal with high blood pressure. The hundreds of times I've heard her say, "Let's drop it," just when we were about to break through onto new ground. Something else fits here, too — though I really don't understand how — that curious habit she's had of turning off the tv five minutes before the end of a drama.

With the preciousness of this life more acute now that she is so close to its end, my guess is that she is afraid it will be over before she has used it as well as she might have; as she might still, given a little more time. (Are you listening, Sara?)

Angie comes in to get Mom ready for bed.

"Angie, is my daughter right in what she's saying?"

"She is," Angie nods. "It's your nervousness."

I ask Angie to make sure the call bell is securely in place, that Mom can reach the water bottle, that the light over her bed is either on or off, whichever way she wants it. As I leave, Mom gives me a kiss goodnight that, while it isn't begrudging, is far from enthusiastic.

I call when I get home. The nurse, recognizing my voice, laughs. "She's fast asleep."

"I was so hard on her tonight," I say.

"Sometimes, you just can't help it."

When I wake up, it's still dark, 3:47 shining its fluorescence from the face of the clock radio. I've been dreaming.

> *Two children have been left by a man in a large room to fend for themselves. I go into the room to find them. The boy-child is gone, probably dead. The girl, a tiny yellow bird, is hiding in her nest made from a cut in the fabric of a chair. How has she survived for this long, alone? Sometimes, she flies out and hides on the floor behind the "curtain" of a piece of furniture. The children originally belonged to Barbra Streisand.*

I think of my mother, alone in her end-of-life process. Barbra Streisand, alone and needing courage, as Yentl:

Papa, can you hear me?
Papa, can you see me?
Papa, can you find me in the night?

A fair-haired baby girl lies at her mother's feet in a basket on the floor of the Wittenberg family's Bronx apartment. The mother, at her sewing machine, is unable, despite this baby's arrival, to erase pictures from her mind of five-year-old Sam, who pulled a pot of boiling water off the stove and died from the scalding.

I think of the many ways Hannah, blonde and blue-eyed, would have been left behind by her older, brown-haired, dark-eyed sisters, Jessie and Theresa and Doris. How lost she must have felt, years later, when she married into the noisy, excitable Bragin family, so different from the quiet, somber, and, likely, depressed Wittenbergs.

How lonely it must have been for her when Irving died, leaving her, at 40, with two children to raise. How, when we were taken in by her sister, Doris, and Joe, there was no one to hear her grief. How unable I am to listen now.

I fall back to sleep and dream again.

I have left my beloved Siamese cat, Judy Blue Eyes, with a man I suddenly realize is unreliable. On my return, I expect to find her dehydrated,

> *maybe even dead. A vulnerable kitten, she is holding onto life until she can be rescued. She is waiting for water. I pour water into my cupped hand, but she doesn't want it, tries to flatten my palm with her paw, which makes the water run out. A young male cat separates himself from her body, crawls under and around my hand to fresh water rushing by in an underground stream to which she follows him.*

I begin to understand that my mother has a fate of her own. Though the details aren't totally clear, it has to do with the loss of her mother, still suffering over the death of her son. Grief, too, over the loss of her own son, the stillborn boy born two years before me.

I, too, have a fate that belongs to me alone.

In my dream, both kittens know about the rushing stream of fresh, cold water waiting to save them. That it's right there, just under the ground, and they are both determined to drink from it.

She's Still There

December 15

"I love your mother," Marla tells me. "She's still there." Marla is the psychologist who has been meeting with Mom on and off during the four-and-a-half years Mom has been living at The Jewish Home.

Marla has counseled me, too — what she thinks can be expected from my mother and what can't. The truth, I'm convinced, lies somewhere between her view and mine. I know, first-hand, my mother's stubbornness; from a kinder viewpoint, her endurance. It's also likely that Marla and I have different views of what's possible for a person, over a lifetime.

I've called Marla because I want to know if there's someone who can talk with Mom, on a regular basis, about what looks to me like her fear of dying; how anxious she gets and the fact that drugs that might otherwise help are now closed off to her, her system too sensitive to counter their sedative effects.

"I saw her yesterday, she was calm," Marla says.

"She was calm, too, when I arrived, but, as soon as she started thinking about going to bed, she turned dark and agitated. She's sure it's oxygen that's keeping her alive."

"What do you think about letting her have the oxygen tubes in her nose but with the oxygen turned off?" Marla asks. "It's an idea Angie has come up with."

"Sure, if that makes her comfortable."

Saying yes gives me a way to surrender to Marla's view of my mother, step out of *my* way that has her deciding on her own to turn away from this latest crutch, returning to greater independence.

Mom and Miriam are sitting alone in the darkened dining room, light from the tv flickering off their faces. It's almost eight o'clock, late for Mom. I say nothing to draw attention to the oxygen. Instead, I tell her about a film I just saw, *Far From Heaven*, that takes place in 1950s Connecticut, close to where we lived. "I think you'd like it, Mom, maybe we could go to see it together." She gives me that "Don't kid yourself" look.

I tell her that everything in the film looks just the way it did when I was in high school: cars shaped like boats, sofas and coffee tables in a style we called "modern," push-up bras and full skirts with crinolines underneath that made waists look smaller than they were, perfectly set hair held in place with lots of spray. I tell her that, unlike anything I knew about in the '50s, it's about a man who finally gives in to his attraction to other men and what happens when his wife is drawn to a black man; the uproar that both situations caused.

My mother shakes her head as if to say, "Can you

believe it?"

I tell her that in 1960, when I was at UCONN, I joined the NAACP. What a big deal it was, how on the cutting edge I felt. I remind her about Diane Minor, the young black woman who, in 1958, was invited to join my Jewish sorority. How proud I felt. How the other sororities looked at us askance.

Earlier that afternoon, I'd spoken with a friend who was home recovering from surgery to remove an ovary. "Even now, Sara, six weeks after the surgery, my thinking processes are still scrambled. Sometimes, my thoughts roll backward."

I think about everything my mother has been through in her 90s. Twice on life-support, three weeks each time, drugs galore to keep her from feeling the pain of the breathing tube. Once she could breathe on her own, more weeks of recovery and having to get used to a new "sitter" in her hospital room every 12 hours, each woman from a different country speaking with a different accent. I think of how I would have to coax her to eat Jello — would she ever be able to swallow real food again, let alone think straight?

And here she is, still available at 93 for a conversation about cultural tensions we lived through fifty years ago.

As I think about the assault of just one surgery on my friend's 50-year-old body and mind — a few hours of anesthesia and three days in the hospital — a re-ordering takes place in me, a new respect for my mother. Whatever she is able to do that resembles normal living suddenly seems like a miracle. I see myself, sitting at my mother's feet, head bowed, as I'd sit at the feet of a Buddha.

It's late. I thank Mom for staying awake. Vickie brings her a small Arrowhead bottle filled halfway with water, a straw sticking out.

"I don't like all these rules about water," Mom says. "At my age, I should be able to have what I want."

"Look what's happening," I say. "You're getting upset over something that right now isn't a problem. You've got water and you're upset about not being able to have water. You're seeing the glass half-empty, not half-full."

She points at me with her chin, then to the water bottle on the table, seeing before I do the humor in what I've said.

Neither half-full nor half-empty, the water bottle is just there, waiting to serve its purpose in sips through the night. And here I am, hanging out with the mother I always wanted to hang out with, her bright sense of humor showing through. So what that it took this long? So what that we are sitting in the darkened dining room of a nursing home, red-haired Miriam asleep with her head on her chest, my 93-year old mother in a wheelchair with an oxygen tank on the back, a cannula in each nostril, the valve turned off?

The Glory Of Yosemite Valley In Winter

December 18-21

When I call, Elissa tells me she's genuinely happy to see my mother again, tells me she remembers her from when Mom first moved to The Jewish Home. I take the smile in Elissa's voice to be an indication that Mom's having a good day — when she is nervous and upset, it's hard to be around her, no matter how much you might have liked her under other circumstances. She says Mom's gained a pound-and-a-half, a good sign. She hands her the phone. I'm relieved Mom remembers where I told her I'd be and is interested to hear what I'm doing.

"You sound better," I say.

"I was in a bad way before you left," she tells me as if I didn't know.

That night, in desperation, I'd given her three tiny tablets of *Arsenicum album*. No, I wasn't trying to poison her! *Arsenicum album* is a homeopathic remedy for nervousness. I explained to her what the tablets were for, held her jaw closed so they could dissolve under her tongue.

Did the remedy work? From the sound of her voice, I'm encouraged.

For four days, I breathe in the beauty of Yosemite Valley, air filled with the sweet sharpness of evergreen.

Stark white beauty so all-encompassing it allows ordinary mortals like me to see as Ansel Adams saw.

Bedtime Story

December 22

First night back, I notice how very old my mother looks. White hair still untrimmed; no makeup to give her face color; the high arms of her wheelchair making her look even smaller than she is.

But she smiles when she sees me.

"They tell me you're feeling better," I say.

"You don't know, Sara, what I put on for you."

"You're *not* feeling better?"

"Maybe I am ... a little."

She asks about Yosemite. I tell her how the tree branches drooped with the weight of wet snow. How the full moon lit the whole Valley with a white glow — the waterfalls, Half Dome, El Capitan. How I could feel the light of the moon filling me.

We're sitting at the door to the combination tv room/library. She points to a book she says she's been looking through, tells me I can take it if I want. Too quickly, I tell her how many unread books are already on my nightstand. (Years later, reminded of that moment, I want to kick myself for not paying attention to what she wanted me to know about *her* life those last few days, the book she wanted me to read.) I pick up a paperback of short stories by Jewish writers and read to her about a man who is rewarded with a bag of gold coins for bringing figs to Emperor Hadrian. The wife of another man in the same town pushes *her* husband to do the same, expecting him to be rewarded equally. But Hadrian has the second man pelted with the figs until he has to turn and run. When the man's wife derides him for his bad luck, he tells her how lucky he was not to have brought peaches or he would have been stoned to death.

Mom listens with eyes closed, breathing easily, resting. I leave her patiently waiting for Angie to come to help her into bed. These few quiet minutes we've spent together over a bedtime story fill me with yet another kind of beauty. I breathe it in.

Horror Story

December 23

Mom looks like a spring rain: pale green slacks, green knit shirt, green fleece jacket. The downpour comes before I can say hello. "I'm not going to the dentist," she says. "There's nothing wrong with my teeth."

It's a little after 9:30; her appointment is for 10:45 and, though the office is nearby, I figured we'd need plenty of time to get there, time for discussions like this.

She tells me her teeth are full of food.

"Do you want me to brush your teeth?" Norma, the aide, asks.

"Of course I do," she spurts.

Norma brings the brush and a kidney-shaped pink plastic basin to catch the water.

"That's not brushing," my mother says.

"Then, you do it," I tell her. "Why aren't you doing it for yourself, anyway?"

Mom has always been diligent about brushing her teeth, so much so the enamel has been worn down in places. "Brush up and down, not back and forth," I tell her.

She brushes, slips her partial dentures back in, smiles at me, says, "I'm so glad you're here." Has brushing given her time to quell her nervousness? Can she now feel the decayed tooth with her tongue, the reason we're going to the dentist in the first place?

We change her jacket to one whose zipper works, remember to bring a hat, find a portable oxygen tank, get someone to wheel her out to the door of the building closest to where I'm parked. I juggle my purse, the oxygen, the envelope with her dental X-rays, her list of meds and her walker.

It's 10:40 when I pull up in front of the medical building, take the chance I won't be towed away in the time it'll take to get Mom into the elevator and down the hallway to the dentist's office.

"This is no good," Mom says. "The elevator's too small."

"Do you feel claustrophobic?" Before she can answer, the doors open.

"I'm dry," she tells the receptionist, who returns with a plastic cup filled with ice water.

"Too cold, I can't drink it."

She hands the water to me. I wait. After a few minutes, give it to her again.

"Too cold."

I ask the receptionist to bring tap water.

The dentist towers over my mother. He's a big friendly-faced man with dark curly hair. A leftie, his stool and tray are all turned around from anything I've seen in dentists' offices before.

He lowers the head of her chair; her head stays raised. I coax her to relax her neck enough to rest her head against the chair. Her scoliosis twists her away from him. He's on her left, she's turned toward the right.

She insists she doesn't want the decayed tooth extracted. "I'm an old lady," she says, "and to tell you the truth I don't think I'm going to live much longer."

The dentist asks me to come into the next room with him. "If we don't extract the tooth, it'll have to be fixed. It'll probably come to three thousand dollars."

I don't know how to talk about this with my mother. She thinks she's taking the simpler route by refusing to have the tooth pulled. While an extraction *will* mean the need for new dentures, opting to keep the tooth means a root canal and a crown.

Whatever she wants is fine with me; it's her money.

The dentist invites me to stay in the room as he works. Intensive care units, breathing tubes and IVs are one thing; a dentist drilling into my mother's decayed tooth is another. I say I'll wait outside.

He's done in less than half-an-hour, having provided some kind of temporary fix. Which, after a 10% discount, comes to $711. He complains about his back, how my mother kept turning away from him. Oh, that inexorable pulling of hers to the right.

Four people follow us into the elevator. On the ground floor, they quickly exit, leaving me to hold the door open and, at the same time, onto Mom so she won't fall.

I've been out in the world enough with my old, old mother — old old is different from just old — to notice the many ways people try to escape seeing the realities of aging.

Once, as we were coming into Mom's regular dentist's office during a pounding rainstorm, his assistant stood frozen inside as I struggled with an umbrella, my stooped-over mother, her walker, and a door that opened out.

By the time we were ready to leave, the assistant was noticing what had to be done. People do wake up. She swung the arm of the dental chair away to make room for the walker. Opened the door that led back out to the waiting room so we could walk through without tripping over each other. And the dentist himself walked outside with us and held the umbrella open over Mom while she slowly made her way to the car, his pale blue smock getting soaked in the process.

Today, we're hardly back in the car when Mom starts explaining to me what went on inside. "What do they call it, that machine they put in your mouth?" Mom asks.

"A drill, do you mean the drill?"

"Not the drill, it's an electrical machine."

She has me scurrying to remember every little detail

of what goes on when you sit down in a dentist's chair. Does she mean the vacuum that pulls away saliva?

"I'm pretty sure you're talking about the drill," I say.

"What is it called?" she asks again.

She's insisting on finding the right word. I'm insisting she means the drill.

"I don't know what you're talking about," I say, losing patience. My voice is getting louder. I'm also trying to drive.

"Don't be stupid, Sara. When you think of the word, you'll see that I'm right."

She won't stop. She can't stop. The hate she's directing at me with her eyes is so powerful I can barely keep my own eyes on the road.

"Be quiet," I say. "I can't talk to you and drive at the same time. It's not safe."

She keeps talking.

I yell at her. "Silent! I need you to be silent!"

She tries but, perceiving the slightest opening in my defense, starts up again.

I grip the wheel with both hands. Clench my jaw. Pull over to the side of the road to call ahead for someone at The Jewish Home to meet us with a wheelchair. I've got to get her out of this car.

"This isn't where I live," she insists, as I pull into the parking lot.

"What's it called when you go to the dentist?" my mother, looking up from the car seat, asks the aide. The aide, a middle-aged Latina, has wheeled the chair right to the edge of the curb, leaving Mom with no room to stand up, maneuver into it.

"Wake up," I want to scream.

Back in the wheelchair and out of the blue, this woman, my mother, turns to me and flashes a smile. "Thank you for taking me," she says.

By the time I've gathered up the oxygen and the walker and manage to get them inside, Mom is sitting at her table in the dining room. She's taken a few bites out of an egg salad sandwich, the beginning of a parade of small plates of food she just barely samples — kugel, stewed fruit, two slices of white bread with a single slice of Muenster cheese inside, coffee, a carton of milk.

I ask how the tooth feels. She insists there was no work done. I ask her to feel for a space that wasn't there before, where the dentist had taken the decayed tooth down to the gum line. She insists again that nothing was done.

Mom pulls up to an aide and starts a conversation, somewhere in the middle, about having gone to the dentist. The aide stares right through her, making no attempt to understand. Mom turns to the social worker, tries to tell *her* what happened but, again, starts in the middle, leaving no way for the social worker to catch up. The social worker looks to me for help. I shake my head, unable to offer anything.

We've been back for about an hour. Mom has finally accepted this is where she lives.

In her room, I show her some new slacks and tops. She doesn't want any of them. It's too much for her to take in. It's been weeks since she's told me about all the things she needs me to get for her. "If you ever do want new clothes, Mom, I'll go shopping again."

On my way out, I run into Marla, tell her about the homeopathic remedy I'd given Mom before I left for Yosemite. How, when I called each day, there were no horror stories or high anxiety. Mom had begun eating again, gained a pound-and-a-half.

"I saw her the morning after you left," Marla says. "She said somebody had put something in her mouth, and she had to get it out of her system through her rectum. She must have been talking about those tablets you gave her."

I feel betrayed.

I wake up during the night, aware of how overwhelmed my mother must feel. How hard she's been trying to hold on. Plain old human stubbornness turning into iron-clad intransigence.

Before we left for the dentist, she'd pointed to a woman she called Angie.

"Angie comes at night, Mom."

"No, that's Angie," she insisted.

I asked the woman her name.

"Leticia," she said. "Your mother calls me Angie."

"Don't kid me," Mom said. "Tell the truth, you're Angie."

"No, Mom, she's Leticia."

"Sara, you don't know," she said, the look on her face saying maybe someday you will. "Her name is Leticia, but everyone calls her Angie. You'll see."

Every day, it's a different nurse, a different aide. No consistent someone to note the huge changes taking place. As if the loss of clarity is something to be expected.

I don't know. Maybe it is.

You Should See How They Celebrate Christmas Here

Christmastime

The temperature gauge on my dashboard is reaching up into the red. I exit the 101, come to a stop in front of Tarzana Convalescent Hospital, watch steam as it seeps out from under the hood to rise in the cool air, creating a silent cloud around me. It's Christmas Eve and my plan, after visiting with Mom, is to meet Keta and Judy for dinner at 7. It's now 5:30. I'd suggested Spumante for its festive feel, tiny white lights strung inside and out.

A few years ago, Keta and Judy and I spent a New Year's Eve there, the New Year's Eve Judy said that any resolution she could make, any wish she could have for herself, would be so much smaller than what might actually come if she simply opened herself to Providence.

I roll down the window. Breathe slowly. Listen to the sounds of hissing. Make up stories about the people passing by in their cars. As I imagine they are making up stories about me, the woman at the side of the road whose car, what a shame, on Christmas Eve, is overheating. I think about how they are on their way home to Spanish-speaking neighborhoods in the northern part of the Valley, their last-minute shopping done, red shopping bags overflowing with fancy bottles of perfume, fluffy fleece jackets, computer games that still need to be wrapped. I see a tree heavy with candles in the corner of a crowded apartment. The tv turned to Telemundo's latest telenovela. Children teasing each other as *abuelas* and *abuelos* look on with amusement and pride.

I call roadside assistance. Think about how, for weeks, I'd been watching the temperature gauge sit above the halfway mark, aware that the engine was running hotter than usual. Playing, literally, with fire.

I think about how lucky I am — so lucky I wouldn't have even thought to wish for it — that the radiator is giving out now instead of three days from now when I'll be driving north through California's hot Central Valley on my way to Carmel Valley, a silent meditation retreat.

A jolly man from triple-A pulls up, fills the empty radiator, assures me the car is safe to drive and that I'll make it to the mechanic's shop the day after Christmas. He suggests I spend a quiet holiday at home.

He follows me to The Jewish Home and I wave to him as I turn into the gate, freeing him to drop down somebody else's chimney.

Mom is in bed, resting peacefully, thanks to a Tylenol. I rub her leg. She opens one eye. Closes it again.

Georgina stops in for a visit.

"There's a check for you in my pocketbook," Mom, who only seems to be sleeping, tells her.

Georgina tells me that Mom wants to help her buy the computer that Helena, eight, wants for Christmas. Georgina tilts her head, smiling her wide smile at Mom. Mom shakes her head yes, happy she'd remembered to ask Bill to write a check for it.

I feed Mom a few sips of the soup that's been waiting on the tray table.

"Let me see you," she says, signaling me with her chin to stand up. Oh, that chin, the power it wields.

She looks at me for a long time, her calm gaze creating a kind of silence in the room. I'm wearing a tangerine knit dress instead of my usual black or brown sweats. Green clogs. Lipstick. "Sara, you're gorgeous," she says.

I tell her I'm meeting Keta and Judy for dinner. She knows them. I've found ways to introduce them to each other — my mother and my friends. My family — and my family.

"You're gorgeous," she repeats. "I've always thought you were gorgeous." She insists on my hearing it.

I celebrate all the way to the restaurant. Finally able to take my place alongside all those other people hurrying home to celebrate, whatever their language, Christmas Eve, the birth of love.

Keta and Judy have ordered a bottle of Ruffino Chianti. The waiter pours me a glass. I tell them about Mom. "You're gorgeous, Sara," she'd said. "I've always thought you were gorgeous."

A thousand tiny lights sparkle through my tears.

Christmas morning, I make a fire in the stone fireplace of this big, old house where I live with Bonnie and Lily. Bonnie and I sit on the couch, a book of carols between us.

Oh, come, all ye faithful.

I've never been able to harmonize, hold my own past the first couple of notes, so easily pulled away from who-I-am-right-now. While it's true that, for weeks, I've been on the edge of jumping out of my skin, as Mom would say, I am also more and more on the edge of being very much present, aware of exactly how it feels to be me, at this particular moment, sitting on this particular couch, alive, breathing, there for each new situation with all its idiosyncrasies. For once, I am able to find the harmony, stay with it, play with it.

Joy to the world.

And when the time comes for me to carry the melody, I will be true to that, too.

Silent night, ho-o-ly night, all is calm, all is bright.

Rosario stops in, gives my half-sleeping Mom, dressed and in bed, her special, adoring, head-tilted smile. "I take good care of your mother," Rosario says. "In forty years, I'll be where she is."

I couldn't wish for a better gift.

I read Mom a Martin Buber story from a book in the drawer of her nightstand. As she drifts back to sleep, I realize how complicated the story must sound to her.

A couple of characters, each with a couple of different motivations for the action about to take place.

Awake again, she wants to get out of bed. "Get that off my chair," she says, meaning the green oxygen tank. "It ties me down." As adamant as she is now about wanting it gone, she has been that adamant about having it there. A few minutes later, she's again wearing the tubes that attach her to the tank.

She tells Rosario that the blue jacket, the one new piece of clothing she said she'd keep, doesn't belong to her. She won't wear it. Frustration carries me out of the room.

I stop back in to tell her I'm on my way to Sandi and Jordan's to celebrate Christmas. "It's not December 25th," she insists. "You'll see, Sara, and then you'll feel stupid. You should see how they celebrate Christmas here."

How can I be leaving her for a week? Mom is practically out of control again. What if they have to admit her back into UCLA?

At Steve's Independent, they lift the radiator out of my car, send it to be flushed. I call Georgina and arrange with her to visit Mom three hours a day while I'm away.

Satisfied that the radiator is once again able to do its job, I tell Mom I'll be driving to Northern California the next day for a Buddhist retreat. She doesn't like it one bit.

Before leaving, I take refuge in the hallway with Eileen, who is screaming. Refuge has many faces. I find a wheelchair and, facing Eileen, navigate my chair backward, pulling Eileen, her knees between mine, up and down the hallway, talking her down into some degree of calm.

"I'll pay you for your work," Shirley, the sometimes troublemaker, says.

The next afternoon, when I stop in to say goodbye, Mom turns away from me, maneuvers herself to the nurses' desk. "I'm right, aren't I?" she says to Vickie. She needs to know she's right. It's about Leticia really being Angie. Norma and Rosario wheel her away to a room set up as a beauty parlor for a much-needed haircut. She leaves me standing there, doesn't look back.

About to enter into eight days of silence, I call Georgina. She tells me Mom is picking at her teeth and refusing to eat. Vickie says she is yelling for water. "Tell Mom I'll come home if she needs me." Vickie tells me Eileen may have been overdosed on Zyprexa.

On Her Way To ... Where?

January 15, 2003

For eight days, hour after hour in the peaceful beauty of Carmel Valley, I sat undisturbed by anything except the incessant chatter of a madwoman's raucous thoughts, my own mind. But stay long enough in the gray boredom of no outer distractions ... and a blessed moment arrives when all those thoughts and the body's aches dissolve into a great spaciousness.

Nothing to do, nowhere to go. You're simply there, aware that you're breathing. A smile animates your face. Tears make their way down your cheeks. Your heart drums out a dance, something about gratefulness for being alive.

Back home, I remain in retreat. I haven't seen Mom since Christmas. It's too hard to relate to everything going on with her. Too hard to take note of every last drama, the occasional success. Too hard to hope. Too hard to grieve. I apologize to Reality for staying away.

No apology is needed, of course. Reality didn't suffer from my need to take a rest, most of which isn't turning out to be restful at all, head pounding whenever I bend over, the little annoyances of my own life stepping back in to take the place of the down-and-dirty dramas of Mom's. I'm lost again in a mind full of thoughts. Where did all that life-giving awareness disappear to? There's a reason meditation is called a practice.

I'm up early this morning, hoping to catch some quiet before construction begins on an addition to the house next door. My view of sky and trees is still there, though latticed by wooden framing. Soon, a wall will rise, reducing the light to just a sliver as it comes peeking around a corner to find its way into my room.

At 6:08, I crawl out of bed. Yes crawl, my bed is a futon on the floor. I splash cold water on my face, pour hot water over leaves of green tea, brush my teeth, slip out of a yellow nightgown into black tights and sweatshirt, climb back under the covers and sit up straight, determined to meditate.

A familiar thought comes: whatever you're doing isn't enough. And then another: besides, you'll probably fall asleep. Before I can catch them, the thoughts become a whole train on its way to the well-known station of despair. I sit through it all, grateful for the few moments when I wake up into knowing I'm simply here, aware that self-judgment is just another thought. I take a deep, sighing breath, my body a bellows. I hear the old house creak, as it continues, after all these years, to settle. Feel, deep in my belly, the forward motion of a car going by. And somewhere in this newfound spaciousness, feel infused with amazement at how simple it can be — self-judgment dissolving into peace.

What happens to those thoughts, I wonder, when we're lucky enough to catch them before we're totally lost, when there's still a chance to stop the train and get off. Does the train lurch on without us? Does it disappear? Poof. Gone. Do thoughts have any substance once we let go of them?

Back at The Jewish Home, Mom has been yelling, striking out at people, refusing to eat, only the occasional can of Resource keeping her alive. I'm told she kicked Norma in the stomach — Norma had been trying to get her out of bed at a time she was intent on staying in. I arrange for her to have a consultation with a psychiatrist and, desperate, give Mom another dose of the homeopathic remedy that had shown some small sign of working. I decide not to tell the psychiatrist about the homeopathic remedy, then I do. I am surprised she is not against it, says she understands my need to find something to help my mother with the agitation that renders her out of control. She suggests a trial of Trazadone to see if it can help Mom through, as she calls it, "the turmoil of her mornings." I have no choice but to agree. A patient who kicks a staff member is immediately labeled combative.

I see how changed my mother's mind is, ideas appearing and refusing to leave. One day, she tells me she must get her teeth attended to, the next that there's absolutely nothing wrong with them. There are the obsessions, too. Mom's so certain that food is getting stuck in her teeth, how can she possibly eat? I see how obsessions can kill.

At dinner, I find her facing away from the table into the center of the dining room. "You're here in time for the big celebration," she tells me. It's true that today is the day all the January birthdays are being celebrated — red and yellow and blue and green balloons rise from her roommate Miriam's chair. When I called, she was deciding if she wanted to go to the party. Now, she's ready for a party she's sure is about to begin, the party that had already taken place that afternoon.

I show her the Fix-A-Dent I stopped to buy, tell her her own dentist, Dr. Treible, thinks it may help with the problem of food getting stuck in her teeth. Her face lights up, but when I ask her to come out into the hall with me so I can apply it to her dentures, she refuses. "I might miss the party."

"Hannah, don't be bad," says Shirley. "Your daughter is trying to help you." I shoot Shirley a rueful smile.

I try to turn Mom's chair toward the hallway; she digs her feet into the floor.

"Mom, you have to cooperate with me."

"Don't be ridiculous," she says.

"If you don't let me do this, there are going to be dire consequences," I hear myself say.

"Let there be," she answers.

"I'm leaving," I tell her as I turn, walk out the door and stomp down the hallway toward her room, the tube of dental adhesive clutched in my hand. What am I doing? Am I really going to leave like this?

Tania stops me in the hallway, asks me to sign a new Do Not Resuscitate order, another for No Intubation. Each time I've had to sign these orders, I've imagined the conditions under which they might be needed, what would happen if they weren't signed. I see a young, muscular paramedic pressing and pounding my mother's tiny chest, her fragile breastbone under his large hands, her thin ribs, the contusions, the stopping, the waiting, the possible starting up of her heart again.

I've imagined the scene in the emergency room, a blue plastic accordion tube being passed down through Mom's mouth and throat into her bronchus, the door to her lungs. The hiss of a breathing machine. Her body flat on a bed in the ICU, tubes going in and coming out of her mouth, her veins, her bladder, her stomach.

Not again!

I sign the papers.

"Tania, she won't let me experiment with her dentures," I say. "Maybe you can help."

Tania wheels Mom, who is now wearing a sheepish grin, into the hall where I am pacing. Mom agrees to take her dentures out. I take them into the bathroom, brush them clean, dry them carefully, dot the pink Fix-A-Dent adhesive into the channel that's meant to hug her gums where teeth have been removed. I help her place them back in without getting adhesive on her fingers. Press up, press down, hold, wait ten seconds, her head all the while pulling away, eyes reaching back to the center of the dining room, sure the party is about to begin.

She is still refusing to eat. I tell her she has to, I have to know if the adhesive is going to hold. There is a lifetime at work here of my wanting her to do things on my schedule, not hers. The only difference is that now she is willing to look crazy as she says no.

Mom and The Redhead

January 16

I slip into the dining room, take a seat behind Mom. From the back of her head, I can tell she isn't paying one whit of attention to Mara, who is leading a meeting of the residents. They've convened to consider, in a democratic way, where they want to go for their once-a-month outing.

But here's the math.

Only six people can go at a time, no more than two in wheelchairs, and at least thirty women live on this floor, almost *all* in wheelchairs. Which comes to an average of one outing every five months per person. More important, the numbers are moot given the slipperiness of these women's various conditions and the fact that most are in their 90s, at least. My mother is unlikely ever to be one of the people going. Ever. And she knows it.

As Mara, the vivacious social worker engaged to Howard, darling of every nonagenarian here, spins on her heel to answer the question of a resident behind her, the ruffles at the cuffs of her print silk blouse and the bell bottoms of her tight khaki pants wave in a self-made wind.

I follow behind Mom as she navigates her wheelchair out of the dining room, into the hall. This way she's learned to propel the chair with her feet makes me want to cry. Those same SAS oxfords that used to take her everywhere she wanted to go on foot, her feet hitting the floor — boom, boom, boom — nothing or no one able to stop her once she got an idea in her head. Burger King for lunch. Afternoons at the Leisure Village pool with her cronies. Roaming the aisles at Von's, leaning, as she was wont to do, arms folded on the handle of her shopping cart. Leading me to ask her, as I was wont to do, to stand up straight, that it would be better for her back.

Now, those same SAS oxfords only tap, tap, tap the ground as they carry her toward some idea of freedom. Boom boom boom being saved for when she is angry.

But boom or tap, neither she nor her feet have lost their resolve. Yes, it makes me want to cry.

"Thank God," she says when she sees me, her eyes darting with question marks, the muscles around her mouth full of fear. "I couldn't imagine what happened to you."

Though she'd seen me through the window, she hadn't seen me slip into the room, sit down behind her. "Where *is* she, where did she *go*?" had grown, in the fertile ground of anxiety, into "My God, what happened to her?"

"Sure I saw you," she says, when I try to calm her down, her worry now turning to anger. I wheel her back into the room, pull my chair up next to hers, take her hand.

"Do you see my roommate?" Mom asks, pointing with her chin to Miriam sitting smack in the center of the room. I nod yes. To which Mom shoots me a knowing glance I don't have a clue how to read.

"The one who always yells at me ... ," she says, partly a question, pointing again with her chin, every few seconds turning back to look at Miriam.

My guess is that my mother has absolutely no idea what to make of this hot-headed redhead who says exactly what she thinks. I can only imagine what goes on with them during the night when Mom, too anxious to wait for her call light to be answered, yells, "Wawdah, I'll die if I don't get wawdah!"

"Shut the hell up," I can hear Miriam yelling back. Or, something even more, shall we say, direct.

I've asked Miriam how they get along.

"I love your mother," she tells me. "If I have to tell her to shut up, I tell her to shut up. Then, it's done. I forget about it."

I doubt if my mother forgets.

My mother has described the childhood home she grew up in as "quiet, too quiet." I see a neat and orderly Bronx apartment where nobody talks unless it is absolutely necessary. Her sisters, Jessie and Theresa and Doris, are already out in the world, working. Their mother, Sarah, leans back in her chair dozing, a copy of "The Forvitz" — *The Jewish Daily Forward* — about to fall off her lap. She is tired after a day of getting up and down from her knees on the floor, straight pins held tight between the same full lips my mother has, as she pins up skirt hems for neighborhood women who can afford to have her do it rather than do it themselves. Her husband, Hyman, a trim man in a vest — maybe he's hung the jacket of his gabardine suit over a straight-backed kitchen chair — has been reading, too, something in English, a glass of tea ("a glezl tay") in his hand, its tall spoon held back between index and middle fingers. Hannah, their chubby, plain-looking blonde daughter sits on the piano bench, playing exercises from a book with a green cover on an old upright, practicing those exercises over and over again into the late-afternoon quiet.

Hannah, whose confident and sure notes on a piano could, still can, easily fill a room, has always played her personal thoughts and feelings close to the vest. With all that practice, she still could never hide her unhappiness. There it was — in the droop of her shoulders, slack jaw, head tilted to one side, faraway look in her eyes.

You could see it, but she wouldn't talk about it. If you were the daughter, this daughter anyway, you'd have to keep asking what was troubling her. You needed to know. Because you needed to cheer her up. You needed her to do things *you* knew she could do when *she* didn't know she had enough energy to get them started on her own. She was your connection to the world. You needed that connection, needed *her*, to be strong and stable. Needed to know she would stay with you, not disappear again into that space behind her eyes. Where deep in your cells you remember, even from when you were a baby, she had a habit of going, leaving you alone. Even when she sat next to your crib, you weren't sure she was really there.

You didn't know how to wake her up enough to get

what you needed. As much as she gave you, and it was a lot, there was something about always having to fight for it that left a hole still waiting to be filled.

Now, here's this redhead every night in a bed not three feet away from your mother, making no bones about telling her exactly what's on her mind. Asking for, no *telling her*, exactly what she wants and when she wants it.

Now! Miriam wants it now!

I don't think my mother is hurt by Miriam's directness so much as shocked. Leaving her with no option but to point with her chin and say, "That's my roommate." Expecting me to get her whole meaning, just like that. Which maybe I do, maybe I don't.

A couple of years ago, something did let loose in the way Mom held herself together. She began to ask for what *she* wanted, began speaking up about things that were bothering her. It was a major advance over complaining; even worse, over retreating into silence. I admired her ability at 91 and 92 to be changing, to be feeling a strong touch of women's lib in her old age. Why not? She'd made it into a new millennium.

Then came the two pneumonias, each leaving her weaker in body and mind than the one before. But alive, still alive.

"Hannah, what a strong constitution you have," people would say. "What a fierce will to live." And you'd see her now small body rising to the occasion, her will made stronger by their acknowledgment.

At some point, this new assertiveness turned into downright demands. As the gravity of old age exerted its inexorable downward pull and she became more and more separate from the outside world she had always gained strength from — "Sara, look at that beautiful tree," she would say — the hold she had on her tried-and-true ways of controlling life loosened, leaving her yelling, hoping there'd be someone to hear.

Miriam hears. And Mom hears Miriam.

Now, as she points her chin in the direction of this redhead who, I'm willing to bet, did not grow up in a quiet Bronx apartment, Mom needs me to understand something about Miriam. Something that's being worked out in her understanding of the world — and her place in it. I may never fully know what is going on inside her head, but I can be here with her as she navigates the new terrain.

Yes. But Not One Moment Sooner

January 17

She calls and introduces herself as Karen, a social worker from a new service at The Jewish Home. Supportive Care, she calls it. She wants to know how I would feel about her starting to see my mother.

One day, there will be another early morning call. To tell me Mom has died; worse, had a stroke, broke a hip. Today, I'm relieved. I've been asking for this, someone to give Mom a chance to talk about whatever it is that has her practicing dying.

"I hate to tell you this," Mom says. "You're not going to like it. But I'm dying."

"Tell me about it," I say.

"Don't laugh," she says. "It's not funny. I'm really dying."

"I'm not laughing, Mom. It's just that right now I see you're very much alive."

"But I almost wasn't. It's a miracle I'm still here."

"Tell me."

"It gets quieter ... and quieter ... and quieter ... ," she says, her voice diminishing to practically no sound at all.

"Then what?"

"Something changes. Someone comes with a glass of

water to save me. Or I open my eyes."

"Now you know what to do next time it happens," I say. "Open your eyes. You'll see that you're still alive."

Oh, dear. Here she is, opening herself up, talking to me about death, and I'm all matter-of-fact and "we-can-fix-*this*-too."

I have wonderings, too. *Is* death just on the other side of opening your eyes from a dream that's come to steal you away? Does real dying happen that one time when you let your eyes stay closed?

"Are you afraid of dying?" I ask.

"Sure I am," she says. I press her to say a little more, but she won't. Or can't.

"I'm not ready to die. I want to live just a little longer."

"Well, here you are."

Karen says she'll be able to give my mother more attention than she's getting now, talk with her a couple of times a month, maybe even once a week. As good as I think that will be, something puts me on guard, something slowly finding its way into the foreground of our conversation.

"Did you know The Jewish Home is developing a hospice program?" she asks.

So that's it!

She assures me that hospice is only part of her job and that, from what she could see when she stuck her head into Mom's room this morning, my mother isn't ready for hospice.

"Who referred her?" I ask, a mother lion rising up slowly from her haunches, front legs firm, back legs on their way to standing.

She assures me my questions are appropriate.

I ask how she feels about encouraging people to stay as independent as they can be. "It's more convenient for the staff for my mother to be in a wheelchair," I say. "They ask her if she wants to walk, she says no and they leave it at that. When I'm with her, I say, 'Here's your walker, let's go.' And she walks. She walks just fine."

I ask Karen to notice how low my mother sits in her wheelchair. "With her arms down at her sides," I say, "the sides of the chair compress her chest, which limits her breathing." I'm a broken record. "And even the alternative isn't good; with her arm lying heavily on a too-high armrest, the nerves on the inside of her arm are being compressed. I've been telling the nurses for weeks that if they don't get her a new chair she's going to end up with a paralyzed arm, then she'll really be in trouble. I'm concerned that, if the staff knows my mother is in this Supportive Care program, their expectations of her will drop lower than they already are. They're overworked. And, granted, my mother is a handful."

I think of Vickie who, as busy as she is, tries. "I keep

telling the aides to take your mother to the bathroom every two hours," Vickie tells me. "I don't want her to get used to the diaper, she'll become incontinent. Sometimes, she refuses."

"I'm my mother's advocate," I tell Karen, hot tears spilling from my eyes. "I've lived with this my whole life, her saying she doesn't want to. Doesn't want to talk, doesn't want to walk, doesn't want to sit in a chair, doesn't want to whatever it is you want her to do. But if you take the time, if you encourage her ..." I have to stop to get my breath back, wait for my throat to open before I can go on.

"She's always been a very independent-slash-dependent person," I continue. "A wonderful mother who's lived through things nobody thought she would live through. Now, she tells me she's not ready to die. I want her to be given every possible chance to live to the very last day of her life. I don't want anyone cutting it short."

"I hear you," Karen says. "I understand."

"I need someone on my side," I say. "It's too big a job for me alone."

We hang up. Sobs a long time coming, come. These sobs, this conversation, important steps on the path Mom and I are walking.

Don't Go, Not Yet

Later

I call ahead to ask Mom if she would like to attend Howard's Shabbat celebration with me. It used to be the highlight of her week at The Jewish Home.

"I couldn't," she says. "I'd spoil it for everybody."

I have a vague sense of what she means. "How about putting your makeup on, just in case?"

I'm surprised to see Bill, tan and trim, just returned from eight days in Hawaii. The kind of handsome that comes with being well-rested. He's shocked at how incoherent Mom sounds, the fear in her eyes that says she's shocked by it, too.

He shakes his head in a way that says, "How sad. What am I supposed to do now?" Love and burden all mixed up together.

"Smile," Mom says, trying to cheer him up. He forces a smile he can only manage for a few seconds.

"I know. You're upset to see how I am," she says, her mother's heart reading the feeling behind his reaction.

"We'll drop in on Howard another time," I say. "Maybe next week."

"I'm wet," Mom says.

Bill and I wait in the hallway while Nancy changes

the diaper. I sit. He stands.

Before the end of the year, I'd sent him a note asking him to write me a check, a gift from Mom's account, to recompense me in part for the work I do with Mom; another check after the first of the year. He didn't answer.

Reverting to practicality, where he feels more stable than on the shaky ground of feelings, he asks what kind of ongoing time arrangement I've made with Georgina.

"None," I say, feeling the need to defend myself. "The hours she put in were only when I was away. If she hadn't stepped in, I wouldn't have been able to go." I remind him of the money I laid out to pay her.

He tells me she'd left him a message. "She went on and on," he says, "how she wants to be paid in cash, that it's too hard for her to cash checks." He says he won't reimburse me until I get a statement from Georgina for the hours she put in.

"Georgina's a poor woman from El Salvador," I want to scream. "She can barely write in English. She doesn't have a checking account. She and her husband are living from hand-to-mouth, supporting two daughters. She comes to visit Mom every day, sometimes twice a day, for no pay at all. Give her the damn money she earned. She isn't General Electric, for heaven's sake."

But I don't say anything. We sit there, each looking away from the other into a world of our own.

Back in Mom's room, I place the walker in front of her. "I can't walk with that," she says. "I've never walked with that."

"C'mon, Mom, your walking is just fine."

She walks half the length of the building. I set three chairs up for us near the entrance. She looks like herself, but her talk belies her looks. She only makes half-sense. A quarter of an hour before dinner, she asks Angie to put her to bed.

"You go to bed *after* dinner," I tell her.

"No, I go before," she says. And makes Angie promise to stay long enough to help her to bed.

Eileen has returned from a few weeks in the Geriatric Psych Ward and, at least for the moment, is quiet and smiling, once more the beautiful woman I knew her to be when she and Mom were both new to The Jewish Home, each living in their own room. She asks me how my husband is. She still means my mother.

Shirley, who Eileen had been driving crazy with constant yelling before the psych ward admission, pulls her wheelchair up next to Eileen to give her a welcome home kiss. She can't quite reach her cheek. I suggest she kiss her hand instead. She does.

Leah, the woman with four teeth that float up out of her lower jaw, comes over to greet my mother as if they're old friends. My mother has just been telling us how crazy

Leah is. Still, she finds the attention seductive. "I love you," my mother tells her.

"That woman is one of the nastiest people I've ever met," Bill says, shaking his head.

I ask Mom to give me her dentures. They come out easily. For the third day in a row, they have no adhesive in them. I take them to her room, brush them, dry them and, coming back to where she and Bill are sitting, dot adhesive on top and bottom, press the dentures into her mouth.

Bill kisses Mom on her forehead and leaves.

In the dining room, there are new seating arrangements. Anna, deaf in her right ear, is seated next to Mom's deaf left ear. Eileen, who's been placed across from Mom, can't find the right word for anything and, if the drugs she's been put on don't work, will soon be screaming again. And Mom? Mom's just plain old refusing to eat, a plate of asparagus, roast chicken and kasha lies untouched in front of her. An ideal dining arrangement!

I feed Mom the tips of the asparagus and a couple of bites of chicken before she closes her mouth tight the way a baby does as the spoon approaches. She can't eat, she says, the food gets stuck in her teeth. I make her an open-faced tuna sandwich, which she eats just fine, until she suddenly stops and pushes it away in favor of dessert. It's the kind of rugelach she used to bake, with cinnamon and sugar. She eats them with enthusiasm. I don't know what to believe anymore.

I leave her in the hallway next to Rachel, who is speaking Yiddish to a Filipina nurse. I remember how Mom and Rachel would sit next to each other every night back in their Transitional Care Unit days. Dinner over, Mom would make a beeline for one of the flowered easy chairs in the lounge. No one else would dare sit in it. When someone new was admitted, maybe they got to sit in it once, until word reached them that the chair belonged to Hannah.

Waiting for the wrong to be made right, Mom would stare at the intruder from one of the straight-back chairs. If she could have forklifted the new person out of that chair with her eyes, she would have done it. I tried to talk her out of being so insistent. "Mom, that chair doesn't belong to you," I'd say to the side of her face, as she continued to stare down the hapless new resident.

Rachel would sit at right angles to Mom in another of those flowered chairs, combing and combing and combing her straight, thick, white hair; put on makeup; bawl me out in Yiddish if I was taking up too much room in their vicinity or if, in her estimation, I was talking too loud. Mom would cluck over how much time and attention Rachel would spend gazing into her hand mirror.

Rachel and Mom eventually moved to the Factor

Building and Rachel, now in a wheelchair, too, is no longer putting on her own makeup. Whenever she catches my eye, she tells me bits and pieces about her years in Auschwitz. Sometimes in Yiddish, sometimes in English.

Mom spots Elizavetta sitting by herself near the nurse who is handing out medications. She motions her to come closer and sing. Elizavetta, who immigrated recently from Romania, has a singing voice as sweet as sugar cubes dissolving in the bottom of a glass of hot tea. I ask her if she wants to sing, she shakes her head no.

"Go get her," my mother orders me. "I don't want her sitting there all alone."

I bring Mom a familiar looking book from the little library across from the nurses' station. *Peace of Mind.* I remember it from the bookcase in our Connecticut apartment, circa 1952. It has her name written inside the front cover. She says she's never seen it. I hand her her reading glasses. But to navigate the two pairs of glasses is more than she can manage. She tries to read with her distance glasses, stares out at me with the ones for reading. Back again. I want to scream. "Read!"

"Don't go, not yet," Mom says. "Stay just a little longer. Don't leave me now."

Lox 'n Bagels

January 18

It's Saturday night dinner at The Jewish Home. On the table in front of Mom sits a hard plastic plate, the kind we used to call Melmac; on it, an egg bagel (minus its paper bag), cream cheese, two slices of tomato, a slice of red onion, a generous slice of lox.

I cut the lox into small squares, press them into the thin layer of cream cheese I've spread on half the bagel. Mom's always liked open-faced sandwiches. Maybe if I prepare one for her, she'll find the interest or the energy to eat.

For a special treat on Sunday mornings in my childhood, we'd have lox and bagels. On extra-special days, the lox would be Nova Scotia. We didn't say *from* Nova Scotia, just Nova Scotia. People I considered to be more worldly — like my friend Ronni's mother and father, Harry and Bertha Shwartz — would shorten the name of the delicacy to Nova. Unlike the salty, cheaper kind of lox we usually had, the kind that seemed old-fashioned to me, whose glisteny white fibers you couldn't saw through with a knife, let alone your teeth, the kind you had to tear apart with your fingers, Nova Scotia lox was so tender you could slice through it with the side of your fork. It would practically melt in your mouth. For the three of us, Mom would buy an eighth or a quarter of a pound. We would each take a small piece and tear it apart, dotting shreds of Nova Scotia lox, just for the taste of it, over the Philadelphia cream cheese, its tough silvery package opened out onto the table.

Now, when people eat lox, even here at The Jewish Home, it always seems to be Nova, served in slices even bigger than the half of a bagel it goes on. You have to fold it over double. It hurts me, still, to see how much gets wasted. Each time Mom refuses to take a bite, Eileen breaks through her aphasia. "Eat!" she says. Exclamation point.

Mom takes a bite.

"I've been wondering, Mom, are you doing what an animal does when it's getting ready to die?"

"Maybe I *am* an animal," she answers. "If I don't eat, I'll die."

Background to all this talk of lox and life, The Three Tenors are singing.

Earlier, Mom had taken her hearing aid out and put it in her pocket. I'd given it to the nurse to put away for safekeeping.

"I want to hear the tenors," Mom says, angry.

I retrieve her hearing aid.

She loves music, would always smile that special smile

of hers at any chance to hear it. Tonight, mad at the world and minus that special smile, she still wants her music.

I turn her chair around so she can see the screen. Mom's mind is elsewhere; not even the sight of Zubin Mehta *kvelling* over Placido Domingo's latest high note at the Baths of Caracalla is enough to break through. "I'm scared," she says. "I'm all alone here."

She's sitting behind a pillar. I place a chair more in the center of things, help her into it. I wonder: how much of feeling alone had to do with sitting behind the pillar and how much with something I'm not privy to?

"Not in front of me," says Lauretta who — surprise! — is dressed in a skirt and sweater, not her usual house-coat.

I move Mom's chair back a little.

"Uch? In front of me?" says a woman who looks like my mother's Aunt Fanny, but whose temperament couldn't be more different. Sweet Aunt Fanny, who lived in The Hebrew Home on Upper Fifth Avenue in New York City, still crocheting afghans at 99, her specialty a raised yellow flower in the center of each colorful square.

Stepping over the edge of my temper, I turn to face into the complaint. "Do you really think I don't want you to see?" I ask the woman.

"All right, all right."

Earlier, Shirley had caught my attention with her eyes

and an upward movement of her head. When your movement elsewhere is limited, it's amazing how much can be communicated with head and neck and eyes. "I've got to snitch," she'd said. I kept walking. Now, she manages to pull me over with a conspiratorial glance and, before she can get a word out (her eyes are glaring), I say, "It would be better, Shirley, if I don't hear what you have to say. I notice that when you tell me things, I go away feeling bad. I don't need any more reason today to feel bad."

She shrugs as if to say, What can you do?

I tell Mom I'm meeting my housemates for a seven o'clock movie. "I'll see you tomorrow."

"I just hope I'll be here," she says.

What Only A Mother Can Give

January 22

Mom and Eileen are sitting side-by-side in front of the nurses' station, each in a wheelchair, each with a tray table in front of her with a mess of food on it. My mother has taken her place alongside Eileen as the other most difficult person on the first floor of the Factor Building.

Mom is quiet tonight, almost calm. I pull up a chair

and talk to her in a soft voice. She leans forward, toward me, to hear. A good sign.

Lately, as I've redoubled my efforts to get her to do things she doesn't want to do — eat, walk — she's receded deeper into the shell she's been laying down around herself. For two months, she's been left to tough it out without drugs that have become too dangerous for her sensitive body, leaving her to find her own creative ways to manage high anxiety. She learned to self-medicate with oxygen her body didn't otherwise need, until the oxygen pushed her over the edge of coherence. She's taken to screaming. When someone doesn't come immediately, she screams. When she can't stand my urgings anymore, she pulls away, literally, using her feet to maneuver the chair. On more than one occasion, she even ordered Bill to leave. She's practicing dying.

But tonight, there's a window again into the mother I knew, maybe into a mother I haven't yet known. She says she's hungry, and actually eats — bites of bread and spoonfuls of egg salad I bring her from the kitchen.

I sit directly in front of her, pull her wheelchair up between my legs. "Mom, you know I'm writing about you. About us."

She opens her eyes wide.

"You told me it was okay. Is it still okay?"

"Why shouldn't it be?"

"It's very personal," I tell her. She's unfazed.

"Maybe it will be published. Maybe you'll get rich."

"I doubt it, not very many writers do."

"But you'll get recognition," she says, her voice going down at the end; a statement, not a question.

"If I do, it'll be because we did this together," I tell her.

We are late bloomers, my mother and I, she in her 90s, me in my 60s. Doing the work of coming together and then separating, what the psychology books say is the work of mother and baby. Mother and toddler. Mother and adolescent. Or, maybe this is how people in real life *actually* do it. Maybe it's never too late.

"I love you so much," she says, taking me in with a soft gaze. "If anything happened to you while I was still alive, I'd die."

Here it is, the sadness and humor of the human condition all wrapped into one thought. "I worry about it," she goes on. "I worry about how you'll be when I die. I love you more than anything. And it's always been that way."

She has to know her work is done. Has to trust I will be able to live without her.

She's finished saying what she needs to say and I don't remember ever feeling closer to her. Then, on the heels of this almost dizzying feeling of having gotten from her what I've always wanted, a sly smile of self-satisfaction comes over me. Bill has been digging his heels in ever harder not to acknowledge me for the time I spend with our mother, refusing to say that what I do allows him to go about his own life in ways he wouldn't be able to otherwise. The deprived and nasty child in me wants revenge.

"You love me more than you love Bill, don't you?"

I want to say it. But I don't.

For one thing, I really don't want to hurt him. He is at least as attached to our mother as I am. Besides, I know it isn't true. And I don't want to ruin this private moment with my mother by opening a door for her to tell me, yet again, what a special place she has in her heart for him, how "good as gold" he is. No. Not tonight.

Tonight, I want to allow what she said — and maybe even felt, at least for a moment — to sink in. That I am what is most precious to her and have always been. At one time, before there were two children to love, it was probably true.

Tonight, by some miracle, my mother has come out of the hardening shell of death to be my mother again and, at last, shower on me, with her whole heart, the kind of loving only a mother can give.

What Will Go Next?

January 24

Smack in the middle of the entryway to the Factor Building, an old woman is sliding out of her wheelchair. A nurse, who tries to make up for her perpetual scowl by wearing small clips in her hair dotted with multi-colored rhinestones, walks by as if nothing is wrong.

"Mom, you can't sit like this," I say.

"Why not? I have to."

"You can sit straight. I know you can."

I get under her right arm, try to lift her. She won't budge.

"You're starting to look like Eileen," I say. And, for just a moment, her eyes show that she knows what I mean. Eileen, who often sits half out of her chair, in this same spot.

I'm immediately sorry I said it, ashamed at being so critical.

I lock the brakes on Mom's chair, hurry to her room to get her walker. I put it in front of the chair, get under her right arm again. Again, she makes herself into dead weight.

The nurse comes back, this time offering to help. With one of us on either side, Mom comes to her feet and, with only the slightest support from the walker, even then only for balance, walks to her room.

"The urine is coming," she says, her attention more on her bladder than on walking. As soon as I help her onto the toilet, urine begins to flow. She's rolled up like a ball. To see her face, I have to kneel down, roll into a ball myself, turn my head so it's facing up.

I've been assured the redness over her tailbone is not a bedsore, and it's true the skin hasn't broken down. But I'm shocked by how tender it looks, how red her skin is along the length of both buttocks. It could be the beginning of real trouble.

"She won't let me give her a shower," Angie says. "It's the only way I can clean that area on her back." She shows me, too, how dry Mom's scalp has become.

"Mom," I say, getting into that almost upside-down position again to plead with her, "you've got to stay clean."

"Don't be ridiculous," she says to me. "I don't need a shower. Besides, I can't stand up."

"Angie says there's a seat in the shower room."

"You'll show her, won't you, Angie?"

I feel shaken. Mom, who prided herself on never sweating under her arms, would use a swish of deodorant anyway. She brushes her teeth to a fault. Has always been aware of the slightest smell of onion or garlic on her breath, or mine. I could always snuggle my nose into her body and be greeted by the fresh smell of soft skin.

Now she's refusing to take a shower. She's not eating. Unless I do a sales job, she doesn't want to walk. What else, I wonder, is about to go?

"I only have a few minutes," I tell her. "I've got to be in Malibu in half-an-hour for a haircut."

Though Mom is still curled up on the toilet with her attention on getting rid of that last drop of urine, she does seem to be giving in a little about the shower.

When I tell the wise and beautiful blonde who cuts my hair that I don't know how much to push my mother at this time in her life, she tells me about her own mother who, since a stroke seven years ago, can't turn in bed by herself, has to use a diaper. "As long as your mother can still walk, can still sit on the toilet, help her to keep doing it. It's awful to be so dependent."

I wonder what the people at The Jewish Home think of me when I insist on Mom walking to meals, being tak-en to the bathroom every two hours so she won't become dependent on a diaper. Am I fighting a losing battle?

Shirley, who has had two strokes and isn't able to walk at all, looks at Mom and, with a frown, pronounces her judgment. "She's lost her will to live."

It's true that Mom is at least thinking about dying, a subject she'd held at arm's length until the UCLA admis-sion less than four months ago. Less than four months ago! There have been so many changes since I came back to LA, this hardest of times for both of us.

Her will to live after the first pneumonia, again after the second, had everyone shaking their heads. "I can count on the fingers of one hand the people who survive what your mother went through," the administrative nurse at Sherman Oaks Hospital told me. "And your mother survived it twice." The intubation. Weeks in the ICU on a breathing machine. Learning to swallow again, to sit in a chair, to walk to the bathroom, even to play the piano.

Her will to live has given us the time we needed — those two years, accelerating into these last months — to do what we wouldn't have had the chance to do otherwise. Come together and, finally, begin to separate. Along the way, each of us becoming more fully who we are.

I didn't have the chance, when I was a child, to say goodbye to my father, who died one morning just like that. I'd organized my life around never being shocked like that again and now here I am, learning how to say goodbye. It's not easy knowing what to do, how to be when someone is dying. It takes practice.

Are You Hearing Little Voices? The Woman Asked

A dream, January 26

Mom calls me into her room. She is absolutely rational. "Who is that person?" she asks. She says a woman had taken her into a small room behind the nurses' station and was asking her questions. "Are you hearing little voices?" the woman asked. "It's okay. Many, many people do." My mother understood that the woman was doing whatever she could to pigeon-hole her as crazy. While I'm at the nurses' station trying to find out who that woman was, another woman in a white coat — young and pretty, with long dark hair — sits down behind us to write in a chart. I've seen her before. I think she's a social worker.

Can I Hold Her As I Let Her Go?

January 27

I wake up in the middle of the night to the hum of a motor inside my chest. I lie quietly and listen. It's happened before — a long, narrow column of vibration that extends through my torso. I'm relieved, this sign of life expanding.

On second thought, no. It must be the anxiety I inherited from Mom. If I make it to her age, will I be as out-of-control as she is? Oh dear.

Wait! Maybe it's not her anxiety I inherited. Maybe I inherited her hiatal hernia, too. That opening in her diaphragm that allows the aorta to slip up and through, and this is how it feels when blood rushes through a crimp in this largest of blood vessels.

I scare myself with thoughts. Thoughts like these that cover over the possibility of goodness, the possibility that my life *is* actually expanding.

It's early morning when Michael, the Activities Director, calls. Michael is a serious middle-aged man who wears Hawaiian shirts and whose eyeglasses sit far down on his nose. He has a special, intimate way of connecting with the women on the first floor of the Factor Building where Mom lives.

"I'm going to put your mother on the phone," he says.

She informs me that I'm dead. That I fell. And died from the fall. She saw it happen. She's distraught. "I was trying to get in touch with Bill," she says. "I wanted him to see you while you were still alive, but I couldn't reach him and you died."

"It's okay, Mom. I'm alive. I've been cooking all morning. Pretty soon, I'll be there to pick you up. We have an appointment with your dentist this afternoon."

She says it can't be true. I'm definitely dead. She saw me. "You'll see, Sara," she insists.

"Mom, you must have had a bad dream. Are your eyes open? Open your eyes. Who are you talking to right now?"

Nothing I say can change her mind. No matter how loud my voice gets. And my voice gets loud as I start to talk over her. I know it won't help. But I can't stop. (As I read this years later, I wish, how I wish, I'd said, "That must have been really scary, to see me die and you couldn't even get in touch with Bill." How I wish that all those times she told me she was dying, I had acknowledged how frightening it must be. Before jumping to quell my own anxiety by denying hers.)

Trying to talk her into the fact that I'm alive feels

familiar. Like all those other times — with my father, with her, with Bill, with my husband Matt — when I felt the need to keep talking, louder and louder, to prove my existence.

I think about the young man in Tiananmen Square who held nothing back in the face of possible annihilation by the tank of State. I've had to hold firm against the steamrollers in my own life, make sure my voice would be heard through the dark cloud of accusation, or irrationality, that seemed to be using up all the air in front of me. Today, in the face of Mom's delirium, I'm fighting for my life.

"Thank God you're still alive," she says, hearing, for a moment, my voice instead of just hers. And then, "You'll see when you get here that what I'm telling you is real."

Michael has literally left me in my mother's hands, my only chance of escape to hang up. I threaten it. She doesn't hear me, her voice, her thoughts obliterating everything.

I notice that the door from my room to the outside of the house is open. The man who lives in the apartment over the carport must have heard every word.

Well, just desserts! Clay is a composer of modern, or minimal, or computer-generated music — whatever you want to call it. Some people would call it noise. Through windows open to the night — his windows, my door — I've sometimes been able to hear past the repetitions and seeming chaos of the music to something essential. Through all the confusions of my life with Mom, crescendoing into the chaos of these last few months, I've never questioned the essential undertone of our love.

"See Mom, I'm alive."

"Don't even talk about it," she says, cutting me short.

She has an appointment this afternoon with her longtime dentist, about thirty miles away, in Camarillo. She says she can't go, she's had too hard a morning. I take her to the toilet. The diaper is heavy with urine and a small, dark bowel movement. Norma comes in to help her get clean. Apologizes for not having her ready. I tell her it's my fault, that I was so busy trying to prove I was alive, I forgot to call back to say I was coming. Norma helps Mom brush her teeth, dusts blush across her cheeks.

Mom is still insisting she can't go. I keep the process moving, the motor inside me revving.

We get her into the passenger seat. She complains it's too hot, her mouth is dry, her eyes are tearing. She insists all the way to Camarillo that she will not go into the dentist's office. I keep driving.

"Remember when I lived here with Matt?" I say as we pass through Woodland Hills.

"What's Matt's daughter's name?" she asks.

"Joanna," I answer. "And here's Westlake."

"We used to go there with Matt," she says, remembering.

It's been ten years since Matt and I separated. She enjoys talking about him. They liked each other, my husband and my mother. Saw something in the other they recognized in themselves. Matt was the first person to tell me how strong my mother was, that she only acted weak.

Back then, her strength presented itself as willful, stubborn. Now, she's fierce.

I point out The Oaks Mall. "You used to drive there to go shopping ..."

"How much longer is winter?" she asks.

I tell her how bitter cold I've heard it is Back East; that, in Florida, the oranges are freezing. Tell her that last night, after a late walk, Lily and I sat outside on our porch. "It was just like a summer's night," I say.

"Lily and Bonnie and I all have old mothers," I tell her.

"There's old and there's old old," Mom says.

"What are you?" I ask.

"Not even old," she says.

I laugh. "Well, in a lot of ways, that's true, isn't it?"

I pull up in front of Dr. Treible's office.

"I'm embarrassed to go in," she says. "I wasn't always like this."

"How do you mean?"

"Old," she says. "I wasn't always so old."

Dr. Treible has an easy way with my mother. He speaks to her with a soft voice. Each time I'm sure she hasn't heard him, it turns out she has.

I tell him she's not eating, says food gets stuck in her teeth. "In the last two months, she's lost eleven pounds."

He sees a place on her upper denture where food may be collecting and cuts it back. Fills a cavity in what's left of the tooth we already know needs a root canal, the tooth she insists is healthy.

"The filling is just for comfort," he says, "to help her start eating again. The tooth may abscess. Sometimes, when you fill a tooth that has decay, an abscess backs up to the bone."

I get Mom back in the car, run over to Vons to get us a tuna sandwich to share, pick up a few slices of Muenster cheese. Mom always had a package of Muenster cheese in her refrigerator, and, until civilization advanced to placing a piece of paper between slices of Muenster cheese, there were ragged edges where she'd try to separate one slice from the other, never having the patience to gently tease them apart.

"This isn't where I eat," she says. "I know this isn't where I eat."

"You're right, Mom, you eat at The Jewish Home. But now you're in my car, and here's a sandwich."

I watch her eat part of the sandwich and a whole slice of cheese, hoping against hope that what Dr. Treible did will work — that she'll forget how preoccupied she's been with her teeth and start eating again.

All the way back to The Jewish Home, she uses the flossing tool he gave her, hissing and clicking air through the spaces between her teeth. No longer water, no longer oxygen, now it's her teeth that take up all her attention.

I play the radio, loud, over her almost non-stop talking.

Floss. Hiss and click. Talk. Floss. Hiss and click. Talk.

I tell her I can't hear what she's saying. She keeps talking anyway.

In the background, on NPR, I hear a story about half-brothers who killed and dismembered their mother. They got the idea of cutting off her head and hands from watching *The Sopranos*. The mother's body has just been identified and a trail has led to the older son.

On the Conejo Grade, the long hill up from Camarillo back toward the San Fernando Valley, my car begins to lose power. Something gives in the engine. The ride becomes rough. "Dear God, don't let me get stuck here with this woman who can't stop talking."

The god of cars and compassion comes through. We make it back.

"This isn't where I live," Mom says, as we enter the parking lot. "It used to be where I live, but I don't live here now."

I don't say a word.

Nancy, the aide, comes out to get my mother. I leave quickly and limp over to Steve's Independent, my long-time Acura mechanic.

When you have a car with 306,000 miles on it, you begin to think like a mechanic. "I think it's the fuel pump," I tell Tom, describing the symptoms.

I pop the hood. He checks the spark plugs, replaces one that appears faulty. Can it be that's all it is? A faulty spark plug? I cross my fingers.

Tom explains that either a piston or valve may have finally succumbed to all the oil the engine's been burning. "What's the best thing it could be?" I ask.

"A worn fuel injector would be a hundred-dollar job," he says. "Six or seven hundred for a valve." He tells me to come back tomorrow, assures me I won't get stuck between now and then.

Going home over the Sepulveda pass, I ride the slow lane. My car gets me where I'm going. That it might not is never far from my mind.

Only much later, after I've pulled myself back together with a cup of good coffee and some time alone in my notebook, do I think again about the vibration I'd felt last night in the center of my chest. I put it together — though I don't know exactly how it fits — with the motor in the center of my car.

That evening, Dr. Smith returns my call.

"She's not eating," I tell him.

"I increased her liquid diet to three times a day," he says. "And changed it to Resource Plus, so I won't have to worry about her not getting enough calories."

"But why isn't she eating?" I ask. "And she's refusing showers."

"I think it's all part of the dementia," he says.

This is the first time he's come right out and said it: dementia.

"Sometimes her thinking is very clear," I say.

"That's how it is with dementia." Is he going to *keep* saying it?

"But this came on acutely," I say, pulling out whatever guns I have to shoot down the enemy word. "Dementia doesn't come on just like that."

"Maybe there's been some organic change," he counters.

"Have you considered that it could be part of a clinical depression?" I ask. No longer just the daughter, no longer just the physical therapist, now the psychotherapist, too.

"I saw her this morning," he says. She didn't seem depressed. She does well with personal attention."

"Not from me," I say. "Lately, she's been worse when I'm around."

I ask whether the uh, dementia could be the result of her having had too much oxygen during the time she was constantly asking for it.

"Her oxygen is very low," he says. "But we can't give it to her because it'll increase her carbon dioxide." Now, he's got me. I've never taken the time to understand how gas exchange actually works in the lungs.

"There's a lot going on with her metabolically," he says.

"I'm surprised she's still alive," I say.

"So am I," he says.

Back home, I tell Bonnie how I'm still looking for something that will restore my mother, or at least her reputation, to the relatively put-together, self-contained woman she was until recently. "The hardest thing for me is when she says she's embarrassed, when she tells me she knows she's not in control anymore and that everyone can see it. I can feel the energy it takes for her to put up a good front."

"Tell her you can see how hard it is for her not to be in control," Bonnie says. "At least, she won't feel so alone. She'll have you with her."

A few days ago, I apologized to Mom for pushing her so hard to walk rather than use the wheelchair. "I guess I don't know what's really going on with you," I say.

"I know you're trying to help," she said. "But sometimes you have to listen to me."

Can I be with my mother's mind the way I'm learning to be with my own? Hold everything that passes through — all my habitual thoughts and fears, all her habitual thoughts and fears — in a space of love? After all, it's just her mind running amok, her mind just a more exaggerated version of mine. Can I return, in the best way I know how, the holding and comforting she's always offered me in the best way *she* knew how?

Leaving The World Behind. Or, The Last Time Mom Eats Mexican Food

February 3

The realization that I need to let my trusty old Acura go has thrown me into a tizzy. I continue to clunk around town on three cylinders waiting for inspiration, what to do next.

I borrow Keta's old purple Nissan to take Mom back to the dentist. Norma, who brings Mom out to meet me, wants to know where she can get *her* car painted purple.

Mom thinks it's my car with new paint.

It's a cool day, the ride out through the San Fernando Valley easy. Mom has brought her sunglasses; she isn't squinting.

"Look at the hills, Sara, they're so green. Didn't anybody tell them it's winter?" Part of her is still Back East where winter means dead grass and leafless trees. Either that or, in the fifteen years she's lived here, she hasn't noticed that, in California, it's in summer, not winter, that the hills turn brown.

I reach over, rest my hand on her thigh. She places her hand on top of mine.

Dr. Treible has completed half the job when Mom says she can't take any more.

I come in, hold her hand. After a rest, she's calm enough for him to seat the temporary crown on the previously decayed tooth.

We leave.

"I'm hungry," she says. "Can we stop somewhere for lunch?"

I get off the 101 in Westlake Village, pull into a handicap space, help her to a seat on the patio of Sharky's Mexican Grill, run back to move the car before it gets a multi-hundred dollar ticket and, finally, get us seated inside, at a window table.

"You said it was going to be sunny," she says. I leave

her there, hoping the sun will come out to prove me right.

I order a fajita bowl for me — salad, roasted vegetables and tofu. A quesadilla for her — flour tortilla folded over onto itself, cheese melted inside. I figure the closest thing to a grilled cheese sandwich can't be all bad. At the salsa bar, I fill two of those cute little pleated cups and bring them back to our table.

"No flavor," she says, biting into the quesadilla.

I smooth on some guacamole and a spoonful of the mildest salsa, a dollop of sour cream on top of that.

"No flavor," she says. "It has no flavor."

I add some of the second, spicier salsa.

"No flavor."

I run back to the salsa bar (yes, by this time I'm running) and return with some moderately hot green salsa, a cup of the hotter red, another heaped with chopped onions and cilantro.

"No flavor."

"No flavor."

"No flavor."

She's eyeing my fajita bowl to which I've added a generous shower of the very hottest salsa.

I give it to her to taste, but not before mixing in whatever I can to cool it down. "Too much flavor" is the last thing I want to hear.

"It's hot," she says, "but no flavor."

I suggest she eat some chips. Which she does. Which leads to her picking her teeth to get out whatever crumbs have gotten stuck. I steel myself not to scream.

I gather up the mess on our table and, not before registering how colorful chaos can be, dump it all into the trash, and get her seated at a table outside while I go for the car.

"I don't think I go for Mexican food anymore," she says. "I think I'll just stick to what I'm used to." This mother of mine who, in so many ways, relished life is, little by little, leaving the world behind.

Back at The Jewish Home, Norma whisks Mom away, sneaking a backward glance at the purple paint job on Keta's car.

Sad

February 4

I can't keep the days straight. Mom's confusion is taking me over. There's been a change, a new pattern developing. She asks to be put into bed in the afternoon. When I arrive, I find her not quite sleeping, not quite awake. When her eyes are open, I see question marks in them.

In bed with her clothes on, she looks tiny under an afghan grown huge. I rub her hand. No response. I rub her leg and hip, feel how bony she's become. Her forehead is lined. Something's troubling her and she's trying to work it out.

I sit in her wheelchair and wait.

She wakes up a little more.

I think about the e-mail I received from Bill this morning, the last in a series of back-and-forths, vitriol easier to spew the farther away you are from having to see the other person's face or hear their voice. The overt message was that he left the check I was waiting for on top of Mom's nightstand; the inner message so ice-cold it made me shiver.

"I threw it out," Mom says.

"Mom, that money was to reimburse me for paying Georgina."

"I know. I don't know why I threw it away."

In the wastebasket, I find the envelope in which I sent my brother the statement he'd asked for, detailing the hours Georgina spent with Mom while I was away. The envelope is torn in half, a torn-in-half check inside. On the back of the envelope, in my brother's pressured, capital-letter printing, there's a five-point note to me, each point containing more anger than the one before. #5. IF YOU HAVE ANY QUESTIONS, DON'T CALL!

"Did you tear it up because of the angry words?"

"I suppose so," she says. "He's good, Sara, he's good."

"He's a good son," I say.

As I'm helping her up, getting her shoes on and tying the laces, she hits me with the beginning salvos of a new obsession. "My shoes are too loose; they're falling off my feet."

I tie the laces tighter, then tighter again, as tears roll down my cheeks, land in splotches on Mom's blue slacks.

"Don't cry, Sara."

"I can't help it, Mom. I feel so hurt. I'm sorry you had to see that note. It's one thing for him to take his anger out on me; it's another thing to make Georgina jump through hoops to be paid for helping you. And for you to have to see it all."

Back home, I tell Bonnie what happened.

"Maybe it's good," she says, "good for her to know the truth."

"But I don't want her to see how unhappy it makes me."

"Maybe it'd do the two of you good to have a big old cry together," Bonnie says. "It's real life, why hide it?"

We haven't had that cry. It's a real question whether I dare tell Mom how it really is for me with my brother. Let it out of the dark from which it escapes only in momentary snarls, rarely tears, before going back into hiding.

I'm done waiting for someone to come along and save

us — that hope I had in the Geriatric Psych Ward that someone would. If anyone is going to grab the two of us by the scruff of the neck, the way a mother cat picks up her kittens and carries them out of danger, it's going to be me. I'll have to take the chance that my imperfect efforts will, one day, allow us to leave the hates and hurts behind, bring us closer to the love I know we have for each other.

Hanging My Hopes On Rouge

February 6

Mom sees me out of the corner of her eye. She goes on talking to Angie, who is helping her into a new jacket. Asks Angie to help her put on her makeup.

"What are you doing up so early?" she asks, looking at her watch. "It's four o'clock, what are you doing here?"

She thinks it's four in the morning and nothing can persuade her it isn't. Not opening the curtains and seeing afternoon light shine in. Not pointing out that everyone else is out and about in the hallway. Nothing.

At a meeting I'd requested to review her care plan, I learn that, as much as I visit nearly every day, there are ways in which my mother is a stranger to me. She is constantly on the move, navigating her now beloved wheelchair out of her room, up and down the hallway, in and out of the dining room. She is only able to sit at the dining table for a few minutes at a time, which means she's barely eating. Mom is discovering ever new ways to be "jumping out of her skin."

With more than an inkling that wanting to keep her alive by keeping her eating is *my* obsession, I suggest she be given more frequent meals. And yogurt. Yes, yogurt! That'll do it! Yogurt is less likely to stick to and between her teeth.

Again, I make my case to the staff that it's only lately she is so agitated and confused and hard-to-manage. That these changes are only temporary and she will return again, as she has before, to her earlier, calmer ways. I ask them if they can join me in holding this as a possibility.

After all, hadn't she asked for help to put on her makeup?

You're A Poet And You Don't Know It

February 7

An enthusiastic volunteer, who speaks very clearly and with a loud voice, is leading a discussion about birthdays. Mom shoots me an angry look.

I pull up a chair next to hers, put my arm around her shoulder, knead the cords at the back of her neck and rock her back and forth from one hip to the other. She turns toward me, smiles.

"Did you have a special birthday?" the volunteer asks.

Lauretta, looking rather together again, in actual clothes, says she was born on December 25th and that nobody ever celebrated her birthday.

"Tell the story about Armistice Day," I say to Mom. She says she doesn't remember. I start it for her.

"It was my mother's ninth birthday," I say. "November 11th, 1918. Everyone in New York City was celebrating the armistice that had just ended World War I."

"I was going to the store with my mother," Mom says, joining in. "To get a piece of herring."

"I bet it was schmaltz herring," the volunteer says, her addition seeming quite unnecessary to me. Wouldn't it have been enough just to listen? Remember this, I tell myself.

Mom says "yes" to schmaltz. I am unconvinced.

"I can see it as if it was yesterday," she continues, then pauses.

"Mom, you said people were hanging out their windows, shouting and throwing things. Was there music?"

She says she's not sure if there was music. Oh no, here I am doing what the volunteer did, getting in the way of a story that's Mom's to tell.

"You thought they were celebrating your birthday?" I continue, unable to stop myself.

She nods her head, eyes filling with the excitement taking place on a busy Bronx street that day. The volunteer says she loves the story, asks if she can tell it to other people. And, in the next breath, is asking about first boyfriends.

A woman who grew up in Detroit tells about the boy she met when she was 13 and married when she was 30. Another woman remembers that her first boyfriend's name was Sam Sunshine.

"Did he ever kiss you?" the volunteer asks.

"Of course," she says, the room suddenly juicy with the memory of first kisses.

Mom says she never had a special boyfriend until she met her husband. I egg her on to tell how they met, how she and her sisters would stop in at his family's store in Old Greenwich, how he would make them black 'n white ice cream sodas at the fountain.

"The whole family worked in the store," Mom says. "My mother-in-law, she was a big, busty woman. She made her own syrup."

Michael breaks in to remind people to sign the card for Mara, the social worker, and Howard, of Sabbath afternoon fame, who are getting married tomorrow.

When I ask Mom what she wants to write, she shrugs it off. "Let it go," she says.

"Mom, you love Howard and Mara. You could say you wish you could play the piano for their wedding." With no hesitation, she maneuvers her way out to the desk and writes, "I wish you could play the piano on such a happy day. Hannah." She writes it in a sure hand, her message colliding with what someone else has written, reminding me of how, in the same way, she bumps into other people's wheelchairs with her own.

I suggest she change the "you" to "I" and that she add her last name, which she does, spelling Epstein with an extra p.

Michael wheels a new resident into the hallway where Mom and I are sitting. Rosella's lips are trembling, her brow furrowed, her eyes wide and scared.

"Leave her here with us," I say to Michael. I put an arm around her shoulders and am impressed with how substantial she feels. I introduce her to Mom, who beams a smile at her. For the moment, Mom is full of social graces. I pat Rosella's shoulder, ask where she lived.

"At the top of Mulholland," she says. "On Roscomare."

"Did you look out over the Valley or the City?"

"Both. We were the first people to build up there. It was 1952."

Miriam rolls in, pushed by her son. They've been out all afternoon; her cheeks are as red as her hair. She has a See's Candy bag in her lap. "Diabetic chocolates," she tells me, biting into one with white nougat inside.

"Miriam, this is Rosella," I say.

"Rosella from the cella," Miriam says and her son, the comedian, laughs out loud.

"You're a poet and you don't know it," my mother adds, turning to face Miriam, get her attention. Miriam doesn't seem to notice.

Some time passes. I say, "Rosella has just moved here."

"Rosella needs a fella." Miriam sings it this time.

Mom comes closer, plants her face directly in front of Miriam's, and sings — my mother who never sings — "You're a poet and you don't know it."

Miriam still doesn't respond.

I'm angry at how Miriam keeps ignoring my mother's attentions.

When I tell Mom it's almost dinnertime and I'm going to leave, her good attitude falls to pieces. She pouts, tries to convince me to stay. She turns and, with her feet, walks her wheelchair away from me and into the dining room where a video of *Damn Yankees* is playing.

"Gwen Verdon," I say to Mom and am happy she remembers the name. "*Damn Yankees*." She remembers that, too. She finds a place where she's not in anyone's way and settles in to watch, finally willing to let me go, this time with a smile.

Later that night, I get a call. "Your mother asked me to call you," the nurse says, handing her the phone.

"I wanted to tell you something," she says, her voice sweet and tired. "It's nothing bad," she assures me.

"What is it, Mom?"

She starts out several times but nothing comes.

"I love you, Mom," I finally say. "You sound tired; I think you'll sleep well tonight."

She's still trying to remember why she wanted to talk to me.

After some silence, I say goodnight, ask her to give the phone back to the nurse.

Defenses Crumbling

February 8

Not ready to face what I'll find at The Jewish Home, I detour to get some coffee. The traffic is heavy. By the time I get to Peet's, it's after four. By the time I get to The Jewish Home, it'll be after dinner and Mom will be more interested in getting into bed than visiting with me.

I decide to call and, depending on how she sounds, I'll either get my Americano to go or, just for today, bow out of the visit she and I have both come to expect.

Elissa, a nurse I can usually depend on — is it that I can depend on her to tell me what I want to hear? — answers the phone.

"How is she?" I ask.

"She's right here in front of me," Elissa says. Which I take to mean okay.

She brings Mom the cell phone, stays with her long enough to help her know which ear to listen with — her good ear, the one with the hearing aid, the hearing aid that, yes, screeches when something comes up close to it, like a cell phone.

"Sara....Sara....Sara....Sara....Sara....Sara.... Sara....Sara....Sara...." Mom intones.

Until I'm the one screeching. "Mom....Mom....

Mom……"

I hang up, my fantasy of sitting down with a coffee shattered.

I retrieve my notebook from the cushy leather chair I was saving and stand looking out the window. I call back and the line, of course, is busy. I imagine Mom, phone to her ear, still repeating my name into the emptiness.

The coffee is dark and bitter. I wait and call again.

Angie answers, gives Mom the phone, then takes it back. She tells me Mom is using it like a walkie-talkie, unable to get the idea of holding the receiver up to her ear. Angie says that, when she arrived for work at three o'clock, she found Mom back in bed, insisting it was four in the morning.

I ask to speak to Elissa.

"What do you want us to do?" Elissa asks.

"I don't want my mother to be put to bed in the afternoon," I say. Then think: what kind of daughter am I, denying my mother the rest she's asking for?

"I don't want to be the only one who understands it doesn't work to put her to bed in the afternoon," I tell Elissa. "She wakes up confused, traveling around in her wheelchair asking everyone for corroboration that it's 4 AM. Though everyone tells her no, she always finds someone else to ask."

What *do* I want? I want someone *there* to figure out what to do.

It's Not Me, Sara. It's Nice Here, But It's Not Me

February 9

Sylvia, the lively Armenian volunteer who, with Michael, plans activities for the women on Factor One — Johnny Mathis, *Damn Yankees*, *The Three Tenors*, manicures on weekends — is taking a cigarette break. "Your mother's over there," she says, pointing to the sunny patio in front of the new Alzheimer's building. Years later, I'll wonder: was Mom willing to accept something I was still fighting?

Mom greets me with a big, if weary, smile. "How strange to see you here," she says as if we had just run into each other after many years apart, as she is sunning herself on the boardwalk in Atlantic City or some other faraway place where we had never been together.

I sit down, pull her wheelchair close to me, her knees between mine.

"How would you like to go for a ride with me?" I ask. "I'd like to look at some cars today and I thought it would be a chance for you to get out for a while."

She likes the idea. "But wait a few minutes," she says.

We sit for a while, quietly talking.

I tell her we'll take the walker, just in case. She is adamant that we won't need it, she's not going to walk anywhere.

I'm driving Keta's purple car 'til she returns from Japan. We drive to Woodland Hills, to the dealership where a friend just bought a used Explorer. The thought of buying a used car right now boggles my mind, fraught as a used car can be with uncertainties at a time when I'm already filled with so many uncertainties about Mom's dying process. Still, I decide to take a look.

I see a two-year-old Ford Focus I'm sure is overpriced. Returning to where Mom is sitting in Keta's car, I point to a new Focus, interestingly enough a purple one, parked next to us. "Mom, this is one of the cars I'm considering." The glare off its shiny surface is too much for her. She pulls her head away.

I find a newsstand, pick up *The Recycler* and the Sunday *Los Angeles Times* for the classifieds, drive to a tree-lined street parallel to Ventura Boulevard to read the ads. The sun is glinting through leaves rippling in a slight breeze. It is a low-in-the-sky, San Fernando Valley sun, and I find the flickering glare disturbing. I start up the car to move a little farther down the street, hoping to find a place with just the right amount of shade.

Mom closes her eyes and falls into a waking dream. She begins to mumble, only a few words clear. "It's not me, Sara," she says when I ask her if she's comfortable sitting in the shade. "Sure, it's nice here, but it's not me."

"Do you want me to take you home, Mom?"

"It's nice, Sara, but it's not me."

I start up the car and turn back toward The Jewish Home. "Remember Topanga Canyon, Mom?"

"Topanga Canyon," she repeats, in a way that says she used to know what the words meant.

When I first lived with Matt, our house was just minutes from here. When she would come from Connecticut to visit, I would take her on the narrow, twisting Topanga Canyon road to the ocean. It was a big adventure for her, a taste of being in the mountains.

I leave her with Norma, who is surprised we're back so soon, take myself to The Pita Kitchen for a late lunch. I have no appetite. I eat anyway.

Parked in an alley behind the glitzy stores of Ventura Boulevard, flush up against two bulging dumpsters, I begin to study the classifieds. Call for details about an Acura Integra for sale, the same year as mine. Someone answers. I hang up.

Legacy

February 11

This could be the painting of a master, maybe Rembrandt. An old woman sitting quietly in front of an undisturbed plate of eggplant topped with tomato sauce, baked acorn squash, green beans; to the side, a nibbled-at plate of green salad; to the other side, a slice of peach pie, the peaches in the pointed part looking as if they've been played with. My mother, at her table in the dining room of The Jewish Home.

"You love acorn squash," I say, still trying to convince her to eat.

"Not today."

I ask her if she'd like something else. "Egg salad? Tuna? Gefilte fish?"

"I had plenty," she says, confusing what she ate for lunch, or what she ate yesterday, or who-knows-when, with now.

We go out into the hallway, and I ask Elissa — her blonde hair is braided into cornrows today — to bring my mother a nutritional drink.

She hands her a box of Strawberry Resource with a straw in it. Mom sips disinterestedly, then holds the box at a tilt so that, each time she moves her hand, slightly squeezing the box, whatever is left in the straw burps out and lands on her fleece jacket. She leans forward to look down the hall, preoccupied with flagging down Angie to help her into bed.

"Mom, Angie will find you," I say. "While I'm here, can you be with me?"

I swivel her chair around so that we are facing each other and she takes me in slowly, all of me, finally landing on my face as if she is taking a photograph that requires an exposure of several seconds.

"Eyebrows," she says. "You should do something with your eyebrows. I can't see them."

"I never seem to have the time, Mom," I tell her. "Besides, I don't have eyebrows."

"You *do*," she says, emphatic that I *do* have eyebrows. That by saying I don't I am implying she hasn't gotten her job done as a mother. What kind of mother would it be who didn't make sure her daughter had eyebrows?

"They need to be a little darker," she continues. This, from a woman who knows; a woman who would never be caught without her red Maybelline pencil. "It'll bring out your eyes," she insists. And, with her feet, swivels the wheelchair away again, on the alert to catch Angie's attention the moment she comes out of the room where she's been helping another woman into bed.

It's 6:20 in the evening.

"Please be with me, Mom," I say, turning her toward me again, this time continuing to hold the arm of the chair so she can't turn away.

"Lipstick. You should wear lipstick," she says.

"I am wearing lipstick."

The truth is that for a couple of weeks now I've been needing a new lipstick, have been digging color out of an old tube with a brush. Today, it was too much trouble, so I put on the too-pale pink lipstick Bonnie had passed on to me as part of the Clinique gift she'd once gotten.

I remember again all those outings we'd shared, Mom and I, to the Clinique counter each gift season; how I'd inevitably talk her into buying a lipstick more muted than the bright pink or coral she was leaning toward; and how, inevitably, once she got it home, she never wore it.

"You're not wearing the right color," she tells me. "It's too light." And turns away again, the force of her will winning out over mine.

"I don't like you avoiding me," I say.

She turns back, this time on her own. "Rouge!" she says, her voice low-pitched and loud. "But just a little. It'll lift your cheekbones."

My hand rises to touch my cheek.

She leans forward, her eyes narrowing as they look directly into mine. "And eyeshadow." She shakes her index finger to make the point, then, with the same finger, points to her own lids. "But not too much," I hear her say, her voice trailing off as she pulls away again. "A little color is enough."

"Mom, if you keep turning away from me, I'm going to leave. Do you want me to leave?"

"It's okay," she says.

It's happened. She's turned some corner beyond which I'm not able to go. I stand up, take a deep breath, plant a quick kiss on the back of her head and hurry out of the building, my hand covering lips that are too light.

B-I-N-G-O!

February 12

Huge raindrops bounce off the tops of cars, the gray surfaces of sidewalks.

I've arranged for a homeopathic doctor, Dr. Zeeb, to see if there's some way she can help my mother feel better. Will she be late because of the rain? Is she the kind of person who will purposely be early on a day like this?

It's a few minutes after one when I arrive at The Jewish Home.

Inside are all the regulars — Vickie, the nurse; some

of the aides; Eileen, who looks up from her chair to ask me how my father is, meaning my mother; some of the residents in wheelchairs, others pushing aluminum walkers, yellow tennis balls on their front legs announcing their arrival.

Mom, in her wheelchair, is at the entrance to the dining room, looking in. Somber, distant, neither here nor there.

A tall blonde woman walks in and we introduce ourselves to each other. I introduce her to my mother, my mother to her.

"Mom, I'll fill Dr. Zeeb in about how things are going, then come to get you so we can all talk together. It'll be just a few minutes."

We go to Mom's room, sit on her bed.

Practically bursting, I tell her everything about my mother's history. The pneumonias. High blood pressure. High anxiety and low sodium, both uncontrolled by medication. Urge incontinence and urinary tract infections. An hiatal hernia that led to an esophageal ulcer. Her lifetime habit of registering nervousness in her belly.

I include snippets of my own story. How I've been so involved with Mom for so long it's as if my body and hers have become inseparable. I tell her about the tree I visit in Malibu Creek State Park, its large branches inextricably intertwined like lovers, each branch, though rising out of the same trunk and roots, still free to feel out its own particular way of moving in the world, its own existence.

"I better go get Mom," I say, aware she will be wondering what we've been doing for so long without her. My fear is confirmed when I see her. She is still sitting at the door to the dining room, looking in. As she sees me coming, the tips of the fingers of her right-hand rise to describe a line, up and down, along the center of her chest.

"I'm nauseous," she says when I apologize for taking so long. As I push her chair down the hallway to her room, I wonder if she will refuse to participate in the conversation.

"Dr. Zeeb is Jewish," I say, hoping to break the ice. "Her mother-in-law asked her to take a look around The Jewish Home while she's here."

Mom, still the gracious hostess, spreads her arms as much as the limited motion in her shoulders will allow and, with a watery smile, says, "Look around."

Admiration rises in me, causing me to sit straighter. A deep breath rushes in.

"How are you?" Dr. Zeeb asks.

"A little nauseous," Mom says, running her fingers again along the length of her breastbone.

"Do you prefer to be warm or cool?" It's one of those questions homeopaths ask.

"I don't know," my mother says.

"You always like to have a sweater or jacket on," I say. "How is your appetite?"

"When I like the food, I eat."

"Mom doesn't like chicken," I say. "They serve it here practically every other meal."

I tell Dr. Zeeb that, in the early 1900s, my mother's father sold homeopathic remedies to drugstores in the Bronx. "Did you take remedies at home?" I ask Mom, hoping to find common ground.

"No."

Mom's reticence strikes me. Might it be that she thinks what we're doing is against the wishes of Dr. Smith? I remember the day I wanted to tape a string of tiny Tibetan prayer flags — red and green and saffron and white and blue — to the wall behind Mom's bed. She asked me to take them home, didn't feel it would be right at The Jewish Home to make a show of any other religion.

"I told Dr. Smith I was going to ask a homeopathic doctor to see if she could offer some extra help," I tell her. "He said it'd be fine."

She nods.

"Is there anything you worry about?" Dr. Zeeb asks.

"Not really," Mom says. "Maybe my health."

"Well, it certainly sounds like you're a very strong woman. I'm glad we've met."

"I'm nauseous," Mom says again, touching her chest.

"Nauseous?"

"Not nauseous for food. Nauseous for breath."

Dr. Zeeb says she'll call me in the morning with some suggestions. Mom and I see her to the front door.

Mom seems troubled. "What will I do next?" she asks, back at the entrance to the dining room.

I see that the afternoon activity is about to begin. "Would you like to play Bingo?"

"What will I do after that?"

"After that, it'll be close to dinnertime," I assure her. But she looks at the clock, sees there will still be time between the end of Bingo and dinner. I remember how she used to talk about killing time.

"I'll get into bed," she says. "But what will I do after dinner?"

"Sleep, I guess. You've been going to bed early."

"But what should I do now?" I can't tell if this is nervousness I'm hearing or a serious question for which she'd like me to give her a serious answer.

"Would you like me to stay and play Bingo with you?"

"If you stay, I'll play," she says, relieved for the moment.

We sit next to each other, each with a big white Bingo card in front of us. Across the table, Lauretta is flashing her usual smile and tending two cards the way women sit in front of two slot machines in Las Vegas. Lauretta, in her housecoat again, confuses my mother no end on days when she wakes up from an afternoon nap not knowing if four o'clock means late afternoon or middle of the night.

Mom reaches forward with her left arm to arrange and rearrange the chips that lie on the table around her card. I thread my left arm through her right. For once she doesn't take my hand and hold it. As my hand lies in her lap, untouched, I feel the emptiness of no-relationship.

"O-72," the caller says.

She and I both have a big black 72 in the upper right-hand corner of our cards.

"O-71."

In the lower right, we each have 71.

An hour passes. When I tell her I'm going to leave, she asks me to stay a little longer.

The next game, she completes a line across the top of her card and, without enthusiasm, repeats the numbers back to the caller.

"Kosher Bingo!" the woman announces, placing three shiny nickels on my mother's card.

"You could use those nickels as chips," I say lightly. She doesn't respond.

Mom's always been happy to tell me about her latest bit of good luck. Today, winning is simply what's happening.

Back East, when she and Bill used to go to "the trotters" at Roosevelt Raceway and Yonkers, she'd invariably pick a winner, sometimes two. On a bus trip with her friend Ida to Laughlin, Nevada, not so long ago when she was still living in her own home, she won $980 playing Keno. Last summer, when I heard on the radio that the winners of a huge lottery jackpot were about to be announced, I rushed back to The Jewish Home, where I'd been visiting with her. I asked her to pick numbers for two cards. On one of them, she picked four out of five and got nine bucks back for her two. Lauretta still hasn't won a hand.

When I stand up to leave, Mom gives me the tiniest little kiss on the lips. And with difficulty, reaches across my card to slide my blue plastic poker chips across the table to come to rest near her own card. She does it without saying a word, a cloud of quiet hovering around her.

Leaving, I see the back of her head through the dining room windows, remember all those other times when she would be facing out and always managed to see me.

"Look! Look At The Hills," She Would Say.

February 13

Eyes wide open, I turn to see the clock. 5:15. I awaken, certain about Mom's dying but not attached to any day or time. I see her sitting in a wheelchair, her body twisted by a stroke. "No!" I say, "don't let it be that." And lie quietly in bed, aware of my own breathing.

At 5:30, the phone rings. "Is this Hannah Epstein's daughter?"

"Yes."

"I'm sorry to tell you this ... "

Of course, I know what he is going to tell me.

"At 5:15 this morning, your mother passed away."

I've always resisted people saying "passed away," thought it was a desire to avoid the truth. But I'm grateful those are his words. What I hear him saying is that the woman who was my mother has passed out of her body. Which, I suppose, is what happens, it's the body that dies.

"When we went in to check on her at two and at four," he continues, "she was sleeping. At 5:15, she had no vital signs. Will you be coming?"

"I'm on my way," I tell him.

My housemate Lily is up early, preparing for a day of teaching Emerson and Wordsworth to high school

English students. She is sitting at the foot of her bed, papers spread out in piles all over the red and yellow Indian bedspread.

She is as shocked at the news as every one of my friends will be. My mother has been so alive for them, those who knew her, and those who knew her through me. Lily opens her arms, takes me in against her soft breasts.

I pull on brown velveteen pants and top, white socks and sneakers.

Bill calls. We agree to meet in our mother's room.

Grasping for something to keep me going as I hurry out of the house to drive to The Jewish Home where Mom's body, I imagine, is fast losing its warmth, I grab an old *LA Weekly* that is open to a blank crossword puzzle on one side and the *Rockie Horoscope* on the other. I take a look at Scorpio, Mom's birth sign. "A rare and wonderful phenomenon is about to occur," it says.

It's six o'clock. NPR's *Morning Edition* is just getting underway. I register something about North Korea having the capacity to strike the western United States with nuclear weapons; that one of the Enron trials is about to begin; that today is Kim Novak's 70th birthday, Jerry Springer's 59th. What a world!

It's pouring. For once, the 405 is empty.

As I drive through the gates of The Jewish Home, I

give myself permission not to look at my mother's dead body. In the hallway, an aide comes into step alongside me. Says that the day before, she had helped my mother get dressed, how easily Mom had stood up and how straight, how perfectly she had made the turn from bed to chair. How Mom had wanted help putting on her makeup, how the aide thought her eyebrow pencil was too light a shade of brown.

The brightness of the overhead light in Mom's room seems like a cruel touch. The curtain between her bed, on the far side near the windows, and Miriam's, is drawn. I'd caught a glimpse of Miriam in the dining room, watching early morning tv.

"Please turn off the light," I say to the aide.

"Turn it off?" she asks. Why is she surprised?

"Turn it off. The light over her bed, too."

I walk in slowly, my attention drawn to a drinking straw on the bathroom floor.

For 52 years, since Daddy died, I've kept watch over my mother to be sure she was still alive. When she and I shared a bedroom, first in Aunt Doris and Uncle Joe's house, then in our own apartment, I'd wake up in the middle of the night and, in the dark, listen for her breathing. Sometimes, in the house in Camarillo, where I stayed with her before her move to The Jewish Home, I'd come in late and, before going to bed myself, would open the door to her bedroom, stand there to watch her breathe. In myriad hospital rooms and ICUs, when pneumonia after pneumonia had left her lungs increasingly unable to do their job, I'd breathe *for* her, doing whatever I could to help establish a normal rhythm.

I've listened for her gentle snore. Watched sheets in summer, blankets in winter rise over the hills and valleys of her body, over the hills and valleys of my own life, this woman I came to love more the older she got.

Despite everything. Because of everything.

"Your mother has passed away," he'd said.

Her eyes are closed. She is lying slightly toward her right side, though nothing like her usual curled-up position, hand under her ear.

She is wearing a light blue hospital gown in a fleurs-de-lys pattern, covered with a sheet that comes to just above her breasts, its top folded over a lightweight pink bedspread.

I feel her left cheek with the back of my right hand. Still warm.

"Oh, Mom. I love you so much," I say quietly.

Not knowing what else to do, I go into the bathroom, pick up the straw and throw it into the wastebasket. Check to see that everything is clean and in order. Take a long look at the toilet seat, remembering what she looked like that day, almost five months ago when this all began.

When she refused to get up, sure that if she got up she would die.

On my way out of the bathroom, the door slams on my thumb. The nail bed turns pink and the thumb begins to throb. As the day wears on, the nail bed turns black. I keep touching the thumb's pad with my index finger, offering it a kind of massage.

Someone has placed two chairs at the side of the bed. I sit in one, lay my head on Mom's belly. Feel the stillness.

I stand up, press my cheek against hers.

I gently fold back the covers. Her right hand has been laid over her left, nails red from the new manicure. Wonder of wonders, not even the hint of a smudge.

I ease the salmon-colored coral cameo from her left ring finger, afraid for a moment it will not come off. I twist it a little; it begins to slide. I put it on my own finger as if I am now wedded to her.

I slip back more of the covers to reveal her legs. Pass my hand down along the outside thigh and calf of her left leg, along the flat front of her foot. Down along the front plane of her right thigh, knee, shin, up and over the bone that protrudes from her instep. Feel the sharpness of a small dark scab over the highest point of the displaced bone. Bend down to kiss it.

I kiss the smooth skin on each foot at that place where the toes begin. Feel along the left arch with the back of my hand, smooth over the downward roundness of the right arch with my palm. Move down toward the foot of the bed, bend to kiss the ball of each foot.

She is wearing a diaper. I skirt over her belly which seems distended. I remember something about death and distension.

I pull the gown away to expose one breast at a time. Her breasts are smaller than I have ever seen them, her large café au lait areolae now almost as pale as the skin around them.

I scurry my right hand under her left breast. It's warmer there than anywhere else I have touched, moisture as fresh as you'd find some early morning on a field of grass. I bend down, kiss the soft skin.

Her right breast has fallen to the side. Pressing lightly with the fingers of my right hand, I lift the skin, scooping the breast up with my left hand, feeling its weight in my cupped palm. I bend to kiss her nipple, feel the moist warmth underneath.

Under the gown is the necklace she's been wearing. The amber charm I'd chosen for her in China, its gold characters, translated for me such a long time ago by the tiny Japanese man at the Tokyo Princess Motel. Good luck on one side, long life on the other.

Recently, when anxiety was threatening to tear her apart, I'd suggested she reach for it. Sometimes, she'd remember, press the charm between her thumb and forefinger.

I slide my left hand under her neck, spread my fingers to support her head. I feel shock at how feathery light her head feels in my hand, her neck offering no resistance to my lifting. I try to slip the chain over her head, an antique gold chain that once traversed her father's vest, holding his watch in his watch pocket. I remember the place where the catch can be opened, slide the chain out from under her neck, re-clasp it and pull it over my own head.

I bring my attention back to her lips and cheeks, pass my hand over the cool skin of her forehead. With my still throbbing thumb, I smooth out the place between her eyes, travel the ridge of her nose.

Her left nostril has collapsed a little. Is it the steady passage of air, I wonder, that keeps our nostrils open in the characteristic way we come to know each other's noses?

I place a tiny bronze statue of Ganesha on the pillow behind her head. I've brought him in from where he sits, easily crosslegged, on the dashboard of my car. Ganesha, the most beloved god of hundreds of millions of Indians, human boy with the head of an elephant, whose job it is to guard against obstacles. May there be no obstacles to the passage of my mother's spirit or soul — I don't know what to call it — into eternity if there is any such thing as eternity. I am in territory totally unknown.

This Ganesha has been right there with my mother during every hospital stay in the last two years. He's seen her through before. Why not now?

I want to see my mother's blue eyes. I'll be able to assure myself she is gone when I see how they've turned from bright and moist to dry and matte, when they look out at me as if from behind the glass of a framed picture that's been treated to prevent the reflection of light.

With my thumb, I pull back the left lid. What I see scares me, her eye as bright and blue as ever.

"Go, Mom," I say. "Go, go, go, go, go. Fly! You're free now. Fly!"

I tell her I'm fine. Bill is fine. We're okay. "Go, please go."

I gently pull back the other lid. Though the eye, of course, doesn't move, she also isn't staring. Some part of her is still here, alive, I could swear it.

I sit back down, place my hand over her hands which are under the covers again — I've rearranged them so the left hand is protecting the right, the more abstract giving cover to the material — and close my own eyes. Feel myself breathing. Gathering up whatever support I might find for whoever is staying around, support for whoever is getting ready to let go, fly away.

Bill arrives. Comes in slowly, gravely, curious like

me to see the physical details of this event we have both feared and staved off, each in our own way, our whole lives.

He touches her gently, fingers slightly hyperextended as I have often noticed them to be. Runs his fingertips over her face, bends down to kiss her.

I make room for him. Tell him whatever I know. We say how peaceful she looks. He kisses her again.

I tell him about yesterday, about the homeopathic doctor and how gracious Mom was to her, though, I would have to say, rather disinterested. How I'd stayed on to play Bingo with Mom and, when I was leaving, Mom leaned over to slide my chips toward her own card. How I'd noticed that her speech was a little slurred and that, later, I'd called the nurse to tell her about it. The nurse had been busy. I said I'd call back and then forgot 'til it was too late, Mom would be sleeping already.

He and I talk about when we want the mortuary to come — not too soon and not too long — and I say I want the *tahara* for Mom, the Orthodox Jewish ritual washing of the body to prepare it for burial. "Mom was always so clean," I say. A woman at the mortuary tells us how it would be done and that, if we decide to do it, Mom will be able to be buried in a shroud.

A shroud? What is a shroud?

Bill doesn't know if it would be right to do the washing, fears it would be hypocritical — Mom was hardly Orthodox. He talks to the rabbi who will perform the service — the same rabbi who married Bill and Lynn. He assures him it will be fine.

I consider the possibility of our burying her in clothes rather than the shroud. A certain much-worn blouse comes to mind — white puckered cotton with stripes of pink and blue, three-quarter sleeves, boat neck. But no makeup. It wouldn't seem right after the bathing. Without makeup, the blouse doesn't seem right either.

"Let's do the shroud," I say, which we are assured is plain cotton or linen, no ornamentation, off-white.

I ask the woman from the mortuary if I can be there for the washing. It isn't allowed, she tells me. Though it's done in a private room, I would have to pass by other bodies. It wouldn't be respectful.

Angie, who is wearing her street clothes, has made a special point to come in early. She tilts her head one way and then the other, allowing Mom's stillness to wash over her. She takes my hand and tells me she'd been the one to help Mom into bed last night. That when she came in later to check on her, Mom had thrown off her nightgown and was trying to sit up on the edge of the bed on her way to the window. "I'm too hot," Mom had said. Angie turned the heat down. Mom asked her to stay and hold her hand. Angie sat with her and, by the time she had to leave at 11, Mom was making her way back to sleep.

We'll never know exactly what happened after that. There was no sign of a struggle, no grimace, her mouth was gently open the way it often was when she slept, snoring lightly. I'm not surprised Mom's dying turned out to be a private affair. She always needed time to let things sink in.

Her body had been carefully washed; she was wearing a fresh hospital gown and a clean diaper. Had her bladder let go of its urine, her bowels their feces when there was no longer a person there sensing fullness? Her usual sweet smell was gone.

The previous few days, she had been somber. Slower than usual. And the fact that her speech had been the tiniest bit slurred the day before? Was it the Trazadone that had been added to help calm her? Were her lungs finally giving up their struggle to keep her oxygen level high enough, carbon dioxide low enough, to maintain life? If I'd remembered to call back and tell the nurse about the slurred speech, Mom might have died in the hospital instead of in her bed, having just held Angie's hand.

Did Plavix, the drug she had been taking for a long time to treat atrial fibrillation, cause a slow seeping of blood into her brain? Or did it stop working, allowing one of those fibrillations to produce a clot, cause her heart to stop?

She'd been practicing for this. "I'm dying, Sara, I'm dying. We wish we didn't have to face it, but we have to, I'm an old lady, I've lived a long life." She'd fight me when I would say I didn't think she was dying then and there. "You'll see," she would say emphatically. "I won't see, but you'll see." The conversation might go back and forth like this for half-an-hour.

"It gets quieter and quieter and quieter," she would tell me, lowering the sound of her voice to show me what she meant. There was some sound, some feeling she was aware of inside herself she wanted me to know about. As if I could hear it, too, if only I would listen carefully enough.

"What gets quieter, Mom? Is it your heart?"

I don't know if she ever said yes. Or if she ever said no. That's how it was with Mom. She resisted being definite. And that's how it was with me. I'd try to force it.

Was it a decrease in the amplitude of her physical heartbeat, together with a more general ebbing of life force, she was becoming aware of? The diminuendo, decrescendo of the music she was?

The sound would get quieter, she would say, until it was on the verge of disappearing completely, and, when that happened, she would be gone.

"What stops it from going all the way?" I would ask.

"It stops when you walk in," she would say. "Or when

Angie comes in to answer the bell." As long as someone was there with her, whoever had been tiptoeing to the exit would turn and come back to live another day.

I wonder what she had been hearing last night before Angie came in, whether something in her had decided, this time, not to press the call button. Mostly, I wonder if she was fully there for the moment when the sound faded away, leaving her, once and for all, in peaceful silence.

It's seven. Vickie has just come on duty. She rushes in. She's known my mother better and longer than anyone here but Evelyn, the aide in the Newman building, who used to give Mom showers when Mom was still in residential care. Mom and Evelyn had developed a special liking for each other.

Despite Evelyn's loving care, that was the time when Mom began to develop one urinary tract infection after another. Leading to the first pneumonia. Which led to the second. Which led to today. Lending some credence to the statistic that five years is how long someone can be expected to live once they've moved to an institution.

Vickie is shocked. Everyone is shocked. Though Mom was 93 and increasingly frail from not eating; though she had come to favor a wheelchair over walking; though she showed the confusion of too little sodium, too much carbon dioxide in her blood; Mom was often radiant, bright light shining through her at a moment's notice.

Vickie looks at Mom for a long time, slowly nodding.

She looks back at me, sees me pressing, at the pace of a beating heart, the pad of my thumb with my index finger. "What happened!" she says, wrapping my hot, throbbing thumb in her cool hand. She brings me a Styrofoam cup filled with ice chips. I plunge my thumb in, continuing to press its pad rhythmically against the ice.

At eight o'clock, Vickie calls Dr. Smith. It was just two weeks earlier he'd told me how amazed he was that Hannah was still alive. Even so, he, too, is shocked.

"How's Sara?" he asks. People who know us will be sure to wonder how I took the news, how I will manage without her.

He gets me on the phone later in the day. He sounds shaken. "I really liked Hannah," he says. "She was a great lady."

Keta, whose car I've been driving, is returning today from Japan. I think about not going to the airport to pick her up, staying here instead.

I talk to Mom. "I'll never get enough of your body," I say. "I'll never get enough of you." I shake my head in wonder at how beautiful she looks.

I realize another hour with her won't make the difference — and I don't want to be here when the men from the mortuary come with their stretcher.

I take a last look at her eyes, which are still bright and

wet. Lean down to hug her shoulders. Get close to her small chest with my own. Brush her nose with my lips. And, pressing her lower jaw closed, kiss her lips.

I ask Vickie to find a way to support her jaw in the up position so, as the muscles harden, her mouth won't be left gaping.

I take one last look at Mom's feet. See them on the pedals of her piano. Right foot on the pedal that strings contiguous notes together. Left foot on the pedal that softens the percussion.

I hear the last notes of "The Moonlight Sonata." Feel the silence that comes just after the music has ended, after the final lifting of her foot from the pedal. The deep silence that's always there. Always been there. Behind everything.

Bill and I hug.

Shirley is sitting in her wheelchair in the hall near the nurses' station. When she sees me, her arms reach out. Her eyes, somewhere between fear and terror, are filled with tears.

"She was my friend," Shirley says. "She was a great lady. How can it be?" She tells me she wants to come to the service. Asks me if I'll still come to visit.

I stay it will be wonderful to have her at the service. Yes, of course, I'll visit.

I stop in the dining room where Elizavetta is playing

with her French toast. Her face is sweet as always, and solemn. Her eyes are tinged with red. "Hannah always asked me to sing," she says. I promise to come back and visit.

The morning traffic is heavy. The rain has stopped and the sky is especially beautiful as it always is in Los Angeles after a good rain. If my mother were in the car with me now, she would be telling me, in amazement, to look. "Look, Sara, look at the hills. They're so beautiful. Hasn't anyone told them it's winter?"

Above a line of low-lying clouds, there is an expanse of sky the medium-blue of my mother's eyes. Below the clouds, a long, narrow strip of pale, watery aqua.

Who Cares?

February 14

On the way to Hillside Memorial Cemetery, my eye is drawn to clouds floating on the glass facade of a shiny new office building. "Who cares?" I say to Keta, who is driving. "Who cares about spending all that time, risking all that money, to put up a new office building?"

I've looked up from reading over the three pages of eulogy I wrote sitting up in bed this morning. Bonnie's boom box is on the floor between my feet.

Last night over dinner, Bill and I, in the high level of cooperation we can be counted on for when the chips are down, came up with a plan for today's graveside service. He had just returned from having a CD burned, one for him and one for me, of Mom playing the piano. Seven years earlier, when Mom was 86, still living in her own home, I'd held a microphone inside the open cover of her baby grand, over the strings, and recorded for Bill, as a birthday present, a tape of Mom going through her repertoire. The CD is from that tape. It would be the glue needed to hold the service together, even if he and I were falling apart.

I'm wearing a pale green turtleneck dress of the softest cotton jersey — an old dress, expensive, from my days twenty years ago in New York. It's a quiet, still dress. I chose it because I feel safe inside its softness, a young bird in a nest of leaves and shed feathers.

Around my neck is the gold chain with its amber charm I'd slipped out from around Mom's neck. Good luck, long life. On my left ring finger is the coral cameo she'd worn every day, except during all the hospital stays when I would wear it for her. I'd show it to her each time I came to visit, reminding her I was only wearing it until she could wear it again, herself. To which she would offer up a wan smile, shake her head yes.

"My mother's dead. Who needs glass office buildings?" I say to Keta. "Who needs glorious days like this?"

Still, I notice, the sun is warm, the sky blue, the wind gently definite.

We're directed to a building just inside and to the left of the cemetery gate. I make my way through a room furnished like a parlor, straight through a door, into a smaller room where an open coffin is waiting.

A small woman is lying inside, peaceful as can be. Her face, surrounded by a bonnet, is pale. Her cheek greets my hand with a special kind of cold — unforgiving, the kind you could get lost in if you're not careful.

When we decided to have Mom dressed in a shroud, no one said anything about a bonnet. It turns out that a shroud, at least this shroud, is a three-piece, cream-colored outfit of cotton or linen. Pajama pants, a pajama top, a bonnet.

With the tip of my finger, I follow the line of lace that runs along each side of the jacket's front opening. There is lace at the wrists and lace ties that cross over the front to keep the jacket closed. I pull back the off-white sheet that tucks Mom into this bed-of-sorts to see the top of the loose pants. I tuck her back in and go out into the parlor to wait for Bill.

He arrives wearing a well-tailored gray-brown suit, crisp shirt and tie. A far cry from the scruffy shorts and t-shirt, worn sneakers, that made up his usual visiting attire. "Mom would approve," I say.

He's brought a few roses. He asks the funeral director, a man in black with a white chrysanthemum in his buttonhole, a truly sincere smile, and eyes that actually make contact, if it's okay for there to be flowers. There's something Bill remembers hearing about Jewish funerals and flowers.

The man pins a black button onto each of us, over our hearts, the button trailing a length of black grosgrain ribbon which he tears up toward the button. Each time I move, I feel the pin where it sticks away from the back of the button scratching the skin above my left breast. I try to flatten it, but it won't flatten. I give in, figuring its job is to keep me here, in my body, rather than into thoughts where I could easily disappear. The same way my throbbing thumb is keeping me here. Scratch, throb. Scratch, throb.

Bill follows me into the small room, walks slowly around the coffin gazing at Mom from every possible angle. We agree how beautiful she looks, how utterly peaceful, how lovely the shroud is, how elegantly simple the coffin. He touches her cheek with the back of his hand.

The coffin is made of smooth, blond wood. It is lined in an off-white slippery fabric that's basted somehow to the sides, the same fabric that tucks her body in. As I feel for how the fabric is attached, some of the basting gives way. I let it be. On the outside of the coffin's cover, which eventually will slide up to offer closure, is a slightly raised Star of David resting within a circle.

"We have to do something about this bonnet," I say to Bill, pointing to how off-center it is, how it comes up slightly higher on the right side of our mother's face.

I know how it happened. In the dark of night, the ritual bathing complete and the body dressed, she began to turn, in her own determined way, toward her right side. Which moved her head slightly within the bonnet as the bonnet stayed put. Her strong desire always to lie on her right side still alive.

I show him how we have to kind of shimmy it around. I'm using my hands around my own head and face, scooching my right hand toward the back, my left hand forward.

We stand behind Mom and carefully lift her head. I slide the right side of the bonnet toward the center back and then let go with my left hand. He continues to hold the weight of her head with his left hand and scrunches the fabric around toward the back of her head with his right, then switches hands to hold the weight of her head with his right hand, sliding the now-bunched fabric with his left hand around to the front. We are so intent on getting the job done without disturbing her hair, without pulling her hair, that, in the middle of it all, we find ourselves laughing. Not anxious laughter, as it could be. But something like the laughter of relief, the relief of discovering how closely we are working, brother and sister together, taking such good care of our mother, even in death. Mom might be laughing with us.

When we are done, her head rests in the center of the bonnet. Not perfect, but better. Her nose, eyebrows so pale as to be almost non-existent (as mine are in the process of becoming, her recent protests to the contrary notwithstanding), each peaches-and-cream cheek fully available to make their impressions on this last mirror, the inside of the lid of her simple pine casket.

I wouldn't be surprised if, even after all of our work, she will once again win out, slowly but surely inching her body over onto its right side, returning the bonnet again to its off-center position. Getting the last laugh.

"Can her head be raised a little?" I ask the funeral director. "I think she could be a little more comfortable. She always used two pillows." I realize how crazy this sounds, but how often do you get to bury your mother?

"If you would just step out and give us a minute," he says. Two men in work uniforms come in and do something or other to raise Mom's head.

"Much better," I say.

Bill and I stand outside the small room as the men are

about to slide the cover of the coffin up over her.

"Wait! Stop!" Bill says. "She's too high. The cover's going to shear her nose off." Even if Bill hadn't always been partial to our mother's nose — who can understand the mysteries of love? — the last thing you would want to remember after you bury your mother would be that you had stood by and watched as her nose was being sheared off.

"Give us another minute," the funeral director says, closing the door again.

Bill bends over, leaning his head to the side to eyeball the coffin, to make sure he can't see the tip of Mom's nose in the space over which the cover will slide. He gives the final okay. We each step forward, take one more look, say one more goodbye.

The coffin is slid into the back of a hearse, and we follow in our cars for the short drive up the hill. This quiet parade, this glorious day, all this attention being paid to our mother. "What a wonderful celebration of her," I say to Keta, as the hearse comes to a stop partway up the hill.

We walk across a green lawn to two rows of white wooden folding chairs. Only later do I realize it is other graves we were walking on, people who came, and left, before us, the names of who they were on bronze plaques lying flat in the grass.

The coffin rests over the grave, a small mountain of earth to its side. The roses lie, stems crossed, on top of the coffin, next to them, a framed photograph of Mom playing her piano. Mom is wearing a blue and white striped blouse with red and pink flowers appliquéd on the front. She is intent on the dog-eared music book in front of her. There's an elegant feel to all of this, something she would have been sure to notice and comment on.

"We're all here to honor the life of Hannah," says the rabbi.

I turn on the CD. We are a small group, and the music draws us together. Bill. Lynn. Georgina. Carol, representing her mother, Taube, and her father, Don, our family's oldest friends. Bonnie and Lily who have both left work early. Keta, of purple car fame. Ginger, in whose guest room I'd stayed when the journey to this day began. Rabbi Weinberg, who, ten years ago, married Bill and Lynn. John, a new friend. Judy, an old friend, who slips into a seat in the second row, having made it in time despite Friday afternoon traffic.

I turn the volume down but not so much that Mom's music can't still be heard as background. Here and there, at particular places in the tributes — and in between — I raise the volume to give Mom her say.

"Eight years ago," I begin, "I asked my mother to sit down at her piano and play, so I could make a tape we would always have, so Bill and I could hear what had been as much a part of our nourishment, growing up, as food. I didn't know then we would be listening to her music now. Or did I?

"Even today, as I look for what words to say to honor her life on earth which, by the way, she thought to be, without any sense of loss, her whole and only life, my mother leads the way. This woman, who so often lived under a gray cloud of depression or 'jumping out of her skin' with anxiety, had chosen, as her first piece to play, a reminder of lightness and joy: Mozart's Twelve Variations on the old French melody we've come to know as *Twinkle, Twinkle Little Star*."

I close my eyes, plant my feet on the ground, feel her support.

"I have loved her body, coming to know it almost as intimately in her old, old age as I must have known it, from the inside, when she was young and carried me in her belly. Starting today, this woman, who has been the ground I stand on, becomes earth again, on its way to stardust. My guess is she'll always be with me — in the beauty of a cloud-filled sky, in the green winter coat of mountains."

Holding back tears, Bill speaks about how Mom raised us after Daddy died, how she sometimes held down three jobs at a time. He remembers the snow storms when she would drive him around so he could cover his paper route. How she'd help him pile his huge set of drums into the trunk of our Pontiac, so he could play Saturday night jobs at local parties. He speaks about her love of the piano. Tells the story of how he surprised her, after she had moved from Connecticut to California and, for the first time in her life, was piano-less, with the Mason & Hamlin baby grand he had found for her. It had the year 1927 burned into the underside of its cover, the same year as Mom's original Mason & Hamlin her piano teacher helped her buy when she was just seventeen.

Bill sits down. The tears he has been holding back come.

We listen to Mom's *Für Elise*.

"After the 1994 earthquake," I say, "and, no less ground-shaking for me, a divorce from Matt, Mom's home became my home base and we began to know each other in new ways."

Beethoven's *Moonlight Sonata* begins with its simple clarity of one note after another. She and the music are holding us in place, holding us together. The wind picks up, making itself known.

Lynn recalls the day Bill brought her to meet Mom — what a gracious and welcoming hostess she was, even though Bill hadn't warned her he was bringing not just a guest, but a girlfriend. "Mom's house was always a place where you knew you would be taken care of," Lynn says.

Georgina opens a window for us to see into the special friendship she and Hannah shared. "Hannah was like another mother to me," she says. Looking directly at me, then at Bill, she recalls Mom telling her, over and over again, how important it was to her for Bill and me to love each other.

Carol talks about how she's heard, all her life, about that special friendship her parents shared with Hannah and Irving when, as two young couples, they lived next to each other in Long Beach. How Irving had held their baby boy for his bris. How Taube had ridden in the ambulance with Hannah as Irving was dying.

"There's so much to celebrate about Hannah," the rabbi says. "A good name. An appreciation for beauty and the ability to pass beauty on through the love of music. The courage it took to give life to two children, after the grief of losing her first-born. Faithfulness to her children. The faithfulness *of* her children."

We stand as Rabbi Weinberg leads us in the Mourner's Kaddish. And brings the service full circle to starlight as he reminds us of the natural order of things, how the body returns to dust, releasing the spirit to live on.

"*Ruach* means both wind and spirit," he says, lifting his arms to bring our attention to the wind, whose presence has become stronger, even insistent. "Can you feel how Hannah is all around us?"

The men who had attended to Mom's comfort in the coffin — who'd raised her head so she could breathe more easily and lowered her body so she could be buried with her nose intact — lower the coffin into the ground. I scoop up a pile of moist earth in my hands, let it sift through my fingers to land on the top of the coffin. Bill uses the shovel. Each person takes part in the ritual of returning Mom's body to the earth.

Bill and I release the roses, two white and one red. They drift down, coming to rest on the coffin in their own order.

As we turn to leave, I feel full — the sparkling day, the music, the simple coffin, the shroud with its lacy bonnet, not perfect but good.

And the wind. The wind.

Time To Hurry Up. Time To Slow Down

Two weeks later

The 5 Freeway runs straight up through California's Central Valley, hundreds of miles through grapevines and fields of cotton, groves of almond trees. It's the road you take when you want to get from LA to San Francisco in a hurry. Plenty of time? You take the coast. I'm on my way to a weekend celebration for Charlotte Selver, who will be 102 in April.

Until now, wherever I was traveling, my mother knew it. Without her, there is no one who has to know where I'm going or when I've arrived. I think about all those person-to-person calls I used to make decades ago. So she could hear my voice letting her know I'd safely reached my destination. So I could hear hers. I shuffle around for my cell phone and call Georgina. Tell her where I am and where I'm going. She understands. In her own way, she relied on Mom's presence in this world, too.

There's so much to understand about dying and yet, when the need for it finally comes, it comes like an avalanche. Along the way, Mom and I did our best to keep our heads above the crashing. An ordinary mother and daughter doing what they could to poke around for pockets of air. Though there were times when we might have tumbled over each other more gracefully, our love never became buried but kept moving us forward, down the hill, picking up substance and speed on our way to the inevitable. On our way to rest.

I think about the stories we tell about what happens after someone dies. "What if life is the purpose of life," a friend says, "and then we sleep?" It's what Mom believed.

It's the Jewish way, too — to devote oneself fully to life here, rather than saving anything up for some hereafter.

A couple of years ago during that first pneumonia, I sat next to Mom's bed, listening to the hiss of the breathing machine that was keeping her alive. Afraid she was going to die, I reached for solace. "Suffering is caused by ignorance," I read in a book by the Dalai Lama. "Ignorance of the reality that each of us is going to die." To hear the truth so clearly and kindly stated was a relief.

We die. And yet.

Inside the car, amidst the whirring of tires on concrete, I feel sad I didn't have more to give. All part of grieving, I suppose.

Outside, a huge sky stretches ahead to the north, behind to the south. And there's Mom, as comfortable as can be and without a worry in the world, lying next to Kwan Yin in the lavender and orange clouds of the western sky.

On my way home, I'll take the coast.

The unlikely love story of a brother and sister

Afterword

On an August day six months after we buried Mom, I call Bill, tell him it's important for me to show him the parts of this book that have to do with him. He knows I've been writing about those last months with Mom. I don't blame him for not showing interest. He knows what I'm likely to say — about him, about him and me.

If I felt hurt by something he said or did, I'd write, "His jaw hardened." Or, "His jaw hardened." Making him, at best, the devil; at worst, a cardboard character. Yet leaving him out would have created a big hole in the story. He's my mother's dear son, for heaven's sake. My baby brother. I had to find a more generous way to include him.

On a trip to Santa Fe, I'd attended a writing workshop. As I looked more deeply into scenes with Bill, I could see the pain that was causing him to act toward me in hurtful ways. Buried in the muck of one of our particularly difficult exchanges, I saw the possibility of an even greater truth: that for almost 60 years, each of us, in our separate devotion to a complicated mother, had been shepherding her in ever-narrowing circles around death's door, all of it taking place on top of unhealed wounds. What was left to us but to defend ourselves against the scraping open of those wounds?

We agree to meet at Panini, a cozy restaurant in Marina Del Rey, halfway between where he and I live. A little closer to where he lives.

I arrive an hour early, choose an inside table with as much privacy as a public place can offer, go over my notes to be absolutely clear on my purpose for the meeting. It's unlikely I'll get his approval. I do want his understanding. I want him to know that this is my story, about a coming together I needed between me and Mom. I wonder: can it also be the groundwork for a coming together between him and me?

I want to tell him about family patterns I believe he and I have been playing out. That for all the goodness we inherited, there was also the sealed-lips stubbornness of the Wittenbergs; the loud self-righteousness of the Bragins and how their hearts literally gave out from it, despite the fact that they could always prove they were right. I want to tell him, too, about something I don't understand, some reason Mom needed to keep him and me apart, no matter how much she insisted all she wanted was for us to be together.

I take the time to become aware of my breathing, the feel of my back against the chair, my feet on the ground.

It's stuff like this, of course, that drives my brother crazy. "Get a job," he says. In more generous moments, "Get a job and then breathe!"

I watch quietly as Bill gives his full attention to the sections having to do with him and me. Anything I would say now — even a quick move on my part, a sigh — could close down the space of understanding.

At times, he stops to explain himself. Other times, he sees no problem at all with what he said or did. There are moments, too, when it looks to me as if, seeing his own pain on the page, he is soothed by the viewpoint I'm offering — that he and I both learned as children to be righteous, defensive, excitable, stubborn. And, yes, hard-jawed. That now it's time to move on. Begin to find our own way with each other, live our own lives. He and I are having one of the first real conversations we have ever had.

We get through half of the pieces, make a date to meet again.

This time, we meet at The Champagne Bakery, a little closer to where I live. We sit outside over cups of good coffee. He reads. I listen to what he has to say. He doesn't ask me to change a thing. What a mensch!

"There is one thing I'd like you to include," he says, his voice soft and quiet. "Mom tried to make me into the big brother. I failed. I tried to do what she wanted, but you wouldn't let me."

I want to take him in my arms and rock him. Grieve with him for all the living we've lost. All the loving.

We talk some more. About him, about me, about Mom. Until we are done.

As he gets up to leave, he leans over and kisses me on the cheek.

"Thank you," I say.

"It was my pleasure," he smiles.

I sit for half-an-hour, stunned. No more important place to be than here. No more important thing to do but feel what it can be like to have a brother.

Our brother-sister project took another seven years to take its next turn.

We saw each other rarely and there was hardly ever a phone call that didn't lead to my slamming down the receiver, my voice rising to a screech, his cold and ungiving.

As grateful as I was for his monetary gifts to me during this time, made out of his own generosity as well as a promise extracted by Mom that he would see to my financial safety, it wasn't enough to do the trick. I had to see, as clearly as I could, the ways I'd failed him as his older sister and own up to them. How I'd avoided him, leaving him alone as a child, even as an adult. Alone and at the wrong end of my judgmental ways.

When the time was finally right, we met again, this

time on the phone, and I could feel him melt as I told him the purpose for my call. After coming clean about the many ways I knew I hadn't been a good big sister, I asked him if there were any other hurts I'd caused him that I might not be aware of. It was as if all the ways he had been hurt by me were right there on the tip of his tongue, waiting, for years, to be expressed. I listened carefully, promised to do better.

He still thinks I'm crazy to do some of the things I do. I still think his politics are nuts, wish he'd answer my e-mails, take better care of his back. But not once, since that conversation, have we have ever come close to hanging up on each other or walking away in anger.

Are you listening, Mom?

Acknowledgments

So many.

My editor, Holly Prado, for respecting that this story was mine, not hers, to tell; at the same time, pruning away much that was extra, all those ands! Michael Richter, whose careful, committed reading and wise suggestions helped me to know, better than I knew myself, what this story, at heart, was about and that it deserved to be told. Cheryl Murfin, for a generous early reading.

Other guides on my writing path. Jerry Della Femina, one of the first to name me writer. Jack Grapes, in whose class I realized that, because I really was a writer, I better keep writing. Nancy Bacal, Connie Josefs and Margot Blair. Monona Wali and the fine writers in E33 at Emeritus — how I love it when you say, "I'm never sure where you're taking me, and I'm never disappointed." My small writing group — Dinah Hatton, Leonia Kurgan, Connie Higginson, Carolyn Maxwell, Laurie Forrest, Tony Garofalo — who helped at crucial moments. Ann Randolph and my improv family, who kept opening the door into creative freedom when my habit might have been to close it. Jerry Stiller and Anne Meara, who allowed me to put words in their mouths, some of them actually funny. Thank you, too, to the deeply knowing, deeply known women in my forever Journal Group. And Leonard Cohen who, upon reading my letter that I wanted to go on tour with him ("I'll cook, be a go-fer, do anything.") said two things: a) "No." and b) "You're a wonderful writer." Yes, Leonard Cohen said I was a wonderful writer!

I'm grateful to Nick Gisonde, Mark Yustein and Richard Nanaumi, art directors extraordinaire, who taught me the value of collaboration and whose taste and talent I've tried to mirror here; a special thank you and big hug to Richard, for more than patient and generous help with title and cover. Amy Schneider at Blue Jay Ink for your endurance and for sharing your story with me. Will Schwalbe (*The End of Your Life Book Club*) for your example and encouragement.

Thank you to Dr. Smith and everyone at the Los Angeles Jewish Home — whatever frustrations I've shared in these pages, your existence was, and is, a godsend.

Without Charlotte Selver, Lee Lesser and my fellow Sensory Awareness leaders and students, I would never have been able to see, hear, taste, touch, feel and know all the life contained in this book. Other teachers in whose footsteps I do my best to travel are Werner Erhard, Krishnamurti, Pema Chodrön, Bill W, Herb K, my fellows on the Twelve Step path, the women who trust me to be their sponsor.

Aunt Fritzi, not even a real aunt, who, on a walk one day when I was five or six, plucked a weed (she called it onion grass) that opened my heart and taste buds to Nature's gifts. Aunt Esther who, when I was eight, gave me a book, the memoir of a young woman in a Japanese internment camp, *Citizen 13660*, that set me on the path of honoring the experiences of my own life. Aunt Theresa, who sewed the dress I wore on *Art Linkletter's House Party*, when I was chosen to be one of those kids who would say things that embarrassed their parents; I didn't disappoint. Aunt Doris and Uncle Joe, who took us in after Daddy died.

Matt, for love and for helping me to know how strong Mom was. Joanna, who insists on calling me friend, not stepmother. A special hug for Georgina, who loved Mom almost as much as I do.

Love beyond words to Hannah and Irving, who trusted life enough to welcome me in. To Bill, lifelong partner in loving and caring for our mother and his partnership now in our getting to know each other. Lynn, for her support in that endeavor.

Finally, thank you to my family of friends as yet unnamed. Not a day goes by when I don't breathe you in.